Social Networking
as a
Criminal Enterprise

Social Networking
as a
Criminal
Enterprise

Edited by

Catherine D. Marcum

Appalachian State University
Boone, North Carolina, USA

George E. Higgins

University of Louisville
Louisville, Kentucky, USA

CRC Press
Taylor & Francis Group
Boca Raton London New York

CRC Press is an imprint of the
Taylor & Francis Group, an **informa** business

CRC Press
Taylor & Francis Group
6000 Broken Sound Parkway NW, Suite 300
Boca Raton, FL 33487-2742

© 2014 by Taylor & Francis Group, LLC
CRC Press is an imprint of Taylor & Francis Group, an Informa business

No claim to original U.S. Government works

Printed on acid-free paper
Version Date: 20140311

International Standard Book Number-13: 978-1-4665-8979-7 (Paperback)

Visit the Taylor & Francis Web site at
http://www.taylorandfrancis.com

and the CRC Press Web site at
http://www.crcpress.com

This book is for Mo, who I hope to be like one day.

Catherine D. Marcum

I dedicate this book to my family.

George E. Higgins

CONTENTS

Preface   xi
Acknowledgments   xiii
About the Editors   xv
List of Contributors   xvii

SECTION I   UNDERSTANDING THE SOCIAL NETWORK

1   History of Social Networking   3
Catherine D. Marcum

2   Creating Identity on Social Network Sites   9
Matt Richie and Tina L. Freiburger

3   Social Networks and Crime: Applying Criminological Theories   27
Brian P. Schaefer

SECTION II   TYPES OF SOCIAL NETWORKING CRIMINALITY

4   Texting and Social Networks   49
Melissa L. Ricketts and Cynthia Koller

5   **Identity Theft and Social Networks**   69
Jordana N. Navarro and Jana L. Jasinski

6   **Wall Posts and Tweets and Blogs, Oh My! A Look at
Cyberbullying via Social Media**   91
Robin M. Kowalski and Gary W. Giumetti

7   **Understanding Digital Piracy Using Social Networks: An
Integrated Theory Approach**   111
George E. Higgins

8   **Patterns of Sexual Victimization of Children and Women in
the Multipurpose Social Networking Sites**   125
Debarati Halder and K. Jaishankar

9   **Case Study: Advancing Research on Hackers Through Social
Network Data**   145
Thomas J. Holt, Olga Smirnova, Deborah Strumsky, and Max Kilger

SECTION III   THE CRIMINAL JUSTICE SYSTEM
AND SOCIAL NETWORKING

10   **Further Examining Officer Perceptions and Support for
Online Community Policing**   167
Adam M. Bossler and Thomas J. Holt

11   **Prosecution and Social Media**   197
Joseph D. Losavio and Michael M. Losavio

12 **Corrections and Social Networking Websites**   221
Catherine D. Marcum and George E. Higgins

Index   231

PREFACE

The birth of social networking did not originate with MySpace or Facebook. In fact, social networking websites began in 1978 based on the innovation of an IBM employee. Since that time, the appearance and use of social networking are changing on a daily basis. The ability to share ideas and communicate are two of the many uses of social networking websites, and they are continuing to evolve in appearance and purpose. With that said, with innovation comes deviance, and the social networking phenomenon has skyrocketed the ability to commit crime online.

The purpose of this book is to provide the reader with a thorough examination of how social networking criminality has affected our criminal justice system. Experts in the field have provided a comprehensive overview of the emergence of social networking, the types of crimes committed, and how the system is handling these offenders. Key concepts, statistics, and legislative histories are discussed in every chapter. It is the desire of the editors to educate and enlighten a wide audience, from those who are completely unfamiliar with the topic as an entirety to individuals who need more specific information on a particular type of social networking criminality. This text should be a useful guide to students, academics, and practitioners alike.

ACKNOWLEDGMENTS

Thank you to Carolyn Spence and the staff at CRC Press for their assistance and patience with the preparation of this manuscript. It was wonderful to work with a group of individuals who shared the same vision for this book. We hope it is a great success.

ABOUT THE EDITORS

Catherine D. Marcum, PhD, is an assistant professor of justice studies at Appalachian State University. She graduated in 2008 from Indiana University of Pennsylvania with a PhD in criminology. Her research interests include cybercrime, sexual victimization, and correctional issues.

George E. Higgins, PhD, is a professor in the Department of Justice Administration at the University of Louisville. He earned his PhD in criminology from Indiana University of Pennsylvania in 2001. He is currently the editor of the *Journal of Criminal Justice Education*. His most recent publications appear or are forthcoming in the *Journal of Criminal Justice, Deviant Behavior, Criminal Justice and Behavior, Youth and Society,* and the *American Journal of Criminal Justice.*

LIST OF CONTRIBUTORS

Adam M. Bossler
Georgia Southern University
Statesboro, Georgia

Tina L. Freiburger
University of
    Wisconsin–Milwaukee
Milwaukee, Wisconsin

Gary W. Giumetti
Quinnipiac University
Hamden, Connecticut

Debarati Halder
Centre for Cyber Victim
    Counseling
Tamil Nadu, India

George E. Higgins
University of Louisville
Louisville, Kentucky

Thomas J. Holt
Michigan State University
East Lansing, Michigan

K. Jaishankar
Manonmaniam Sundaranar
    University
Tamil Nadu, India

Jana L. Jasinski
University of Central Florida
Orlando, Florida

Max Kilger
Michigan State University
East Lansing, Michigan

Cynthia Koller
Shippensburg University
Shippensburg, Pennsylvania

Robin M. Kowalski
Clemson University
Clemson, South Carolina

Joseph D. Losavio
Johns Hopkins University
Baltimore, Maryland

Michael M. Losavio
University of Louisville
Louisville, Kentucky

Catherine D. Marcum
Appalachian State University
Boone, North Carolina

Jordana N. Navarro
Tennessee Technological
    University
Cookeville, Tennessee

Matt Richie
University of
  Wisconsin–Milwaukee
Milwaukee, Wisconsin

Melissa L. Ricketts
Shippensburg University
Shippensburg, Pennsylvania

Brian P. Schaefer
University of Louisville
Louisville, Kentucky

Olga Smirnova
East Carolina University
Greenville, North Carolina

Deborah Strumsky
University of North Carolina at
  Charlotte
Charlotte, North Carolina

Understanding the Social Network

CHAPTER 1

History of Social Networking

Catherine D. Marcum

Appalachian State University

Contents

Development of the Social Networking Website   4
Social Networking and Crime   6
References   8

In this age of smartphones, touch screens, and lightning-fast WiFi, we often take for granted that these technologies were not always available to us. Today's teens have never lived in a world with rotary telephones, VHS players, and cassette tapes. If fact, the screech of dial-up broadband is a foreign concept, and the Internet has always been an available, quick method of retrieving information. However, the Internet did not become a presence in our homes until a little over 20 years ago.

The first recorded notes birthing the idea of the Internet were written in 1962 by J.C.R. Licklider of the Massachusetts Institute of Technology (Licklider & Clark, 1962, as cited in Leiner et al., 2003). In 1964, fellow MIT colleague Leonard Kleinrock persuaded Lawrence Roberts that using packets in networking, rather than the commonly used circuits, would produce a more efficient connection. The next year, Roberts tested this idea by connecting a TX-2 computer in Massachusetts with a Q-32 machine in California, by using a low-speed dial-up telephone line. While the confirmation that computers could work together to retrieve information and run programs was sealed, the use of circuits was determined as not time efficient for transferring information. This test evolved into Roberts's ARPANET; one of its major components was the packet switches called Interface Message Processors (IMPs). IMPs, the ancestor of Internet routers, were used by computers to connect to ARPANET with a high-speed serial interface. By the end of the year, four independent host computers were successfully connected into ARPANET (Leiner et al., 2003).

ARPANET quickly evolved into what is now known as the Internet. By the 1980s, more vendors were incorporating Transmission Control Protocol/Internet Protocol (TCP/IP) into their products, which in turn heightened interest among private Internet users (Leiner et al., 2003). By the early 1990s, use of the Internet became popular for private use in homes, and as of today, over 2 billion individuals worldwide are using the Internet to shop, bank, and most importantly, communicate. The medium of communication on the Internet is often referred to collectively as social technology (Lamb & Johnson, 2006). Social technology generally refers to computer-mediated communication (CMC) devices that connect people for personal and professional information sharing. One of the most popular CMCs, email, has continued to be a main source of communication for personal use, institutions of education, corporations, and so on. CMCs, such as instant messaging and chat rooms, were immensely popular in the late 1990s and early 2000s but have decreased in usage. However, the CMC that has exploded in popularity is the social networking website.

☐ Development of the Social Networking Website

As mentioned previously, the Internet did not become a mainstay in the private household until the 1990s. We often assume that the social networking website as we know it (e.g., Facebook or Twitter) was not invented until the early 21st century. However, the birth of the social networking website can be traced back to 1978 by IBM employee Ward Christensen (Chicago Magazine, 2011). His computerized bulletin board system (CBBS) was inspired by a pushpin bulletin board at IBM where employees posted 3 × 5 cards with messages. Employees could advertise, ask questions, or post ideas for new products. Christensen and Randy Suess developed a virtual bulletin board that allowed members to get information about meetings and other announcements. The CBBS utilized Ward's MODEM File Transfer Protocol. While the CBBS did not automatically link the world together with information sharing, it was the beginning of a fantastic idea. In the early 1980s, Microsoft Disk Operating System improved standardization, and bulletin boards became more streamlined. Modem speeds improved and bulletin boards attracted more members.

The development of commercial Internet service providers (ISPs), such as AOL and EarthLink, allowed anyone with a telephone line to use the Internet. Once exclusive bulletin boards became overrun and populated with multiple members, providers began to develop areas online for the general public to use as public forums. One of the most successful online areas early on was the Beverly Hills Internet (BHI), where users chose several specialized neighborhoods to calls home. "Residents" developed virtual personas within BHI and crowded chat rooms, photo galleries, and member pages. In 1995, BHI changed its name to GeoCities, and two years later claimed more than 1 million members (CNN.com, 1999). During this same time period, Cornell students Todd Krizelman and Stephan Paternot built their own virtual world called theglobe.com. Just like GeoCities, theglobe.com allowed users to personalize their content and interact with other users that shared their interests. With an original initial public offering (IPO) of $850 that quickly fell to $4 million in only 3 years, theglobe.com was predestined for failure before it could begin.

While theglobe.com was a financial failure, Krizelman and Paternot's idea of linking individuals by likes and dislikes struck a chord in the online world. Other websites attempted the same goal, but failed due to lack of funding provided by membership. However, in 1995, Randal Conrads created Classmates.com to allow graduates to rekindle relationships with friends, romances, and people from the past. Although originally a free service, Classmates.com began to charge a subscription fee to the tens of millions of users who wanted to find past school acquaintances. This subscription fee was an innovation for this type of website. Although there were varying degrees of success, as well as reports of spam and overcharging, it became a business model for future sites (Strickland, 2009).

The short-lived SixDegrees.com was predecessor to the social networking website that we know today. Users were connected by rings based on the strength of the connection between them. While it failed due to lack of funding, the focus on relationships with others influenced Jonathan Abrams to launch Friendster.com in 2003. Utilizing the positive aspects of its ancestors, Friendster.com soared in popularity and quickly had 3 million users in 6 months. Friendster.com actually coined the word *friend* as a verb, not Facebook, as many assume. The downfall of Friendster.com was due to the site's servers trying to handle the traffic and causing slow usage. Sadly, Abrams refused Google's $30 million offer to buy the site in November 2003 and the site began to lose users.

Right before the Google offer, Los Angeles-based eUniverse employees were planning a mutiny on Friendster.com. All 250 employees were asked to join a new website and bring at least 10 of their friends with them. Using a large bank account and huge database, Chris Deolf and Tom Anderson created the first major contender in the social networking world, MySpace (Stenovec, 2011). MySpace was touted as a place of self-expression and complete control for the user in regard to content, photographs, and videos. Millions of users came to MySpace to establish a virtual identity. Rather than charging a monthly subscription fee to users, MySpace generated revenue with an ad generation system that placed banners on individual sites. While individuals are updating their MySpace pages or looking at the friends' pages, they see small advertisements for products or services. After MySpace was sold to Rupert Murdoch's News Corp in 2005, the site expanded by adding an instant messaging service (MySpaceIM), video sharing (MySpaceTV), and personal advertisements (MySpace Classified).

The second major contender for social networking website king is Facebook. Facebook actually began as Facesmash, a physical appearance rating website created by Mark Zuckerberg and three other Harvard classmates. The "hot or not" ranking site placed two student pictures beside each other and asked the participant to rank the more attractive person. As it quickly became very popular, Zuckerberg opened up thefacebook.com pages at other universities such as Stanford and Yale. In August 2005, it became Facebook.com and expanded at first to high school networks, then to the entire planet on September 2006. As of September 2012, Zuckerberg and staff celebrated the joining of Facebook's 1 billionth user. It is now used by individuals as a personal website to connect with old friends and share ideas and pictures. Businesses and organizations utilize Facebook to advertise services and share information.

☐ Social Networking and Crime

Obviously the popularity of social networking is evident, as it has become as mainstream as email usage. However, social networking websites can also offer individuals the ability to engage in deviant and criminal acts in addition to legitimate socialization. For example, an offender can perform identity theft by simply logging into a person's Facebook page without permission and stealing personal information to use later on to open up a checking account or credit card. Or, an individual can log into another friend's Twitter account and post harassing comments about another friend. The purpose of this text is to explore how the emergence of social networking has affected criminality online, as well as its detriment to the criminal justice system. The book is separated into three sections, which are discussed below.

The first section, titled "Understanding the Social Network," features three chapters. Chapter 1, the current chapter, serves an introduction to the history of the social networking website and its emergence on the Internet scene. Furthermore, this chapter introduces the layout of the book and the content of the remaining chapters. Chapter 2 discusses the process of developing an identity with social networking. This text will explore how the Internet allows a user to expand his or her current offline identity, or create a new virtual persona. Finally, Chapter 3 explains different schools of criminological theory and how they relate to criminality on social networking websites.

The second section of the book, "Types of Social Networking Criminality," investigates the different forms of criminal behavior that can be performed utilizing social networking websites. Chapter 4 examines criminality via texting, such as continuous, harassing messages from peers or fraudulent requests for personal information. Contemporary media examples involve law enforcement officers who have sent inappropriate text messages to youth. Chapter 5 examines identity theft, which explores the methods of stealing the identifying information and using it for financial gain. Theft of just a few pieces of personal information can result in long-lasting damage to individuals. Chapter 6 examines hacking on social networking websites, which is the unauthorized access of a website for destructive intentions or theft of information. The social networking website Twitter has been the victim of several hacking attempts.

Next, Chapters 7 and 8 explore criminality often involving adolescents as the offender and victim population: cyberbullying and digital piracy. Cyberbullying is the use of the Internet to intimidate, harass, or harm individuals. Chapter 7 investigates how young people are using social networking websites to torment other friends or peers at school. Digital piracy is the unauthorized downloading of copyrighted material, such as music or movies. Chapter 8 examines how these websites can allow easy, free access to software or newly released albums. Lastly, Chapter 9 delves into sexual victimization online, such as the distribution of child pornography or sexual solicitation of youth via social networking websites.

The final section of the book, "The Criminal Justice System and Social Networking," investigates the effect of social networking website criminality on the criminal justice system. Chapter 10 explores how law enforcement has handled the influx of these crimes. Furthermore, techniques and training have had to be adjusted as a result of this new wave of technology. Chapter 11 discusses the effect on how the prosecution of social networking criminality has evolved, such as including extremely intricate evidence and technological experts. Finally, Chapter 12 discusses how the U.S. corrections system and its staff have been affected by these types of offenders. Technology itself has changed not only the face of the offender incarcerated, but also how these individuals interact while inside prison walls.

It is the desire of the editors of this book to provide a thorough examination of how social networking has affected the criminal justice system and expanded the field of criminality. The contributions of experts in the field will provide this for the reader.

☐ References

Chicago Magazine. (2011). *How CBBS and robot wisdom made the web as we know it*. Retrieved September 6, 2013, from http://www. chicagomag.com/Chicago-Magazine/The-312/February-2011/How-CBBS-and-Robot-Wisdom-Made-the-Web-as-We-Know-It/

CNN.com (1999, January 28). *Yahoo buys Geocities*. Retrieved from http://money. cnn.com/1999/01/28/technology/yahoo_a/

Lamb, A., & Johnson, L. (2006). Want to be my friend? What you need to know about social technologies. *Teacher Librarian, 34*(1), 55–57.

Leiner, B., Cerf, V., Clark, D., Kahn, R., Kleinrock, L., Lynch, D., Postel, J., Roberts, L., & Wolff, S. (2003). A brief history of the Internet. *Internet Society*. Retrieved June 7, 2007, from http://www.isoc.org/internet/history/brief.shtml

Stenovec, T. (2011, June 29). MySpace history: A timeline of social network's biggest moments. *Huffington Post Tech*. Retrieved from http://www. huffingtonpost.com/2011/06/29/myspace-history-timeline_n_887059. html#s299496title=August_2003_Myspace

Strickland, J. (2009, October 12). *How Classmates.com works*. Retrieved from http://computer.howstuffworks.com/internet/socialnetworking/networks/ classmates-com.htm

Creating Identity on Social Network Sites

Matt Richie and Tina L. Freiburger

University of Wisconsin–Milwaukee

Contents

Creating a Social Network Identity	11
Actual Personality or Self-Idealization	13
Context Collapse and Lowest Common Denominator	15
Motivations	17
The Unknown, Loneliness, and Social Support	17
Demographic Patterns	18
Disclosure, Privacy, and Victimization	19
Conclusion	22
References	23

Given the vast array of Internet users and the lack of regulation on Internet use, users have the ability to become whoever they want to online. *Catfish*, a popular show on MTV, uses this as its premise. Individuals, who find a partner online, are followed by cameras as they try to locate and meet the person face-to-face. Despite the fact that they have never met the person in real life, the individuals depicted in the series believe that they are in a serious relationship with the other person; some are even engaged to be married. Upon locating the person, however, they find that the person they knew online is not the same person in real life. The person they meet face-to-face is often less attractive, less successful, and less exciting than the individual that was depicted online. In some cases, the person was even of a different sex or someone that the person knew in real life who was simply pretending to be someone else. While this makes for good entertainment, it leads to larger questions regarding online identities and how individuals use the Internet to create completely new identities, to embellish upon their real identities, and how identities can be created to deceive and even victimize others.

Using lies and deception to benefit oneself and to take advantage of others dates back much further than the Internet. The Internet, however, has made it easier for people to do this without detection. This is especially true with social network sites (SNSs). With their widespread use, SNSs have become an integral part of modern communication and have changed people's social experiences. In the first fiscal quarter of 2013, Facebook (2013) alone reported 1.11 billion monthly users. When discrepancies in Facebook's user count (accounts for pets, brands, and spam) are accounted for, Facebook still has an estimated 889.3 million users (Kleinman, 2013). In addition to a large number of users, individuals are spending most of their Internet time on these social network sites. In fact, social networking accounts for approximately 23% of Internet users' online time (Nielsen Wire, 2012). With this kind of volume, it is easy to see how users can misuse these sites by creating fake profiles to deceive others, and to see how these fake profiles are undetected. In addition, it is important to consider how these sites can impact users' feelings about themselves and others.

Because of the quantity of data that is generated from the large number of users and the frequent use of SNSs by these users, some question whether it is possible to analyze these sites. Despite the obstacles that are created by having such a large amount of data, Williams and Merten (2008) argue that the data SNSs yield can be systematically analyzed with both quantitative and qualitative designs, and did so in their study regarding adolescent blogs and parental intervention. Thus, the study of SNSs is moving past the anecdotal evidentiary period and into an era of scientific discovery on how users interact with each other on these sites, how they present themselves, and how individuals adapt to a new form of communication. An additional avenue of inquiry has been the way in which social networks have shaped individuals' identities and how individuals use social networks to create identities.

Goffman (1959) argues that individuals perform identity in every aspect of their life. With so many individuals participating in SNSs, Merchant (2006) argues that these sites are actually a new way for people to perform identity. The use of SNSs to shape identity is an important topic to examine in relation to cybercrimes and cyber victimizations. This chapter will review how individuals perform identity on SNSs. The first section discusses how sites allow users to create a social network identity. In the second section, a brief description is provided of SNSs, focusing primarily on Facebook and Twitter. The third section discusses whether users portray themselves accurately or if they are showcasing an idealized image for other users. The fourth section explains how users interact with their audience on SNSs. The fifth section discusses motivations for participation in SNSs. Lastly, the sixth section presents a discussion on privacy issues and the disclosure norms users have adopted, as well as a discussion on victimization.

☐ Creating a Social Network Identity

Although creating fake identities is typically viewed as deviant on most popular modern sites, the use of profiles to create nonrealistic identities was accepted and even considered the norm when online communication was in its infancy. According to Robinson (2007) the earliest literature on online communication focused on multiuser domains (MUDs) or role-playing games (RPGs). Within these domains, users created characters that were meant for the various RPGs; these characters were not intended to be an accurate representation of who the user was offline. Creating an online persona different from one's real self was part of the online experience on these sites. It was largely a way for users to share their fantasies and fantasy selves with others. It was not seen as deceptive; rather, it was encouraged and expected.

Participation in MUDs and RPGs was restricted to only a small part of the population using the Internet (Robinson, 2007, p.103). Kendall (1999) reports that the majority of MUD users were the stereotypical nerd, who were more than likely categorized as misfits by their peers. MUDs and RPGs were tools for their users to create an online identity in hopes of fitting in with similar individuals within an online community. As the Internet became more available to people, MUDs and RPGs saw a decrease in popularity. With this decrease, there was an increase in SNSs that allowed users to display their masterself on the site. Sites like Facebook, MySpace, Xanga, and Friendster encourage users to display their actual identities.

There are a multitude of SNSs, but the user framework of these networking sites is fairly standardized. Users are first asked to create a profile. Here they can display as much or as little information as they wish. Typically, when creating a profile, the user is asked to provide a brief description of who they are and a profile picture. There is no requirement that the information provided by the user be accurate, nor that the picture be of the actual user. The picture can be an image of any number of things, as long as it is consistent with the appropriateness standards set by the system administrator (Boyd & Ellison, 2008). SNSs do not typically make efforts to verify the information provided by the user; therefore, it is easy for individuals to set up inaccurate profiles.

Once users have created their profile, they can decide how accessible they want their virtual self to be. The way in which this is done varies by site. For example, Twitter allows its users protected status over their postings. In order to see a protected user's tweets, individuals must be approved by the owner of the profile. Facebook also offers a number of ways to protect a user's privacy. For instance, users can select which individuals are allowed to view specific aspects of their profile. The sites have system defaults for user privacy, but the majority of control over disclosure rests in the user's hands (Boyd & Ellison, 2008).

Arguably the final part of creating a profile on SNSs is linking one's profile to other users' profiles. Similar to privacy issues, the way relationships on SNSs are formed varies by site. Sites like Facebook require both users to agree with the relationship, essentially stating that the two users are now friends and have access to each other's profile and information. Other sites, such as Twitter, do not require this mutual decision. Rather, users "follow" other users to see what they are posting. Furthermore, it is not uncommon for there to be discrepancies in the number of followers and the number of people the user is following. For example, at the time of this writing the singer and musician Katy Perry has over 41 million followers but only follows 123 users on Twitter. The terms *friend* and *follower* should not be understood in their everyday sense; rather, they are terms that explain to users who is linked to whom on that specific SNS (Boyd & Ellison, 2008).

Once a profile has been established and has developed an online community, whether it be friends or followers, users can communicate with each other on the site. Many SNSs offer users the opportunity to communicate in both a public and a private setting. Facebook profiles contain a "wall" on which the profile owner or their friends can post. Twitter does not allow users to post on other users' profiles, but an individual can link another user to a post. These are both public settings where other users can see what has been posted.

Facebook and Twitter also offer a way for users to communicate privately through the use of personal and direct messages, respectively. Although Facebook requires a mutual agreement to link, this can still lead to unwanted attention from other users. Unless a user makes his or her profile private, individuals who are not their "friends" can view their information, posts, and pictures; they are also able to send messages to that person. In addition, even if a user restricts access to these sections of their profiles to friends, there is no error-proof way of ensuring the individual they link to is who that person represents himself or herself to be online.

☐ **Actual Personality or Self-Idealization**

Goffman's (1959) dramaturgical work divides human behavior into a front stage and a backstage where the audience is society. Front stage is where individuals are expected to perform for their audience. When individuals are on the front stage, they project an idealized image for their audience. However, when individuals are in the backstage, they are unpolished humans. The backstage is where individuals are their true selves and can act without the fear of rejection from their audience. A debate in SNS research, that has not received much attention, is whether users are portraying an accurate representation of themselves or if a user's profile is an idealized version of who they wish they were. The idealized virtual identity hypothesis argues that users present themselves on SNSs as idealized versions of their personalities and interests, rather than who they are offline (Back et al., 2010). The extended real-life hypothesis argues that users portray an accurate representation of themselves online and use their profile to communicate their true feelings and interests (Back et al., 2010).

Manago, Graham, Greenfield, and Salimkhan (2008) found support for the idealized virtual identity hypothesis through their use of same-sex focus groups comprised of undergraduate students who were also MySpace users. A common theme with respondents was that they enjoyed the ability to present themselves in ways that may have been contrary to who they were offline. Respondents also stated that they had taken advantage of this by displaying information that was different or more idealized than who they were offline. Furthermore, their findings indicate that SNSs help facilitate identity exploration among college students. With this exploration, users can test different identities without the limitations of the physical world and present a working identity. Essentially, their offline personality is not always meant to be the same as their online personality; rather, this is a period of transition for the individual and his or her identity. In this instance, the idealized version is not meant to deceive other users; rather, it should be seen as an individual finding out who he or she is.

In contrast to the idealized virtual identity hypothesis, Vazire and Gosling (2004) found that information on personal websites is an accurate representation of the individual. In their study, they randomly selected personal websites and had the authors of the sites fill out a personality questionnaire. After these were collected, 11 individuals rated their personality solely based on their personal website. Their results indicate that not only can personal websites display a great deal of information about an individual, but also the impressions formed by other users can be almost as accurate as observing an individual offline. It should be noted that Vazire and Gosling (2004) found evidence of ideal-self measures for both extraversion and agreeableness in their study. However, the evidence for accurate representation was stronger than the evidence for ideal-self overall.

A study conducted by Back et al. (2010) tested the two hypotheses against each other with an international group of participants (one sample from America and one sample from Germany). Facebook was used for the American sample and StudiVZ was used in the German sample for analysis. Interestingly, no significant differences existed between samples, suggesting that users in America and Germany do not differ on how they present themselves. The analysis of observer ratings and ideal-self ratings indicated that impressions yielded from the profiles were true for the owner of the profile more so than the owner's ideal self-image. Furthermore, their results found no support for the idealized virtual identity hypothesis and strong support for the extended real-life hypothesis.

The findings presented here on MySpace and Facebook certainly make sense with the extant research on the two SNSs. Hargittai (2008) argues that individuals use SNSs to connect with their already existing and offline network of peers. Prior research (Byrne, 2008; Ellison, Steinfeld, & Lampe, 2007; Ross et al., 2009) supports this claim and found that Facebook users tend to exhibit an offline-to-online relationship, meaning that users are typically friends offline before they are Facebook friends. In this instance, displaying an idealized image does not make sense because other users will know who this person really is and possibly criticize him or her for being disingenuous or unauthentic. In a different way, we could expect early MySpace users to put forth an idealized image of themselves, as MySpace was initially created for aspiring musicians and music groups (Manago et al., 2008). Assuming these individuals and groups joined the site as a way of marketing themselves to a larger audience, it makes sense that they would want to put the most ideal image of themselves out there.

There is a very real possibility that both hypotheses are true for individuals, and it is the situation that dictates which path they take. Someone with a Facebook account may exhibit evidence of the extended real-life hypothesis, posting pictures of friends, discussing the weekend's activities, or expressing their anger over a poor grade. However, when they log on to Twitter their behavior may lean toward the idealized virtual identity hypothesis by tweeting relevant and pertinent articles from their field. In many ways, it is dependent upon the user's audience and how he or she wishes to appear to it.

☐ Context Collapse and Lowest Common Denominator

Individuals tend to believe that they are the same person in every context of their life. However, individuals perform different identities when interacting with different groups of people (Merchant, 2006). For instance, when attending religious services individuals tend to behave in a quiet and respectful manner. However, under different circumstances, such as the local watering hole, individuals may act boisterous and obnoxious. To switch the behavior with the context would certainly create problems for this individual. Boyd (2007) argues that learning this behavior and context dynamic is a crucial social skill that is developed and honed over time. SNSs like Facebook and MySpace complicate this because users are often linked to many different groups of people at once, essentially creating an environment of collapsed contexts. Using the above example, the individual may be linked to members of the religious organization and his drinking buddies on a SNS. Hogan (2010) argues that the decision to post or share things on SNSs is not based on a calculation of who might see his or her profile. Rather, the user must make this decision based on two groups of people: those who will accept this version of the user and those who may have difficulty accepting this version of the user. Furthermore, the user must account for a hidden audience that may not see what he or she is sharing but could gain access to it (Hogan, 2010).

DiMicco and Millen (2007) found evidence of collapsed contexts in their study of users working for a large software development company. After the preliminary analysis was conducted, users were separated into three groups. The first group was the most active on SNSs and reported using the site to stay in touch with high school and college friends. Users' profiles in this group posted mostly about popular interests, friends, and family. Their posts were mostly informal and focused on weekend activities as well as political, religious, and social affiliations. The second group was less active on SNSs and was more instrumental in using the site. In contrast to the playful images found on the first group's profiles, most of the images found in the second group's profiles were pictures of the user in formal business attire. As could be expected, their posts and information on their profiles were different from those of the first group as well. Most of the respondents had little information on their profile, and what information was provided was mostly work related. The third group had the least information, and the users were described as individuals who may have recently been talked into using SNSs and quickly abandoned them once the pressure subsided. Members of this group could have become more active after the study had been concluded, but during the data collection phase these users were relatively new and arguably apprehensive about SNSs. Essentially, the third group displayed what they were comfortable putting out there for their online community, as did the first and second groups. In this respect, the groups are all quite similar; users of SNSs display what they wish others to see.

Remembering that the behaviors displayed by the user online must match the context of various situations, a lowest common denominator culture is adopted by users to ensure that what they are sharing on SNSs is appropriate and does not violate norms or expectations of the user (Hogan, 2010).

The collapsed context idea is similar to the lowest common denominator culture, but the two present themselves in different ways. Users face collapsed context when they are communicating with individuals in different groups in their life, both on- and offline. On a SNS, such as Facebook or MySpace, users realize their behavior has to fit multiple contexts, so they employ the lowest common denominator culture as to not inadvertently offend another user. However, in online niche communities where the context is not collapsed, users are less likely to use the same definition for what is normatively acceptable. Hogan (2010) argues that users may have a clean Facebook profile but have a number of sexually explicit pictures on websites featuring adult content. Furthermore, an individual may not discuss his or her sexual orientation or political preference on MySpace but be an avid blogger on manhunt.com or stormfront.org, where he or she feels comfortable discussing his or her sexual orientation or extreme political views. Users may not feel comfortable disclosing these pictures or views with SNS that is collapsed like Facebook or MySpace because others would deem what they are sharing as inappropriate.

☐ Motivations

Barker (2009) found that the number one reason individuals use SNSs is to communicate and socialize with their peers. This finding is consistent with the purpose of these sites, as they are designed for such a purpose. Not all sites are the same, however, and some may encourage additional user motivations. This section summarizes the existing literature on why individuals use SNSs and how user participation varies.

The Unknown, Loneliness, and Social Support

Individuals tend to avoid places that they perceive to be unsavory or unfamiliar, and the Internet is no different in this respect. When individuals perceive the Internet to be a warm and welcoming social environment, they are more likely to use SNSs (Papacharissi & Rubin, 2000). SNSs are especially important for individuals who are particularly inept with face-to-face communication; these sites provide a different avenue to communicate with their peers as well as begin and maintain relationships. Papacharissi and Rubin (2000) found that these specific individuals prefer online communication. Furthermore, prior research has shown that individuals use SNSs to actually overcome their shyness, see how others react to their personality and interests, as well as develop relationships (Valkenburg, Schouten, & Peter, 2005).

A discussion on why individuals struggle with face-to-face communication is outside the scope of this chapter. Rather, a simpler explanation is because of the proximity of users, these individuals may not see their peers as much as others do. Barker (2009) found that adolescents that are older and are somewhat isolated from their peers prefer to use SNSs to communicate with them. This finding is consistent with Leung's (2011) study that found individuals experiencing loneliness or a lack of social support prefer communicating on SNSs. Leung (2011) also found differences between age groups. Youth between the ages of 9 and 14, or preteens, who are experiencing loneliness prefer online communication. Teenagers, or youth between the ages of 15 and 19, who lack social support also prefer using SNSs to communicate with their peers.

With these findings in mind, the difference appears to be a combination of autonomy and additional responsibilities. The preteen sample most likely does not have the independence to see their friends and socialize like the individuals in the teenager or older adolescent sample have. To remedy their loneliness, they log in to SNSs to communicate with their peers. Individuals in the two older samples have probably been granted more freedom in their day-to-day activities, but like anything else, freedom comes at a cost. It is at this point in life that older adolescents and teenagers begin to enter the workforce and begin thinking about life after high school. These additional responsibilities can overwhelm an adolescent and can result in perceptions of lacking social support. If an adolescent is experiencing these feelings, he or she will most likely turn to friends for support, and with SNSs providing instant access to an individual's peers, the choice is obvious.

Demographic Patterns

Of course, not all SNS users are lonely or lacking support from their family or friends. Individuals have different motivations as to why they participate in SNSs, and existing research shows that motivations to participate are strongly related to ethnoracial and socioeconomic status.

Individuals tend to socialize with those that are most like them (Marsden, 1987; Verbugge, 1977); SNSs and their users are no exception to this phenomenon. Hargittai (2008) found evidence of this in her analysis of young adults and four different SNSs (Facebook, Friendster, MySpace, and Xanga) and argues that SNSs partially facilitate the formation of young adult peer groups. Participant experiences and demographics were not significant at the aggregate level, but when disaggregated by site, clear patterns emerged (Hargittai, 2008). For instance, Hispanics were more likely to use MySpace than Whites. Furthermore, Asians and Asian Americans were more likely to use sites like Xanga and Friendster than White respondents. The university in which the study was conducted had a large immigrant population from Southeast Asia, where Xanga has a fairly large presence (Boyd & Ellison, 2008, as cited in Hargittai, 2008). Xanga may have allowed Asian and Asian American respondents to keep in touch with friends or family in these countries. With these findings in mind, we can make the case that Verbugge's (1977) hypothesis is accurate at least as far as race and ethnicity is concerned.

Parental education attainment has been used as a proxy measure for socioeconomic status in prior literature (Lamborn, Mounts, Steinberg, & Dornbusch, 1991; McCarthy & Casey, 2008). Hargittai (2008) found that parental education attainment is a significant predictor of SNS user preference. Users who have parents with higher education attainment were more likely to use Facebook, and users with lower parental education attainment prefer MySpace. At the time of this writing, both Facebook and MySpace are free sites that anyone can use. Why then does there appear to be a divide based on socioeconomic status? The simple answer is that Verbugge's (1977) hypothesis also applies to socioeconomic status.

A final note of interest in regard to Hargittai's (2008) study is that it offers partial support for the extended real-life hypothesis. Mesch and Beker (2010) discuss how the Internet can grant users a fair amount of anonymity because individuals have more control over what they disclose when compared to offline communication. Disclosure in this sense refers to nonverbal cues, such as race and ethnicity, that can lead individuals to make assumptions about other individuals that may not be accurate (Walther, 1996). The next section will discuss disclosure and privacy risks on SNSs.

☐ Disclosure, Privacy, and Victimization

Online victimization is a major issue in today's society (Koops, Leenes, Meints, van der Meulen, & Jaquet-Chiffelle, 2009; Wilson, Gosling, & Graham, 2012). For instance, the site MySpace experienced a panic regarding the notion that pedophiles could be victimizing younger MySpace users (Raynes-Goldie, 2010). It was later unveiled that much of the sensationalism was a farce, but MySpace never quite recovered from the pedophilia scare (Marwick, 2008). However, even if pedophiles are not a large population on SNSs, there are still plenty of ways users can be victimized. Wilson and colleagues (2012) cite a number of privacy risks associated with SNS use, ranging from damaged reputation from gossip or rumors to harassment and unwanted contact to hacking and identity theft.

Koops and colleagues (2009) cite 17 different ways an individual's identity can be overtaken by another individual. It is worth noting that all 17 methods involve the Internet or a computer to commit the crime. The reason for this innovation in crime is arguably the transition from face-to-face transactions to human-to-machine transactions and the use of unique citizen numbers, such as social security numbers (Koops et al., 2009). Unfortunately, much of the research on identity theft is anecdotal or the data are ill-equipped to assess how prevalent and detrimental identity theft has become.

With all of these online risks, it has become difficult for administrators to balance the intended experience with the potential for victimization. Certainly, site administrators have an incentive to keep restrictions at a minimum so that users can share as much or as little as they wish (Wilson et al., 2012). However, at the same time administrators are mindful and proactive about preventing another MySpace pedophile scare (Koops et al., 2009; Wilson et al., 2012). Facebook has tried to alleviate concerns by instituting a privacy protection plan; unfortunately, there are still numerous privacy issues on the site (Anthonysamy, Rashid, & Greenwood, 2011).

Mesch and Beker (2010) argue that the definition of privacy rests with the control and disclosure of personal information. With SNSs, users have a great deal of control over their personal information, especially with nonverbal cues of one's identity. As stated earlier, SNSs can mask the gender or race and ethnicity of an individual if the user wishes to keep this information to himself or herself. However, prior research shows that users typically disclose their gender (Bond, 2009) and ethnoracial identity (Grasmuck, Martin, & Zhao, 2009) with a fair amount of regularity. The question then becomes what are the differences in disclosure among SNS users and how does it affect victimization?

Gross and Acquisti (2005) are credited with the first large-scale examination of privacy on SNSs. The study was conducted at Carnegie Mellon University with more than 4,000 participants. Their results indicate that users were largely unconcerned with privacy (Gross and Acquisti, 2005). Barnes (2006) argues that there is a privacy paradox regarding SNSs, in the sense that teenagers are unaware of the public nature of the Internet, whereas adults are very much aware of the Internet's public nature. This is evident by Acquisti and Gross's (2006) findings that individuals who value privacy often disclose a great deal of personal information on SNSs.

More recent research has indicated that the privacy trend has started to shift to users becoming more private with their use of SNSs (Fogel & Nehmad, 2009; Lewis, Kaufman, Gonzalez, Wimmer, & Christakis, 2008b). Dey, Jelveh, and Ross (2012) conducted a large-scale study in New York City and found that SNS users have become more conscious of what they disclose on SNSs. Interestingly, they argue that media attention regarding the risks of online communication is the reason for users becoming more proactive with what they post on SNSs.

Lewis, Kaufman, and Christakis (2008a) argue that SNSs, like most new technologies, will go through a certain pattern. When SNSs are first released, there is a great deal of ambiguity on what the norms of disclosure are on the site. However, when negative consequences are experienced, such as the loss of a job opportunity or identity theft, users reassess the norms of disclosure. Of course, this regulation phase only takes place if the majority of users are made aware of these new consequences (Lewis et al., 2008a).

Assuming that the majority of SNS users have now arrived at the regulation phase, it is important to discuss the existing research on privacy and victimization. Mesch and Beker (2010) found that offline norms of disclosure are different from online norms of disclosure. These findings offer support for the idealized virtual identity hypothesis, but other studies have yielded contrary results. For instance, there appears to be a gender gap in disclosure, with females disclosing more than males (Bond, 2009). This finding is consistent with existing literature that has found women disclose more than men (Highlen & Gillis, 1978; Petronio & Martin, 1986). At this point, the findings of gender and disclosure are mixed, and future research should examine this and ethnoracial differences in disclosure further.

In the regulation phase, individuals can still choose to have public or private profiles. Every SNS user wants to avoid victimization, but what motivates users to protect their profile? Lewis and colleagues (2008a) found that users are more likely to have private profiles if their peers have private profiles or if they are more active on SNSs. Furthermore, female users are more likely to have private profiles (Lewis et al., 2008b). In theory, users with private profiles would be less likely to be victimized online. Unfortunately, having a private profile was not shown to significantly reduce online victimization (Henson, Reyns, & Fisher, 2011). In a similar sense, having protective software on one's computer actually makes users more likely to be victimized online (Bossler, Holt, & May, 2012). Finally, users that were more active on SNSs, had more than one SNS account, and granted strangers access to their account were more likely to be victimized (Henson et al., 2011).

Thus far, we have used discussed victimization in general terms, but what types of victimization are specific to SNS usage? Certainly with the MySpace pedophile scare, the public might expect sexual assault, rape, or at least child enticement to be near the top of this list, despite these claims being unfounded. Wolak, Finkelhor, Mitchell, and Ybarra (2008) argue that this assumption is inaccurate and find that the most common Internet-initiated sex crime is nonforcible statutory rape. When individuals violate age-of-consent laws, they are unlikely to view themselves as an offender or victim (Wolak et al., 2008). This argument is supported by their analysis of arrests for Internet-initiated sex crimes made by federal, state, and local law enforcement agencies in 2000. Of the 6,594 arrests made for statutory rape (95% were nonforcible), 500 were facilitated, at least in part, by the Internet. If their analysis is accurate, then 7% of all statutory rape arrests were initiated via the Internet. The data for this analysis were from 2000, so it is possible that the figures for present day have increased, but it is unlikely.

A more recent analysis found that users were more likely to encounter threats and stalkers offline rather than over the Internet (Kennedy & Taylor, 2010). Furthermore, Sengupta and Chaudhuri (2011) failed to find a significant existence of cyberbullying among a sample of teenagers and argue that the concern for this social problem is mostly due to media hype. These findings not only offer evidence for the infrequency of Internet-initiated violence, but also indicate that victimizations are more likely to occur through offline relationships. This may be due to television programs like *Catfish* or *To Catch a Predator*, or offenders may be more aware of the public nature of the Internet. If their victims have access to what they are posting on SNSs, why wouldn't the authorities be able to gain access to their virtual paper trail? This by no means implies that sexual violence does not happen through the use of the Internet or that victims' credibility should be challenged because of the infrequency of these incidents.

It is possible that the majority of crimes initiated by the Internet are less serious than sexual assault and rape and are rarely committed by violent individuals (Wolak et al., 2008). Prior research has found that sexual harassment and unwanted sexual advances are more prominent on the Internet than offline (Kennedy & Taylor, 2010; Mitchell, Finkelhor, & Wolak, 2001). Users are also more likely to be pestered or bothered by other users on the Internet than in offline situations (Kennedy & Taylor, 2010). These incidents are arguably more problematic because they often go unreported to the local authorities (Finn, 2004). Users may feel that either this is a normal occurrence on the Internet or the unwanted attention is not sufficient to get the authorities involved and may result in a backlash if their complaint is not taken seriously. Researchers in the future should test the prevalence of online victimization and offer recommendations to prevent victimization.

☐ Conclusion

Brad Paisley released a song in 2007 entitled "Online" where the protagonist claims to be so much cooler when he is logged into MySpace. Certainly, there are users similar to Mr. Paisley's protagonist, but the research reviewed here shows that the majority of users present a more accurate portrait of who they are. SNS use is a complex undertaking for individuals. Users must decide what and how much to disclose, whether their presentation will be accurate or idealized, who their audience consists of, and how they will interact with them, while constantly being mindful of victimization and identity theft. Despite all of these factors, SNS usage continues to gain popularity in many demographics. This is most likely due to the fact that these sites facilitate communication between users who would not otherwise be able to stay in touch. In an ever-expanding world, SNSs have the potential to bring friends and families closer than ever before.

☐ **References**

Acquisti, A., & Gross, R. (2006). Imagined communities: Awareness, information sharing and privacy on the Facebook. In *Proceedings of Privacy Enhancing Technologies Workshop* (pp. 36–58). Cambridge, England: Springer.

Anthonysamy, P., Rashid, A., & Greenwood, P. (2011). *Do privacy policies reflect the privacy controls on social networks?* Presented at 2011 IEEE International Conference on Privacy, Security, Risk, and Trust, and IEEE International Conference on Social Computing.

Back, M. D., Stopfer, J. M., Vazire, S., Gaddis, S., Schmukle, S. C., Egloff, B., & Gosling, S. D. (2010). Facebook profiles reflect actual personality, not self-idealization. *Psychological Sciences, 20*(10), 1–3.

Barker, V. (2009). Older adolescents' motivations for social network site use: The influence of gender, group identity, and collective self-esteem. *CyberPsychology & Behavior, 12*(2), 209–213.

Barnes, S. B. (2006). A privacy paradox: Social networking in the United States. *First Monday, 9*(4). Retrieved from http://firstmonday.org/ojs/index.php/fm/article/view Article/1394/1312%2523#b1

Bond, B. J. (2009). He posted, she posted: Gender differences in self-disclosure on social network sites. *Rocky Mountain Communication Review, 6*(2), 29–37.

Bossler, A. M., Holt, T. J., & May, D. C. (2012). Predicting online harassment victimization among a juvenile population. *Youth & Society, 44*(4), 500–523.

Boyd, D. (2007). Why youth ♥ social network sites: The role of networked publics in teenage social life. In D. Buckingham (Ed.), *Youth, identity, and digital media* (pp. 119–142). Cambridge, MA: MIT Press.

Boyd, D. M., & Ellison, N. B. (2008). Social network sites: Definition, history, and scholarship. *Journal of Computer-Mediated Communication, 13*(1), 210–230.

Byrne, D. N. (2008). Public discourse, community concerns, and civic engagement: Exploring black social networking traditions on BlackPlanet.com. *Journal of Computer-Mediated Communication, 13*(1), 319–340.

Dey, R., Jelveh, Z., & Ross, K. (2012). *Facebook users have become much more private: A large-scale study.* Presented at 4th IEEE International Workshop on Security and Social Networking (SESOC), Lugano, Switzerland.

DiMicco, J. M., & Millen, D. R. (2007). Identity management: Multiple presentations of self in Facebook. *Group 2007,* 383–386.

Ellison, N. B., Steinfeld, C., & Lampe, C. (2007). The benefits of Facebook "friends": Social capital and college students' use of online social network sites. *Journal of Computer-Mediated Communication, 12*(4), 1143–1168.

Facebook. (2013). *Facebook reports first quarter 2013 results.* Retrieved from http://investor. fb.com/releasedetail.cfm?ReleaseID=761090

Finn, J. (2004). A survey of online harassment at a university campus. *Journal of Interpersonal Violence, 19*(4), 468–483.

Fogel, J., & Nehmad, E. (2009). Internet social network communities: Risk taking, trust, and privacy concerns. *Computers in Human Behavior, 25,* 153–160.

Goffman, E. (1959). *The presentation of self in everyday life.* New York, NY: Doubleday.

Grasmuck, S., Martin, J., & Zhao, S. (2009). Ethno-racial identity displays on Facebook. *Journal of Computer-Mediated Communication, 15*(1), 158–188.

Gross, R., & Acquisti, A. (2005). *Information revelation and privacy in online social networks (The Facebook case)*. Pre-proceedings version. ACM Workshop on Privacy in the Electronic Society (WPES).

Hargittai, E. (2008). Whose space? Differences among users and non-users of social network sites. *Journal of Computer-Mediated Communication, 13*(1), 276–297.

Henson, B., Reyns, B. W., & Fisher, B. S. (2011). Security in the 21st century: Examining the link between online social network activity, privacy, and interpersonal victimization. *Criminal Justice Review, 36*(3), 253–268.

Highlen, P. S., & Gillis, S. F. (1978). Effects of situational factors, sex, and attitude on affective self-disclosure and anxiety. *Journal of Counseling Psychology, 25*, 270–276.

Hogan, B. (2010). The presentation of self in the age of social media: Distinguishing performances and exhibitions online. *Bulleting of Science, Technology, & Society, 30*(6), 377–386.

Kendall, L. (1999). "The nerd within": Mass media and the negotiation of identity among computer-using men. *Journal of Men's Studies, 7*(3), 353.

Kennedy, M. A., & Taylor, M. A. (2010). Online harassment and victimization of college students. *Justice Policy Journal, 7*(1), 1–21.

Kleinman, A. (2013, May 17). Facebook user numbers are off: 10 percent of reported users are not human. *The Huffington Post.* Retrieved from http://www.huffingtonpost.com/2013/05/17/facebook-user-numbers_n_3292316.html

Koops, B., Leenes, R., Meints, M., van der Meulen, N., & Jaquet-Chiffelle, D. (2009). A typology of identity-related crime: Conceptual, technical, and legal issues. *Information, Communication & Society, 12*(1), 1–24.

Lamborn, S. D., Mounts, N. S., Steinberg, L., & Dornbusch, S. M. (1991). Patterns of competence and adjustment among adolescents from authoritative, authoritarian, indulgent, and neglectful families. *Child Development, 62*(5), 1049–1065.

Leung, L. (2011). Loneliness, social support, and preference for online social interaction: The mediating effects of identity experimentation online among children and adolescents. *Chinese Journal of Communication, 4*(4), 381–399.

Lewis, K., Kaufman, J., & Christakis, N. (2008a). The taste for privacy: An analysis of college student privacy settings in an online social network. *Journal of Computer-Mediated Communication, 14*, 79–100.

Lewis, K., Kaufman, J., Gonzalez, M., Wimmer, A., & Christakis, N. (2008b). Taste, ties, and time: A new dataset using Facebook.com. *Social Networks, 30*, 330–342.

Manago, A. M., Graham, M. B., Greenfield, P. M., & Salimkhan, G. (2008). Self-presentation and gender on MySpace. *Journal of Applied Developmental Psychology, 29*, 446–458.

Marsden, P. V. (1987). Core discussion networks of Americans. *American Sociological Review, 52*(1), 122–131.

Marwick, A. E. (2008). To catch a predator? The MySpace moral panic. *First Monday, 13*(6). Retrieved from http://firstmonday.org/ojs/index.php/fm/article/view/2152/1966

McCarthy, B., & Casey, T. (2008). Love, sex, and crime: Adolescent romantic relationships and offending. *American Sociological Review, 73*, 944–969.

Merchant, G. (2006). Identity, social networks and online communication. *E-Learning*, 3(2), 235–244.

Mesch, G. S., & Beker, G. (2010). Are norms of disclosure of online and offline personal information associated with the disclosure of personal information online? *Human Communication Research, 36*, 570–592.

Mitchell, K. J., Finkelhor, D., & Wolak, J. (2001). Risk factors for and impact of online sexual solicitation of youth. *Journal of the American Medical Association, 285*(3), 3011–3014.

Nielsen Wire. (2012). *State of the media: The social media report.* Retrieved from http://www.nielsen.com/us/en/reports/2012/state-of-the-media-the-social-media-report-2012.html

Papacharissi, Z., & Rubin, A. M. (2000). Predictors of Internet use. *Journal of Broadcasting & Electronic Media, 44*(2), 175–196.

Petronio, S., & Martin, J. N. (1986). Ramifications of revealing private information: A gender gap. *Journal of Clinical Psychology, 42*, 499–506.

Raynes-Goldie, K. (2010). Aliases, creeping, and wall cleaning: Understanding privacy in the age of Facebook. *First Monday, 15*(1). Retrieved from http://firstmonday.org/ojs/index.php/fm/article/viewArticle/2775/2432#p3

Robinson, L. (2007). The cyberself: The self-ing project goes online, symbolic interaction in the digital age. *New Media & Society, 9*(1), 93–110.

Ross, C., Orr, E. S., Sisic, M., Arseneault, J. M., Simmering, M. G., & Orr, R. R. (2009). Personality and motivations associated with Facebook use. *Computers in Human Behavior, 25*, 578–586.

Sengupta, A., & Chaudhuri, A. (2011). Are social networking sites a source of online harassment for teens? Evidence from survey data. *Children and Youth Services Review, 33*, 284–290.

Valkenburg, P. M., Schouten, A. P., & Peter, J. (2005). Adolescents' identity experiments on the Internet. *New Media & Society, 7*(3), 383–402.

Vazire, S., & Gosling, S. D. (2004). E-perceptions: Personality impressions based on personal websites. *Journal of Personality and Social Psychology, 87*, 123–132.

Verbugge, L. M. (1977). The structure of adult friendship choices. *Social Forces, 56*(2), 576–597.

Walther, J. (1996). Computer mediated communication: Impersonal, interpersonal and hyperpersonal interaction. *Communication Research, 23*, 3–43.

Williams, A. L., & Merten, M. J. (2008). A review of online social networking profiles by adolescents: Implications for future research and intervention. *Adolescence, 43*(170), 253–274.

Wilson, R. E., Gosling, S. D., & Graham, L. T. (2012). A review of Facebook research in the social sciences. *Perspectives on Psychological Sciences, 7*(3), 203–220.

Wolak, J., Finkelhor, D., Mitchell, K. J., & Ybarra, M. L. (2008). Online "predators" and their victims: Myths, realities, and implications for prevention and treatment. *American Psychologist, 63*(2), 111–128.

Social Networks and Crime
Applying Criminological Theories

Brian P. Schaefer

University of Louisville

Contents

What Is Theory?	29
Criminological Theories of Cybercrime	31
Rational Choice	31
Deterrence	32
Lifestyle/Routine Activities Theory	33
Social Learning	35
Strain Theory	36
Social Bonds	37
Self-Control	38
Techniques of Neutralization	39
Conclusion	40
References	42

The Internet has grown to become a fact of life for people worldwide, and it offers a new avenue of research for social scientists. Cyberspace, online social networks, and computer-mediated communication systems test traditional criminological research, introducing new forms of crime and providing additional opportunities to commit crime (Yar, 2006). In addition, the Internet provides new challenges for social control, formal and informal. The previous 20 years have seen a growing concern regarding crime on the Internet, commonly known as cybercrime (Thomas & Loader, 2000). Past research has examined the nature and prevalence of cybercrime as well as the predictors of victimization and offending on the Internet on a wide range of subjects (Bossler & Holt, 2010; Higgins, 2005; Higgins, Wolfe, & Marcum, 2008; Jaishankar, Halder, & Ramdoss, 2009).

Despite the extant research literature, making sense of cybercrime still presents significant challenges for criminologists. The primary challenge in studying cybercrime is that the term lacks a clear definition. Cybercrime does not refer to a specific type of crime (i.e., residential burglary), but rather refers to a range of illicit activities that occur in cyberspace. The breadth of acts that can fall under cybercrime led Wall (2001, p. 2) to suggest that cybercrime "has no specific reference in law." These activities can range from hacking to digital piracy to child pornography to victimization. Thomas and Loader (2000, p. 3) define cybercrime as those "computer-mediated activities which are either illegal or considered illicit by certain parties and which can be conducted through global electronic networks." This definition provides additional precision, but Yar (2006, p. 22) goes further by distinguishing between "computer-assisted crime" and "computer-focused crime" (e.g., hacking). Of particular interest for this book is cybercrime that occurs within social networks.

In its simplest form, an online social network exists when people or organizations are connected through a computer system. The form of these connections can be based on friendship, work, or information exchange (Garton, Haythornwaite, & Wellman, 1997). A specific definition of a social network system is provided by Boyd and Ellison (2007, p. 211), who define a social network system as "web-based services that allow individuals to (1) construct a public or semi-public profile within a bounded system, (2) articulate a list of other users with whom they share a connection, and (3) view and traverse their list of connections and those made by others within the system." Social networks have existed since 1997, and there are currently thousands of social networks around the world, such as Facebook (Boyd & Ellison, 2007). Social networks and their associated websites offer social scientists an important research area to understand the social impacts of these networks, including crime (Boyd & Ellison, 2007; Steinfield, Ellison, & Lampe, 2008). A key element to understanding cybercrime is identifying or developing theoretical frameworks that can assist researchers in understanding the changing nature and scope of offending and victimization in a highly mediated society (Steinfield et al., 2008).

This chapter provides an overview of several criminological theories that can be used to explain the prevalence of crime on the Internet. To accomplish this task, the chapter first discusses the importance of theory and its definition. Next, the chapter discusses eight theoretical frameworks that can be, or have been, applied to cybercrime. Finally, the chapter concludes by offering future directions in theorizing crime in social networks.

☐ What Is Theory?

A strong theoretical infrastructure is necessary for all social science disciplines. In the context of explaining cybercrime, theories provide the researcher with a tool to explain why and how cybercrime occurs. To use theory, or theorize, is to simply ask why. All individuals have ideas about why some things occur or why certain people behave in certain ways, or how the things that occur are related to our behaviors. This simple form of thinking about relationships is not generally considered theory, but why not? What differentiates our day-to-day explanations from theory? After all, our common thought process and theory both seek to explain certain phenomena. The difference between speculating why and theorizing is that theory is a process of linking observations in a logical manner in order to understand a particular phenomenon. In other words, we use theory to make sense of the world, and a systematic theory can expose the working systems that we take for granted (Kraska & Brent, 2011).

Theory, unlike our day-to-day explanations, needs to be communicated to a wider audience in order to be influential. Communication to a broader audience requires defining the concepts of the theory, and clearly stating the relationships between the concepts to form propositions (Kraska & Neuman, 2008). Theory can be defined as "a system of interconnected ideas that condenses and organizes knowledge for purposes of understanding and/or explanation" (Kraska & Neuman, 2008, p. 88). The most well known conception of theory is the scientific view. Scientific theory wants to explain or predict phenomena. Scientific theories are intended to be testable. For a scientific theory, the associations among the concepts must make sense and must be related to each other. Scientific theory is made up of three elements: concepts, definitions, and relationships.

A theory's concepts are its building blocks. Concepts are an abstract idea of the particular phenomenon under study. Concepts vary in their degree of abstractness, with some pertaining to concrete phenomena (e.g., age), while some refer to general properties (e.g., gender). Strong theories have concepts that are clearly defined in a way that a fellow researcher can identify the phenomenon to which the concept refers. The most important aspect of a concept is that it conveys the same meaning to everyone (Kraska & Neuman, 2008).

Once the concepts of a theory are identified and developed, a theory must explain the relationships between these concepts. A scientific theory contains a set of assertions that link concepts with each other. Theory, then, is simply a systematic way of stating our ideas on the how and why of social phenomena. A theory with clearly stated propositions can be used by a researcher to direct his or her research. Clearly stated hypotheses allow researchers to test their theories to determine whether the theory is valid. Therefore, theory must be stated in a systematic way to convey the same meaning to scholars who wish to use the ideas. Without this, our ideas would have little value to scientific development because one of our requirements for scientific knowledge accumulation is that we must be able to replicate that knowledge any one scholar may acquire (Kraska & Neuman, 2008).

There are several criteria used to determine if the theory is testable. A theory must make logical sense, have clearly stated and measurable concepts, have propositions that are logically consistent, have a wide scope, and be parsimonious (Akers & Sellers, 2004). Theories that meet these criteria are then able to be tested, in order to determine if current theories are valid. Validity refers to the findings of empirical support for the theory after testing the hypotheses in a manner consistent with the theory (Kraska & Neuman, 2008). Typically, researchers use quantitative methods to replicate or validate theories. This form of research is robust because others can replicate the methods with different groups or behaviors, and quantitative studies allow for random sampling and large sample sizes. The downside of using quantitative methods to test theories is the method lacks the personal involvement or interpretive depth. The qualitative tradition of research can be used to acquire deeper understanding by interpreting observations, interviews, or text (Kraska & Neuman, 2008; Tewksbury, 2009). The qualitative tradition allows the researcher to understand why a behavior was performed from the actor's perspective; however, it lacks the generalizability found in quantitative assessments.

Theories offer several tangible benefits to researchers. First, it is impossible for theoryless research to be conducted (Kraska & Brent, 2011); no matter how applied the research may be, theory is still needed to interpret the findings. For instance, the statistical link between Internet usage and criminal activity requires a theory to explain its relationship. Second, theory enhances our understanding. Finally, theory informs and guides practice. Theoretical driven research can develop strategies for effectively dealing with a wide range of behaviors, including cybercrime. The following sections of this chapter provide several empirically validated criminological theories that can explain criminal behavior within social networks. The concepts and propositions of each theory will be presented, along with its application to cybercrime and its empirical status.

☐ Criminological Theories of Cybercrime

Rational Choice

Rational choice theorists argue that offenders are rational individuals. That is, offenders seek to maximize their pleasure while minimizing their pain (McCarthy, 2002). Theorists do not assume that offenders are completely rational; rather, they recognize that offenders have limited or bounded rationality, which involves some consideration of the cost and benefits, but this calculation is conducted with incomplete or inaccurate information (Clarke & Cornish, 1985; Cornish & Clarke, 1986). Within the rational choice literature, the costs of crime are defined broadly. These costs include both formal and informal sanctions. Formal sanctions include fines or imprisonment handed down by the criminal justice system. Informal sanctions include feeling guilt or shame from committing a crime (Clarke & Cornish, 1985). There are also a wide range of benefits of crime, including money, status, and thrills/excitement. Empirical evidence indicates that most studies find that crime does occur when costs are perceived as low and the benefits are high (McCarthy, 2002); however, the research on rational choice theory has not examined cybercrime.

Research into rational choice theory suggests that a complete explanation of crime requires an explanation of how offenders get involved with crime and how they decide to commit crime. Criminal involvement deals with the decision to become involved in crime, that is, the rationalizations for needing to get involved in criminal activity. Criminal events involve the decision to commit a specific criminal act. Criminal event decisions are where an offender decides to commit a cybercrime rather than burglary. Most crime theories focus on the decision to become involved in crime but do not deal with the facts influencing the decision to commit a particular crime. These factors often have to do with the immediate circumstances and situation of the individual. Rational choice theory has directed much attention to these circumstances and situations and has thereby supplemented the approach of the leading crime theories. Much of the research stimulated by rational choice theory, in fact, focuses on the factors that offenders consider when they are thinking about committing a particular crime. Rational choice theorists argue that it is necessary to develop a crime-specific focus when examining crime, because the cost and benefits of committing different types of crime may vary. For instance, the cost and benefits of robbing someone will be different than the costs and benefits of illegally downloading a movie. Research into the situational factors has been applied to various crimes (Tunnell, 1992; Wright & Decker, 1994), but there is little research that examines the motivations for committing a particular cybercrime. Steinmetz and Tunnell (2013) in a study of online pirates found multiple motivations for illegally downloading information. These motivations included the desire to share content, the desire to sample or test new media, and the desire to undermine copyright laws. Steinmetz and Tunnell's study is indicative of the need to understand why offenders commit cybercrime, in order to develop policies aimed toward reducing crime.

Deterrence

The second criminological theory that can be applied to cybercrime is deterrence theory. Similar to rational choice, deterrence theorists argue that humans are rational creatures. As such, if the costs of committing crime are high, then individuals will not commit crime. The U.S. criminal justice system relies on deterrence theory to gain compliance with the law. The criminal justice system seeks to prevent crime by increasing the costs of committing crime, and thus influencing the rational calculus. Deterrence comes in two forms, specific and general (Nagin, 1998). Specific deterrence seeks to reduce the likelihood of crime by punishing the individual who committed the crime. For instance, when an offender is sentenced to prison for committing a homicide, the goal of the sentence is to punish the offender in a way where he or she will be deterred from ever committing the crime again. General deterrence operates by deterring those individuals who have not been punished or committed a crime. General deterrence seeks to ensure that when an opportunity for crime is presented to an individual, he or she takes into account the legal repercussions of his or her actions.

Deterrence theory takes on two forms, classical and contemporary. Classical deterrence theory posits that individuals commit crime when the benefits of crime outweigh the costs of crime. A key cost for deterrence is the legal punishment of crime, such as arrest, captivity, or fines. In order to increase the deterrent effects of punishment, Beccaria (1764/1996) argued that punishment must be swift, certain, and severe. Certainty refers to the probability of getting caught and receiving a punishment. Celerity refers to how quickly a punishment is applied following the commission of a crime. Finally, severity refers to the how harsh the punishment is. According to classical deterrence theory, a punishment is more likely to deter crime when it is certain, severe, and swift. Research indicates that the threat of certainty is more important than severity, and that celerity rarely has an impact on crime (Nagin, 1998; Pogarsky, 2002). Classical deterrence theory focuses on the objective and formal legal punishments of crime; however, contemporary deterrence theory has revealed there are also informal punishments of crime (Nagin, 1998).

Contemporary deterrence theory moves beyond formal punishment and incorporates informal punishment. Informal punishment includes measures such as shame, guilt, and embarrassment associated with committing crime. Grasmick and Bursik (1990) explored the influence of personal relationships and an individual's conscience, as well as personal embarrassment and shame, on multiple crimes. They found that shame was a powerful deterrent for multiple crimes, and more importantly, they found that shame was a stronger predictor than legal sanctions. Research consistently shows that informal sanctions have stronger deterrent effects than formal sanctions (Nagin & Pogarsky, 2001).

Deterrence theorists would suggest that cybercrime can be prevented by increasing the certainty and severity of the punishments of crime; in addition, the associated guilt or shame of cybercrime can reduce crime. Deterrence theory has been applied to cybercrime. One of the first studies examining deterrence theory and cybercrime was Sherizen (1995), who found that computer crime can be deterred. Multiple researchers have subsequently examined the link between deterrence theory and cybercrime, including digital piracy (Higgins & Makin, 2004a, 2004b; Wolfe, Higgins, & Marcum, 2008). Wolfe and his colleagues (2008) in a study of digital piracy of music found that guilt was an important correlate of digital piracy. In addition, the authors found the threat of viruses is a significant deterrent.

Lifestyle/Routine Activities Theory

Routine activities theory and lifestyle exposure theory developed in tandem (Cohen & Felson, 1979; Hindelang, Gottfredson, & Garofalo, 1978). The lifestyle/routine activities theory suggests that opportunities for criminal offending or victimization arise out of an individual's everyday routines and lifestyles. That is, an individual's day-to-day activities expose himself or herself to the risk of victimization. The main assumption of routine activities theory is that for a crime to occur, there must be a motivated offender, a suitable target, and a place where the offender and target can interact (Cohen & Felson, 1979). When an offender comes together with a target at a particular place, and there is a lack of guardianship, then a crime is likely to occur. Cohen and Felson (1979) visualized their theory in a triangle, where each side of the triangle represents the three components: target, offender, and place. If any of the sides of the triangle change in prevalence, then there can be a corresponding increase or decrease in criminal opportunities. The original conception of a routine activities approach to explaining criminal behavior assumed that crime occurs in a physical space; however, recently researchers have argued that a lifestyle/routine activities approach can be applied to cyberspace (Reyns, Henson, & Fisher, 2011).

Applying lifestyle/routine activities theory to crime on the Internet presents theoretical challenges regarding whether or not an offender comes into contact with his or her victim. A few scholars have applied routine activities theory to cyberspace, but these scholars do explain the lack of interaction in physical space (Marcum, 2009; Pratt, Holtfreter, & Reisig, 2010); other academics have debated the applicability of routine activities theory to cybercrime (see Grabosky, 2001; Yar, 2005a). Eck and Clarke (2003) argued that routine activities theory could be applied to cybercrime if a systems problem approach were taken. Eck and Clarke argued that offenders do not come into physical contact with their victims; however, they do interact with those victims through a system or network, such as Facebook or a torrent site. The system or network becomes the medium for the interaction between the offender and victim and allows routine activities theory to be applied to cyberspace.

Reyns and his colleagues (2011) applied Eck and Clarke's (2003) conception of routine activities and the Internet to cyberstalking victimization. Their study found that routine activities theory has a significant relationship with online victimization. Their study revealed that each component of routine activities theory—motivated offender, suitable target, and lack of capable guardian—is related to various forms of victimization, a finding consistent with prior research (Bossler & Holt, 2010; Marcum, 2009; Ngo & Paternoster, 2011). The research provides empirical support that routine activities theory can be applied to cybercrime; however, further conceptualization of the measurement of routine activities theory applied to cyberspace is needed. For instance, the concept of a capable guardian could still be measured by parental overview of a child on the Internet, or it could refer to the presence of antivirus software. Future research is still needed to understand effective guardianship in cyberspace, as well as what constitutes an attractive target.

Social Learning

Social learning theory was developed by Edwin Sutherland (1947). Sutherland argued that deviance is learned through interaction with peers, and it is through these relationships that attitudes favorable or unfavorable to crime emerge. Sutherland argued that a person becomes delinquent because of an excess of definitions favorable to the violation of law over definitions unfavorable to violations of law. Burgess and Akers (1966) revised Sutherland's theory to include differential reinforcement in the model, and Akers (1998) revised the theory further to include imitation. Contemporary social learning theory contains four elements in the learning process: differential association, definitions, imitation, and differential reinforcement. Akers argues that these four elements play a role in the learning of pro-social as well as antisocial behavior. The social learning research literature indicates that differential association is the most significant factor in the learning process. Differential association refers to the interaction of an individual with his or her primary (i.e., family or friends) or secondary (i.e., school or church) groups. An individual learns his or her motivations, rationalizations, drives, and the techniques for committing crimes while interacting with peers. In addition, it is through social interaction with peers that the individual learns his or her definitions, or beliefs, favorable or unfavorable to committing crime. The learning process is also influenced by imitation, or mimicking the behavior of people an individual interacts with. Finally, the learning process is influenced through reinforcement. Akers (1998) argues that each individual is differentially reinforced; that is, the costs or benefits of certain behavior vary among individuals. At certain times an individual may be rewarded for a particular criminal behavior (e.g., receiving free movies through illegal downloading) and that person will continue that behavior. There is a large amount of research examining the relationship between social learning theory and cybercrime, in particular digital piracy.

Early research into the relationship between digital piracy and social learning theory, conducted by Skinner and Fream (1997), found support for the link between definitions, differential association, and crime. Subsequent research has found that differential association and definitions are related to the physical sharing of software piracy (Higgins & Makin, 2004a)—as opposed to online sharing—and that these two components are related to piracy for personal use (Higgins & Makin, 2004b). These studies have implications for the application of social learning theory to cybercrime, in that criminal activity related to the Internet does not have to manifest online; rather, an individual can download music, burn it to a CD, and then share the files. Higgins, Fell, and Wilson (2006) were able to generate a causal model for the relationship between social learning and digital piracy and found that learning had a direct effect on piracy. Finally, in a study of multiple theoretical frameworks, Morris and Higgins (2009) found differential association to be a significant predictor of retrospective and prospective digital piracy, while controlling for other theories. The aforementioned studies focused on digital piracy; however, other research has found social learning theory to be a predictor of other forms of cybercrime or cyber-deviance, including using a wireless Internet connection without authorization (Holt, Burruss, & Bossler, 2010) and cyberstalking (Fox, Nobles, & Akers, 2011).

Strain Theory

Varieties of strain theory have existed for over a hundred years, and these theories consistently find empirical support (Durkheim, 1897/1965; Merton, 1938). One of the original strain theories was created by Merton (1938), who extended Durkheim's anomie theory, arguing that strain occurs due to the disjunction between ends and means of achieving socially approved means to success and legitimate goals, which is caused by American society. American culture heavily emphasizes economic success while relatively indifferent to the means used to achieve success. Merton (1938) documented five modes of adaptations that occur due to the disjunction between goals and means, with innovators having the highest crime rate.

Robert Agnew (1985, 1992) provides a more recent strain theory, where he argues that crime occurs when individuals fail to cope with the emotional stressors caused by stress. Agnew (2006, p. 4) "argues there are three primary causes of strain: the presence of negatively-valued stimuli; the loss of positively-valued stimuli, and the failure to achieve positively-valued goals." According to Agnew, the strain itself does not cause delinquency; rather, the strain causes negative emotional responses, which if not dealt with appropriately can increase the likelihood of crime. Agnew suggests that individuals use coping strategies to alleviate the strain emotional responses, but if the coping mechanism fails, then crime is more likely. Agnew emphasized two forms of emotional responses that are more likely to lead to crime: anger and depression (Agnew, 1992, 2006).

A third form of strain theory was developed by Konty (2005), who created a micro-anomie theory. Konty (2005, p. 111) indicates that micro-anomie is the "individual level imbalance between social-interest and self-interest and can be measured by calculating the differences between the self-enhancing values and self-transcending values." Konty continues on by arguing that the United States emphasizes self-enhancing values over self-transcending values, which results in individuals who are more egocentric. As a result, Konty suggests that individuals who are self-interested are more likely to turn to crime to increase rewards. An important caveat in Konty's micro-anomie theory is that self-interest does not always lead to criminal behavior; rather, it is more likely because those who are self-interested see an increase in the rewards of crime.

These three variations of strain theories can all be applied to deviant or criminal behavior on the Internet. For instance, Merton would argue that those individuals who have the desire to buy a new movie but lack the financial means may turn to the Internet to illegally download the movie. Further, Agnew's (1992) general strain theory would suggest that an individual who breaks up with his or her significant other may develop anger and turn to the Internet to stalk his or her former partner. Finally, Konty's (2005) micro-anomie theory proposes that those individuals who are self-interested are potentially more likely to use a wireless connection without permission, rather than purchase their own Internet subscription. The empirical research examining the impact of strain on forms of cybercrime is limited, but in a study by Morris and Higgins (2009), they found limited support for Konty's (2005) theory of micro-anomie. Morris and Higgins (2009) found that micro-anomie had a significant but limited effect on retrospective and prospective models of digital piracy.

Social Bonds

Hirschi (1969), in his theory of social control, argues that crime occurs as a result of weak social bonds. Hirschi contends that an individual who possesses strong social bonds to conventional society will be less likely to engage in criminal or deviant activity. Hirschi identified four types of social bonds: attachment, commitment, involvement, and belief. An individual's attachment to society refers to the affective bonds to his or her parents, school, and friends. An individual who has strong attachments is more likely to be supervised by his or her parents and exposed to pro-social values (Chui & Chan, 2012). An individual's commitment refers to his or her desire to achieve societal norms, such as going to college or getting a good job (Booth, Farrell, & Varano, 2008). The level of involvement references an individual's participation in pro-social activities such as extracurricular school programs or other social activities. An increase in involvement is thought to reduce the amount of unstructured supervision an individual has, thus decreasing the likelihood of deviant activity. Finally, belief is defined as the attitudes an individual possesses toward societal norms and rules. An individual that believes committing crime is wrong will be less likely to participate in deviant activity.

Few studies have applied Hirschi's (1969) social bond theory to cybercrime; however, its insight could be valuable. Williams (2006) applies social bond theory to examine systems of social control in cyberspace. Williams argues that online offenders are less committed to maintaining their online identity and reputation, and consequently less attached to the online community. As a result, offenders are more likely to commit deviant activities. Williams's (2006) research implicates the role of parents, peers, and school play in influencing an individual's behavior, and how these individuals can develop identities online. His research goes beyond notions that social control occurs in the physical realm, and notes the importance of understanding how social control emerges in the virtual world. It is possible that social bonds can be developed and maintained in cyberspace by parents limiting their children's time on the Internet or implementing parental blocks on deviant websites. There is a need to examine how the Internet potentially impacts the development and influence of social bonds, in particular, how social institutions (schools), parents, and peers influence an individual's beliefs (positively or negatively) in online communities.

Self-Control

Self-control theory, developed by Gottfredson and Hirschi (1990), is one of the more common theories applied to cybercrime. Gottfredson and Hirschi (1990) argue that deviance can be best explained by individual-level differences in levels of self-control, and that an individual's level of self-control is stable over time. Gottfredson and Hirschi (1990) contend that individuals with low self-control are unable to see the consequences of their decisions. Further, they suggest that individuals with low self-control share six common characteristics: they are impulsive, lack empathy, are risky, and prefer easy, simple, and physical tasks. Individuals with low self-control are more likely to commit a criminal act when an opportunity presents itself. Gottfredson and Hirschi (1990) also argue that low self-control explains all forms of crime, including analogous acts of deviance, such as smoking. Gottfredson and Hirschi (1990) identify poor parenting as the cause of low self-control. They suggest that parents who do not show affection to their children or who do not recognize and punish deviant behavior will raise children who are poorly socialized and unable to delay gratification. Hirschi (2004) later argued that researchers must examine individuals with high self-control in conjunction with individuals with low self-control. Hirschi (2004) characterized individuals with high self-control as having strong social bonds, which allowed them to see the consequences of deviant behavior.

From a self-control perspective, individuals with low self-control are more likely to participate in criminal activity, including cybercrime. A large amount of research studies have examined the relationship between self-control and online piracy. There is considerable support for the relationship between low self-control and digital piracy. Higgins and Makin (2004a, 2004b) found self-control to have a relationship with digital piracy; however, both these studies indicate that the effect of self-control is weakened by the influence of peers. The influence of peer associations in congruence with self-control was also found by Higgins (2005; Higgins et al., 2006). Finally, Morris and Higgins (2009), controlling for multiple theories, found that low self-control had a significant effect on video piracy (retrospectively). And they also found that in the prospective models (willingness to commit crime) were significant predictors of movie downloading. Further research is needed regarding the relationship between low self-control and other forms of cybercrime, as self-control theory is found to be a strong predictor of many forms of deviant behavior (Pratt & Cullen, 2000).

Techniques of Neutralization

The most common form of neutralization theory was developed by Sykes and Matza (1957). Sykes and Matza (1957) argued that individuals can justify their participation in criminal behavior using one or more of five techniques: the denial of responsibility, the denial of injury, the denial of victim, the condemnation of condemners, and an appeal to higher loyalties. Sykes and Matza suggest that by using one of these neutralization techniques, an individual can convince himself or herself that his or her behavior is acceptable, no matter what the conventional norms are. In other words, the techniques of neutralization can be used when an individual is faced with two conflicting value systems. Denial of responsibility permits offenders to avoid or reduce the disapproval from others or themselves by blaming "forces outside of the individual and beyond his control" (Sykes and Matza, 1957, p. 667). The denial of injury involves negating any harm that may have occurred, as Sykes and Matza (1957, p. 667) note that for an offender, "wrongfulness may turn on the question of whether or not anyone has clearly been hurt by his deviance." The third neutralization technique, the denial of victim, can refer to the notion that it is a "victimless crime," or that the person is deserving of the injury. The condemnation of condemners involves shifting "the focus of attention from [the offender's] own deviant acts to the motives and behavior of those who disapprove of his violations" (Sykes and Matza, 1957, p. 668). From this perspective, the offenders do not outright deny their behavior was wrong; rather, they believe it was justified due to the behavior of their victim. The final technique used to neutralize an offender's behavior is the appeal to higher loyalties. The offender appeals to higher loyalties by negating the demands of the larger society and giving primacy to the needs of the individual or social group his or her actions represent. Research supporting the techniques of neutralization is mixed; however, the research that provides negative support often does not provide complete measurement of the theory (Maruna & Copes, 2007).

Researchers have examined the relationship between the techniques of neutralization and cybercrime, especially in reference to various forms of digital piracy. One of the first studies to examine neutralization and piracy was conducted by Hinduja (2007), and he found weak support between neutralization and software piracy. Ingram and Hinduja (2008) examined the relationship between neutralization theory and online music piracy and found that four of the five techniques of neutralization (condemnation of the condemners had no significant relationship) had a significant relationship with the illegal downloading of music. In a later study, Morris and Higgins (2009) found support for neutralization theory in digital piracy, while also controlling for self-control, social learning, and deterrence theories. Finally, Steinmetz and Tunnell (2013), in qualitative study of online pirates, found evidence of all five techniques of neutralization present among hackers.

☐ Conclusion

Cybercrime and other forms of illicit activities present significant challenges to criminologists. There are still questions as to whether cybercrime consists largely of crime that predates the Internet (i.e., theft) that takes on new forms on the Internet, or if there are completely new crimes that have developed with the rise of the Internet. If the former is true, then there are several criminological theories that can be applied to understand crime and deviant behavior on the Internet. If the latter is true, then social scientists must identify these new types of crimes and develop new theories or adapt current theories to explain these behaviors. Regardless of the types or form of crime that exist in cyberspace, it is a necessity to have valid theoretical frameworks to explain cybercrime. This chapter presented seven empirically valid criminological theories that can explain cybercrime without adaptation, and one theory, routine activities theory, that has been adapted to explain cybercrime. These theories offer a strong starting point to examine the correlations of criminal offending or victimization on the Internet.

This chapter does not suggest that the eight theories provided offer a complete collection of theories that can be used to explain cybercrime. There are several other criminological, social, or psychological theories that could be applied. For instance, future research into cybercrime could benefit from the use of developmental theories (Moffit, 1993; Sampson & Laub, 1993, 2003) to examine whether offenders change their online behavior over time. In addition, the eight theories provided in this chapter still need to be tested on types of cybercrime beyond digital piracy, such as cyberstalking, hackers, and identity thieves, among others. As a whole, the application of criminological theories to cybercrime is still in its infancy, and there is still a lot social scientists do not understand about the Internet.

There are two areas of research in particular that are needed. First, the definition of cybercrime and its prevalence needs to be refined. Several scholars note the vagueness of cybercrime definitions (Thomas & Loader, 2000; Wall, 2001; Yar, 2006). In particular, Yar (2005a) challenges the assumed severity of movie piracy. Yar (2005b) suggests that the perceived crime wave associated with movie piracy is a result of lobbying efforts and criminal justice agendas. The work of Yar implicates the need to examine the development of laws and criminal justice responses to online crime and whether new forms of social control are a product of need or political maneuverings. This line of research has begun to develop, with researchers arguing that crime control agencies are creating a web of surveillance on the Internet and violating individuals' right to privacy (Fuchs, 2011; Wall & Monahan, 2011).

A second research need regarding cybercrime is an increase in qualitative research to examine whether current theories provide meaningful representations of deviant activity occurring on the Internet. The work of Steinmetz and Tunnell (2013) and Holt and Copes (2010) shows how current criminological theories can be applied to cybercrime; however, these two studies represent the very few available qualitative studies of online deviance. Cybercrime research will greatly benefit from additional qualitative research examining the motivations, techniques, and drives of digital pirates, as well as seeking out hard-to-reach populations such as hackers, human traffickers, sexual deviants, or identity thieves. The qualitative research can develop new grounded theories or refine current criminological theories to improve the discipline's understanding of cybercrime.

As a whole, research into crime in social networks or cybercrime has increased substantially in the past few years. The Internet continues to evolve and impact society in new ways. As technology advances there are new opportunities for criminal activity that will need to be studied for the purposes of understanding the phenomena and developing effective policies to reduce the criminal activity. No matter how technology changes society, social scientists will need valid theoretical frameworks to understand the relationship between the Internet, society, and deviance. This chapter provides eight valid criminological theories that can be applied to explain cybercrime and encourages researchers to refine existing and develop new theoretical frameworks to further our understanding of cybercrime.

☐ References

Agnew, R. (1985). A revised strain theory of delinquency. *Social Forces, 64*, 151–167.

Agnew, R. (1992). Foundation for a general strain theory of crime and delinquency. *Criminology, 30*, 47–87.

Agnew, R. (2006). *Pressured into crime: An overview of general strain theory.* Los Angeles: Roxbury.

Akers, R.L. (1998). *Social learning and social structure: A general theory of crime and deviance.* Boston: Northeastern University Press.

Akers, R.L., & Sellers, C. (2004). *Criminological theories: Introduction, evaluation, and application* (4th ed.). Los Angeles: Roxbury.

Beccaria, C. (1764). *On crimes and punishment.* New York: Marsilio Publishers.

Booth, J.A., Farrell, A., & Varano, S.P. (2008). Social control, serious delinquency, and risky behavior: A gendered analysis. *Crime and Delinquency, 54*(3), 423–456.

Bossler, A.M., & Holt, T.J. (2010). The effect of self-control on victimization in the cyberworld. *Journal of Criminal Justice, 38*, 227–236.

Boyd, D.M., & Ellison, N. (2007). Social network sites: Definition, history, and scholarship. *Journal of Computer-Mediated Communications, 13*, 210–230.

Burgess, R.L., & Akers, R.L. (1966). A differential association-reinforcement theory of criminal behavior. *Social Problems, 14*, 128–147.

Chui, W.H., & Chan, H.C.O. (2012). An empirical investigation of social bonds and juvenile delinquency in Hong Kong. *Child Youth Care Forum, 41*, 371–386.

Clarke, R.V., & Cornish, D.B. (1985). Modeling offenders' decisions: A framework for research and policy. In M. Tonry & N. Morris (Eds.), *Crime and justice: A review of research* (Vol. 6). Chicago: University of Chicago Press.

Cohen, L.E., & Felson, M. (1979). Social change and crime rate trends: A routine activity approach. *American Sociological Review, 44*, 588–608.

Cornish, D.B., & Clarke, R.V. (1986). *The reasoning criminal: Rational choice perspectives on offending.* New York: Springer-Verlag.

Durkheim, E. (1965). *The divisions of labor in society* (G. Simpson, Trans.). New York: Free Press. (Original work published 1897)

Eck, J.E., & Clarke, R.V. (2003). *Classifying common police problems: A routine activity approach* (Crime Prevention Studies, Vol. 16, pp. 7–39). Monsey, NY: Criminal Justice Press.

Fox, K.A., Nobles, M.R., & Akers, R.L. (2011). Is stalking a learned phenomenon? An empirical test of social learning theory. *Journal of Criminal Justice, 39*(1), 39–47.

Fuchs, C. (2011). Web 2.0, presumption, and surveillance. *Surveillance & Society*, *8*(3), 288–309.

Garton, L., Haythornthwaite, C., & Wellman, B. (1997). Studying online social networks. *Journal of Computer-Mediated Communication*, *3*(1), 1–20.

Gottfredson, M.R., & Hirschi, T. (1990). *A general theory of crime*. Stanford, CA: Stanford University Press.

Grabosky, P. (2001). Virtual criminality: Old wine in new bottles? *Social & Legal Studies*, *10*, 243–249.

Grasmick, H.G., & Bursik, R.J. (1990). Conscience, significant others, and rational choice: Extending the deterrence model. *Law & Society*, *24*, 837–861.

Higgins, G.E. (2005). Can low self-control help with the understanding of the software piracy problem? *Deviant Behavior*, *26*, 1–24.

Higgins, G.E., Fell, B.D., & Wilson, A.L. (2006). Digital piracy: Assessing the contributions of an integrated self-control theory and social learning theory using structural equation modeling. *Criminal Justice Studies*, *19*, 3–22.

Higgins, G.E., & Makin, D.A. (2004a). Self-control, deviant peers, and software piracy. *Psychological Reports*, *95*, 921–931.

Higgins, G.E., & Makin, D.A. (2004b). Does social learning theory condition the effects of low self-control on college students' software piracy? *Journal of Economic Crime Management*, *2*, 1–22.

Higgins, G.E., Wolfe, S.E., & Marcum, C.D. (2008). Music piracy and neutralization: A preliminary trajectory analysis from short-term longitudinal data. *International Journal of Cyber Criminology*, *2*(2), 324–336.

Hindelang, M.J., Gottfredson, M.R., & Garofalo, J. (1978). *Victims of personal crime: An empirical foundation for a theory of personal victimization*. Cambridge, MA: Ballinger.

Hinduja, S. (2007). Neutralization theory and online software piracy: An empirical analysis. *Ethics and Information Technology*, *9*, 187–204.

Hirschi, T. (1969). *Causes of delinquency*. Berkeley: University of California Press.

Hirschi, T. (2004). Self-control and crime. In R.F. Baumeister & K.D. Vohs (Eds.), *Handbook of self-regulation: Research, theory, and applications* (pp. 537–552). New York: Guilford Press.

Holt, T.J., Burruss, G.W., & Bossler, A.M. (2010). Social learning and cyber-deviance: Examining the importance of a full social learning model in the virtual world. *Journal of Crime and Justice*, *33*(2), 31–61.

Holt, T., & Copes, H. (2010). Transferring subcultural knowledge on-line: Practices and beliefs of persistent digital pirates. *Deviant Behavior*, *31*, 625–654.

Ingram, J.R., & Hinduja, S. (2008). Neutralizing music piracy: An empirical examination. *Deviant Behavior*, *29*, 334–366.

Jaishankar, K., Halder, D., & Ramdoss, S. (2009). Pedophilia, pornography, and stalking: Analyzing child victimization on the Internet. In F. Schmalleger & M. Pittaro (Eds.), *Crimes of the Internet* (pp. 43–65). Upper Saddle River, NJ: Pearson Education.

Konty, M. (2005). Microanomie: The cognitive foundations of the relationship between anomie and deviance. *Criminology*, *43*, 107–131.

Kraska, P.B., & Brent, J.J. (2011). *Theorizing criminal justice: Eight essential orientations* (2nd ed.). Long Grove, IL: Waveland Press.

Kraska, P.B., & Neuman, W.L. (2008). *Criminal justice and criminology: Research methods*. Boston: Pearson.

Marcum, C.D. (2009). *Adolescent online victimization: A test of routine activities theory.* El Paso, TX: LFB Scholarly.

Maruna, S., & Copes, H. (2005). What have we learned from five decades of neutralization research? *Crime & Justice: An Annual Review of Research, 32,* 221–320.

McCarthy, B. (2002). New economics of sociological criminology. *Annual Review of Sociology, 38,* 417–442.

Moffitt, T. (1993). Adolescence-limited and life course persistent antisocial behavior: A developmental taxonomy. *Psychological Review, 100*(4), 674–701.

Merton, R.K. (1938). *Social theory and social structure.* New York: Free Press.

Morris, R.G., & Higgins, G.E. (2009). Neutralizing potential and self-reported digital piracy: A multitheoretical exploration among college undergraduates. *Criminal Justice Review, 34*(2), 173–195.

Nagin, D.S. (1998). Criminal deterrence research at the outset of the twenty-first century. *Crime and Justice, 23,* 1–42.

Nagin, D.S., & Pogarsky, G. (2001). Integrating celerity, impulsivity, and extralegal sanction threats into a model of general deterrence: Theory and evidence. *Criminology, 39*(4), 865–892.

Ngo, F.T., & Paternoster, R. (2011). Cybercrime victimization: An examination of individual and situational level factors. *International Journal of Cyber Criminology, 5*(1), 773–793.

Pogarsky, G. (2002). Identifying deterrable offenders: Implications for research on deterrence. *Justice Quarterly, 19*(3), 431–452.

Pratt, T.C., & Cullen, F.T. (2000). The empirical status of Gottfredson and Hirschi's general theory of crime: A meta-analysis. *Criminology, 38*(3), 931–964.

Pratt, T.C., Holtfreter, K., & Reisig, M.D. (2010). Routine online activity and Internet fraud targeting: Extending the generality of routine activity theory. *Journal of Research in Crime and Delinquency, 47,* 267–296.

Reyns, B.W., Henson, B., & Fisher, B.S. (2011). Being pursued online: Applying cyberlifestyle-routine activities theory to cyberstalking victimization. *Criminal Justice and Behavior, 38*(11), 1149–1169.

Sampson, R., & Laub, J. (1993). *Crime in the making: Pathways and turning points through life.* Cambridge, MA: Harvard University Press.

Sampson, R., & Laub, J. (2003). Life-course desisters? Trajectories of crime among delinquent boys followed to age 70. *Criminology, 41,* 301–339.

Sherizen, S. (1995). Can computer crime be deterred? *Security Journal, 6,* 177–181.

Skinner, W.F., & Fream, A.M. (1997). A social learning theory analysis of computer crime among college students. *Journal of Research in Crime and Delinquency, 34,* 495–518.

Steinfield, C., Ellison, N.B., & Lampe, C. (2008). Social capital, self-esteem, and use of online social network sites: A longitudinal analysis. *Journal of Applied Developmental Psychology, 29,* 434–445.

Steinmetz, K.F., & Tunnell, K.D. (2013). Under the pixelated Jolly Roger: A study of on-line pirates. *Deviant Behavior, 34*(1), 53–67.

Sykes, G., & Matza, D. (1957). Techniques of neutralization: A theory of delinquency. *American Sociological Review, 22,* 664–670.

Sutherland, E. (1947). *Principles of criminology.* Philadelphia: Lippincott.

Tewksbury, R. (2009). Qualitative versus quantitative methods: Understanding why qualitative methods are superior for criminology and criminal justice. *Journal of Theoretical and Philosophical Criminology, 1*, 38–58.

Thomas, D., & Loader, B. (2000). Introduction—Cybercrime: Law enforcement, security and surveillance in the information age. In D. Thomas & B. Loader (Eds.), *Cybercrime: Law enforcement, security and surveillance in the information age.* London: Routledge.

Tunnell, K.D. (1992). *Choosing crime: The criminal calculus of property offenders.* Chicago: Nelson-Hall Publishers.

Wall, D.S. (2001). *Cybercrimes and the Internet.* New York: Routledge.

Wall, T., & Monahan, T. (2011). Surveillance and violence from afar: The politics of drones and liminal security-scapes. *Theoretical Criminology, 15*(3), 239–254.

Williams, M. (2006). *Virtually criminal: Crime, deviance, and regulation online.* New York: Routledge.

Wolfe, S.E., Higgins, G.E., & Marcum, C.D. (2008). Deterrence and digital piracy: A preliminary examination of the role of viruses. *Social Science Computer Review*, 317–333.

Wright, R.T., & Decker, S. (1994). *Burglars on the job: Streetlife and residential break-ins.* Boston: Northeastern University Press.

Yar, M. (2005a). The novelty of 'cybercrime': An assessment in light of routine activity theory. *European Journal of Criminology, 2*(4), 407–427.

Yar, M. (2005b). The global 'epidemic' of movie 'piracy': Crime-wave or social construction? *Media Culture Society, 27*, 677–696.

Yar, M. (2006). *Cybercrime and society.* London: Sage.

SECTION II

Types of Social Networking Criminality

CHAPTER

Texting and Social Networks

Melissa L. Ricketts and Cynthia Koller

Shippensburg University

Contents

Evolution of Texting   51
Texting Deviance   51
   Spam Messaging   52
   Sexting   53
   Texting While Driving   57
Regulating, Investigating, and Sanctioning Criminal Communications   58
   Policing   61
Conclusion   63
Discussion Questions   64
Key Terms and Concepts   64
References   65

"Merry Christmas." This was the content of the first-ever short message service text sent via computer to a mobile phone in the United Kingdom in 1992 (Stern, 2012). Within five years, an estimated average of 1.2 million text messages were being sent each month in the United States; by

2012, this monthly average had grown to over 171 billion (CTIA, 2013). It is clear that the rapid diffusion of texting and other social media tools, such as iMessage, Instagram, Twitter, and Facebook, are reshaping the world as we know it in the 21st century. The ease of access to and use of these evolutionary modes of communication grants everyone, from children to senior citizens, virtually unrestricted mobile contact with others, with few physical or spatial barriers. By mid-year 2013 over 90% of American adults owned a cellular phone, up from 65% in 2004 (Pew Research Center, 2013). Although many of these owners do not partake in texting, and the majority of electronic media device use is arguably for generic and mundane personal, social, or business communication, there is a growing trend among individuals to utilize these tools in an illegal manner or to coordinate illegal activities.

The types of deviance being committed in the electronic world are not new varieties of crime. Identity theft, bullying, extortion, stalking, vandalism, trespassing, fraud, and conspiracy—to name a few—are activities that were coordinated and prevalent before criminals had access to instant messaging and social networking channels (Stonecypher, 2011). However, as indicated throughout this book, the introduction of these advancing communication channels into mainstream society presents new challenges for the prevention of victimization and the preservation of individual and public liberty and security. As most institutions of informal and formal social control (e.g., the family, schools, employers, law enforcement, and the courts) are struggling to manage these new predicaments, the issues presented by these contemporary technologies deserve closer inspection.

This first section of this chapter explores the evolution of texting as a computerized social networking tool and its impact on personal communications. The chapter then moves to an examination of how texting facilitates the planning and achievement of criminal goals and objectives. This section highlights some of the more common forms of texting deviance, including spam messaging, sexting, and texting while driving. The final section outlines the U.S. government's role in regulating cellular phone communications and the legislation and control of the illicit use of social communication technology. The importance of this type of review cannot be overstated; structured and extensive deviant networks are inherent in the criminal enterprise (FBI, 2013) and are fast becoming more commonplace in the electronic world; texting/social networking communication modes are fast becoming substantial variables in understanding this growing phenomenon of social networking criminality.

☐ Evolution of Texting

The evolution of text messaging over the past 20 years has been simply staggering. With a potential reach of more than 5 billion people across the globe and an impressive 98% of messages being opened and read, texting has grown to become the leading personal messaging service in the world, which is used by all demographics and age groups (Pew Research Center, 2013). Just a few years ago, to text someone involved a triple-tap format where you actually had to hit the keys multiple times for a letter to come up. Texting technology progressed to full keyboards, and more recently virtual keyboards, which are keyboards that actually appear on the device itself via touch mechanism. The newest evolution in texting is swipe technology, which can be used on more modern devices where you can simply swipe your finger across the screen in a continuous motion to create words, without lifting your finger. Swipe technology has doubled texting speed, with an average of 40 words per minute (Henry, 2011).

While text messages average around 190 bytes and 160 characters (Henry, 2011), and are not the most elaborate method of communication, this form of interaction is widely employed across age groups and cultures because of its simplicity, the conciseness and efficiency of relaying messages, and its compatibility with every mobile device. Six billion short message service (SMS) messages are sent every day in the United States (O'Grady, 2012), and over 2.2 trillion are sent a year (globally, 8.6 trillion text messages are sent each year) (O'Grady, 2012). Since the first text message was sent over 20 years ago, the mobile phone has undoubtedly enabled a truly networked society. But what remains constant, driving online and mobile communication, is people's strong desire to connect with peers anywhere, anytime; to stay in touch, express themselves, and share experiences—sometimes at the expense of others.

☐ Texting Deviance

Cellular phone texting and electronic social network communication channels provide countless individuals with opportunities to engage in virtually unregulated conversations with one another.

These conversations are not restricted to legitimate and pro-social activities, however, as criminals likewise use these same communication networks to facilitate their illegitimate and antisocial activities. For example, inmates of the Baltimore City Detention Center used smuggled cellphones to coordinate illegal transactions and communications within the center and with outside parties (FBI, 2013). The 2013 indictment of correctional officers and institutionalized gang members alleges text messages were utilized to inform inmates of pending shakedowns (cell searches) as well as to coordinate other criminal activities, including "drug trafficking, robbery, assault, extortion, bribery, witness retaliation, money laundering, and obstruction of justice" (FBI, 2013). The Baltimore case illustrates the growing problem with jail/prison contraband and how technology diminishes traditional institutional controls.

Advances in technology also provide expanded capabilities for offenders to engage in both simple and progressively more sophisticated crimes, including spam messaging, sexting, and texting while driving.

Spam Messaging

Unwanted telephone solicitations and email spam are irritants that phone and computer users are all too familiar with. But with the advent of text messaging, the problem with unsolicited communications has grown exponentially. The Federal Trade Commission (FTC) asserts:

> Text message spam is to your cellphone what email spam is to your personal computer. Both may try to get you to reveal personal information. Text message spam is a triple threat: It often uses the promise of free gifts or product offers to get you to reveal personal information; it can lead to unwanted charges on your cellphone bill; and it can slow cellphone performance. (FTC, 2013a)

By 2009, Americans received some 2.2 billion text messages that they identified as spam; by 2011 that had doubled to 4.5 billion (Oremus, 2012).

The latest wave of text scams is orchestrated by a sprawling network of mainly U.S.-based e-crooks and semilegal websites that use confusing privacy notices and fine-print consent forms to separate users from their personal and financial information. This practice, known as smishing, typically begins with a text that may invite recipients to test and keep an unreleased but popular name brand phone. The spam message will ask users to follow links that require the disclosure of personal information (e.g., name, date of birth, phone number, and mailing address) before they can claim their prize. A few clicks later, users are asked to enter their credit card number so they can be charged an $8.99 shipping fee. By the time users notice they never received their phone, the website will be gone, and their name, phone number, and credit card number will have entered the vast and lucrative underground market where such information is traded.

The reason behind the increase in cellphone spamming incidents can be attributed to the low cost for spammers (e.g., unlimited texting for a prepaid phone costs about $20 per month), and the yield of high rewards due to the ability to target millions of people. Take the following, for example:

> According to the FTC complaint, the defendant behind the operation, Phillip A. Flora, sent millions of text messages, pitching loan modification assistance, debt relief, and other services. In one 40-day period, Flora sent more than 5.5 million spam text messages, a "mind boggling" rate of about 85 per minute, every minute of every day, according to additional court documents filed by the agency. The FTC alleges that consumers lose money as a result of Flora's spam text messaging because many of them get stuck paying fees to their mobile carriers to receive the unwanted text messages. (FTC, 2013b)

The cost of receiving constant spam can add up quickly for the consumer, with typical fees ranging from 20 to 25 cents per received text (Fahlman, 2002). Smishing scams that solicit more personal information from cellphone users can cost unassuming victims substantially more, not to mention the time needed to recoup one's identity.

While perpetrators of cellphone spam and smishing schemes typically have financial motives, there are other types of criminal behavior facilitated by cellphone users that target the emotional and psychological well-being of their victims. With the relatively new ability to send messages, images, and videos through technology, people of all ages are taking advantage of this ability to connect socially to others. Unfortunately, it has also led to the evolution of potentially destructive behaviors such as sexting and texting while driving.

Sexting

The term *sexting* has been used in a range of ways, but it generally concerns the digital recording of naked, seminaked, sexually suggestive, or explicit images and their distribution by email, mobile phone messaging, or through the Internet on social network sites, such as Facebook, MySpace, and YouTube (Lee, Crofts, Salter, Milivojevic, & McGovern, 2013). Recent research indicates three main reasons that nude or seminude images are sent: (1) to initiate sexual activity between partners (i.e., boyfriend or girlfriend), (2) as an experimental phase of their sexuality prior to ever having sexual intercourse, and (3) as a way to enhance current sexual relationships (Lenhart, 2009). Sexting, while seemingly harmless for some, can lead to more dangerous behavior and can become an addictive behavior when used in excess. The recent misguided use of a cellphone by former New York Representative Anthony Weiner has turned the spotlight on adult sexting. NFL quarterback Brett Favre also experienced significant backlash for sending sexually explicit images in 2010. Both the Weiner and Favre fiascos demonstrate how the illicit use of technology can have negative personal, social, political, and professional consequences, even when the behavior is not prohibited by law.

Although typically perceived as a practice by teenagers and young adults in our society, the reality is that older adults, both single and married, routinely use text messaging to send provocative images and messages. A Pew Research Center's Internet and American Life Project survey found about 6% of adult cellphone owners admit to sending a sexually suggestive nude or nearly nude photo or video (Smith & Brenner, 2012). About 15% of cellphone owners said they have received a sexually suggestive message of someone they know on their phone. In addition, adults also admit to forwarding sexually suggestive photos or videos of someone who they know on their phone. While this behavior is generally legal for adults (but still risky), it is not legal for minors, and can have serious consequences.

While sexting does seem to occur among a notable minority of adolescents, there are no consistent and reliable findings at this time to estimate the true prevalence of the problem (Lounsbury, Mitchell, & Finkelhor, 2011). The literature suggests two overarching concerns: (1) that youth may be creating illegal child pornography, exposing them to possibly serious legal sanctions (see the case study in Box 4.1), and (2) youth may be jeopardizing futures by putting compromising, ineradicable images into cyberspace that could be available to potential employers, academic institutions, and family members. Sexting images may also provide a weapon for cyberbullies—bullies who torment their victims over digital channels.

Cyberbullying can instill fear in those who are its victims and is more of a problem than regular bullying in that it is not bound by face-to-face interactions; anyone can be a perpetrator or victim of cyberbullying nearly anywhere there is cellphone service (Pyzalski, 2012). The consequences of cyberbullying can be severe. In the past five years, at least two teenagers have killed themselves after suffering cyberbullying, which included the unauthorized sharing of their own sexually suggestive images (Lampe, 2013).

BOX 4.1 Stuebenville, Ohio, Juvenile Case

COLUMBUS, Ohio—Ohio Attorney General Mike DeWine gave the following statement at a news conference held after the verdicts were read in the Steubenville rape trial:

Good morning. I'm Ohio Attorney General Mike DeWine. First, let me make a comment about the verdict. A prosecutor's most important duty is to seek justice. I believe with these verdicts that justice has been done. However, this is not a happy time for anyone. Every rape is a tragedy. This is a tragedy. Before I explain what will happen next in our investigation, I think it is important to recap how and why my office got involved in this investigation and prosecution.

- On August 16, 2012, the Steubenville Police Department asked the Attorney General's Bureau of Criminal Investigation (BCI) to assist in processing the scene of a rape that occurred at a home in Wintersville, OH. Our agent immediately responded and processed the scene.

- On August 17, 2012, the Police Department contacted BCI again and asked for our assistance in analyzing cellphones collected from the main suspects in the rape investigation and to process other forensic evidence.

- On August 24, 2012, Jefferson County Prosecutor Jane Hanlin filed three charges against a juvenile—rape, kidnapping, and dissemination of nudity-oriented materials of a juvenile. On that same day, Prosecutor Hanlin also filed charges of rape and kidnapping against a second juvenile.

- On August 27, 2012, Prosecutor Hanlin moved the Court to bind the juveniles over to be treated as adults. On that same day, Prosecutor Hanlin formerly requested assistance from the Ohio Attorney General's office in the prosecution of the two juveniles. Thereafter, the Common Pleas Court appointed my office as the prosecutor in this matter. I then directed attorneys Marianne Hemmeter and Brian Deckert in our Special Prosecutions Section to handle the case.

(Continued)

BOX 4.1 Stuebenville, Ohio, Juvenile Case (Continued)

- On October 12, 2012, the juvenile court of Jefferson County held a probable cause hearing for the two juveniles. At that time, the Court determined that the two were and are amenable to rehabilitation in the juvenile court system and therefore denied the motion to try them as adults.

As this case evolved, I assembled a team of 15 Special Agents from BCI to determine if any other crimes were committed. I also assigned former Greene County Prosecutor and current Senior Advisor and Assistant Attorney General William Schenck to this team. As part of our investigation, BCI agents identified 43 individuals who attended at least one of the two parties. Investigators interviewed 27 of these individuals, while 16 refused to cooperate (giving various reasons). Investigators also interviewed the owners of the residence where one of the two parties occurred. Our investigators further interviewed the principal, superintendent, and 27 football coaches from Steubenville High School.

To date, investigators have completed a total of 56 interviews. Additionally, cybercrime specialists at BCI analyzed 13 phones. From those phones, investigators reviewed and analyzed 396,270 text messages; 308,586 photos/pictures; 940 video clips; 3,188 phone calls; and 16,422 contacts listed in phones.

Let me turn now to where we go from here. As I have indicated, we have been involved in an extensive investigation seeking to learn if any other individuals committed any crimes. While we have interviewed almost 60 individuals, 16 people refused to talk to our investigators. I have reached the conclusion that this investigation cannot be completed— that we cannot bring finality to this matter—without the convening of a Grand Jury. Therefore, I am asking the Jefferson County Common Pleas Court to convene a Grand Jury to meet on or about April 15, 2013. My prosecutors will present evidence to this Grand Jury for it to determine if other crimes have been committed. I anticipate numerous witnesses will be called to testify. The Grand Jury could meet for a number of days, and, I should point out, that the convening of a Grand Jury does not necessarily mean that indictments will be returned or that charges will be filed. However, indictments could be returned and charges could be filed. A Grand Jury is an investigative tool that is uniquely suited to ensure fairness and to complete this investigation. And this community needs assurance that no stone has been left unturned in our search for the truth.

BOX 4.1 Stuebenville, Ohio, Juvenile Case (Continued)

I would like to take a moment to talk—not just as Attorney General, but as a parent and grandparent. This has been particularly hard for the victim and her family. As I said already, any rape is a tragedy. But, it is even more of a tragedy when that victim is continually re-victimized in the social media. This community has suffered and been through a lot. This is a good community, with good people. I personally feel for this community and what the citizens have been through, and I know that it desperately needs to be able to put this matter behind it and begin to move forward. Everything that has happened in Steubenville has been very difficult—very, very sad—and very tragic. But let me be clear—this is not just a Steubenville problem. This is a societal problem.

What happened here is shocking, and it is appalling. But what's even more shocking and appalling is that crimes of sexual assault are occurring every Friday night and every Saturday night in big and small communities all across this country. And there comes a point, where we must say, "Enough! This has to stop!" Among some people, there seems to be an unbelievable casualness about rape and about sex. It is a cavalier attitude—a belief that somehow there isn't anything wrong with any of this. Rape is not a recreational activity. We, as a society, have an obligation do more to educate our young people about rape. They need to know it is a horrible crime of violence. And it is simply not okay.

Source: http://www.nbc4i.com/story/21664769/dewine-issues-statement-on-steubenville-rape-investigation.

Texting While Driving

In today's fast-paced high-tech community, many people have forgotten that driving is a tremendous responsibility. In recent years, distracted driving has changed with the development of the technology age. Along with traditional distracted behaviors, such as eating, drinking, and using the radio, drivers now have additional means of distraction in the form of mobile phones. In a 2011 study of high school drivers, Olsen, Shults, and Eaton (2013) found that nearly one-half of teenage drivers admit to texting while driving (TWD), and TWD was found to be closely associated with other risky driver behaviors (e.g., not wearing a seatbelt, driving under the influence of alcohol). Drivers of all ages assume they can handle TWD and remain safe; however, there are many dangers associated with this behavior. The National Highway Traffic Safety Administration

(NHTSA) estimates that drivers are over 20% more likely to have vehicle accidents when they are using an electronic device while they are operating a motor vehicle (NHTSA, 2010). Individuals who use electronic devices while operating a motor vehicle have difficulty staying mentally alert and are more likely to be distracted by a text-based conversation. This results in slower reflex response times, thus compromising a driver's ability to perceive or avoid danger, or to stop the motor vehicle when an accident is about to happen. The distraction caused by TWD only needs to be a few seconds long to become potentially deadly.

Current research suggests TWD is a growing trend that is quickly becoming one of the country's top killers (Governors Highway Safety Association, 2011; NHTSA, 2010; Ranney, 2008; Trombley, 2010). According to Wilms (2012), texting in cars and trucks causes over 3,000 deaths and 330,000 injuries per year. The NHTSA (2012), while alleging that driving a vehicle while texting is six times more dangerous than driving while intoxicated, further reports that TWD is the leading cause of accidents and deaths of teenage drivers. The NHTSA explains that sending or receiving a text takes a driver's eyes from the road for an average of 4.6 seconds, the equivalent—when traveling at 55 mph—of driving the length of an entire football field while blindfolded. Additionally, depending upon location, individuals can get into legal trouble for using handheld devices or sending messages while driving: "Text messaging is banned for all drivers in 41 states and the District of Columbia" (Insurance Institute for Highway Safety, 2013).

The need and desire to be in constant communication with others has left people vulnerable to spam, smishing, sexting, cyberbullying, and texting while driving. Consequently, many individuals have suffered physical, emotional, and psychological damages, or even loss of life. The studies and highly publicized incidents depicting the dangers of cellphones have created many concerns throughout the country. In response, there has been a debate over whether the government should (and to what degree) impose legal sanctions and regulate the use of cellphones.

☐ Regulating, Investigating, and Sanctioning Criminal Communications

It is beyond belief that when the Communications Act of 1934 was enacted during the Progressive New Deal era that U.S. President Franklin D. Roosevelt ever imagined, some 60 years later, technology would begin to advance to the point in which ordinary people could make calls and send messages to one another via portable wireless communication devices. The original act was designed to promote national security and consumer protections through federal regulatory oversight of existing and emerging commercial radio and wire communications systems, with the centralized authority for these tasks being delegated to the newly created Federal Communications Commission (Communications Act of 1934). Although the act clearly restricted the commission's authority to impede on First Amendment free speech rights, it did establish some communication parameters, such as "no person within the jurisdiction of the United States shall utter any obscene, indecent, or profane language by means of radio communication" (Sec. 326, Communications Act of 1934). The act also provided the federal government with wider investigative latitude (both at home and abroad) in its pursuit of national defense and security.

Changes were made to the original act legislation over the following decades, and again under the Uniting and Strengthening America by Providing Appropriate Tools Required to Intercept and Obstruct Terrorism (Patriot) Act of 2001. Of special note, the Patriot Act expanded the authority of law enforcement to monitor and intercept communications in the investigation of suspected domestic and international terrorism. For example, money laundering by criminal enterprises is a substantiated conduit for the funding of terrorist activities (International Monetary Fund, 2013); the ability to conduct surveillance into the communications (i.e., wire, oral, and electronic) of parties suspected of these activities was significantly increased through the Patriot Act. Although most communications among individuals do not rise to the level of terrorist or organized crime activity, it is demonstrated throughout this book that significant threats to the economic, emotional, or physical safety of the public can still be coordinated by individuals through the use of advancing technological devices and networks. How to legislate, deter, and respond to these varied activities is of considerable interest and concern to all components of the justice system. For example, local jurisdictions face communication control problems, such as during incidents precipitated by destructive flash mobs, or as evidenced in an attempt by the Bay Area Rapid Transit to disrupt a potential civil disturbance.

Legislating crime typically requires an informed dialogue and at least a general public consensus as to what constitutes deviant behavior. The advent of cellular and computer technology presents new opportunities to engage in this type of discourse, and the criminalization of sexting is the subject of one such contemporary debate. For instance, parents, school administrators, and the justice system continue to grapple with the applicability of the Child Pornography Prevention Act of 1996 (CPPA) to sexting (Herman, 2010). Although the CPPA addressed the contribution of technology to the proliferation of electronically distributed child pornography, it did not originally appreciate or compensate for the fact that minors would one day be so involved in the manufacture and dissemination of sexually explicit material, oftentimes of themselves.

Similarly, the Controlling the Assault of Nonsolicited Pornography and Marketing (CAN-SPAM) Act of 2003 also indirectly applies to sexting. One of the intents of the CAN-SPAM Act was to protect computer users from the unwanted receipt of pornographic content emails, but how is "possession" of child pornography interpreted with respect to the receipt of an unsolicited sext? Herman (2010) discusses this issue, noting that certain applications of the CPPA (i.e., Illinois Child Pornography Act) provide vague guidance as to understanding the voluntariness of possession of a sexually explicit photo of a minor. Depending on how someone interprets the legislation, teenagers who receive or forward sext messages could be subject to prosecution under multiple felony-level state and federal laws (Herman, 2010). As the dialogue continues, states have continued to revise sexting laws. For example, Pennsylvania's new legislation regulating teenage sexting demonstrates some improvement in that "the new law creates a tiered system for adjudicating sexting cases that differentiates between those who make bad decisions and those who have bad intentions" (CBS, 2013).

Without minimizing the severity of child pornography, Herman (2010, p. 192) contends, "A teenager's ability to snap a picture and send it in seconds without reflection gives rise to new legal issues for society and the legal community." Wood (2010) also expresses concerns with this conundrum, pointing out that "it is a venerable common law principle that the class of persons a statute is meant to protect should not be subject to punishment under the statute" (p. 171). Citing other questionable statutes and their interpretation, Wood argues for restraint in the discretionary application of the CPPA and similar legislation when processing criminal and civil sexting cases. Wood notes that changes are being made to sexting laws (e.g., felony classifications being downgraded to misdemeanors), but as long as society continues to struggle with privacy rights and teenage sexuality, it is unlikely that this debate will end anytime soon. McLaughlin (2010, p. 181) suggests statutes that are designed "to be flexible enough to consider the age of the actor, the age of the person depicted, the intent of the actor, the degree of publication and to protect a limited zone of teen sexual privacy." In the meantime, the justice system, including law enforcement agencies, will need to proceed with the laws and tools they have at their disposal.

Policing

Evolving computerized and mobile technologies are also changing the face of policing, from department and emergency communication systems, to the surveillance and investigation of criminal activity. Simply stated, the same tools that facilitate criminal communications also enable law enforcement to engage in new crime prevention efforts (International Association of Chiefs of Police, 2012), to locate, monitor, and apprehend offenders, and to prepare cases for prosecution. The International Association of Chiefs of Police (IACP) suggests a social media strategy in which law enforcement agencies can use a variety of tactics to "promote and enhance crime prevention efforts," including:

1. Posting crime prevention tips

2. Supporting neighborhood watch groups

3. Promoting crime prevention events

4. Developing a crime prevention blog

5. Hosting a crime prevention web chat

6. Creating a crime prevention podcast

These activities illustrate how capitalizing on the public's everyday use of texting and other social media tools provides "opportunities for law enforcement agencies to proactively reach out and connect with citizens" (IACP, 2012). Yet the ability of police officers to possess devices and engage in their own social networking (on and off duty) presents another set of concerns and consequences for effective police management. For instance, Schmidt (2010) notes that the court testimony of police officers is increasingly coming under scrutiny; countless officers have been discredited due to questionable personal social networking activities.

In addition to crime prevention and the management of officer communications, law enforcement officials are also exploiting social media to investigate crime, identify perpetrators, and build cases for prosecution. For example, reporting on the results of a March 2012 survey of 1,200 law enforcement officials, LexisNexis (2012) indicated:

The survey revealed that currently four out of five respondents use various social media platforms to assist in investigations and found agencies serving smaller populations and with fewer sworn personnel (<50) use social media more, while state agencies tend to use it less (71%) than local (82%) and federal (81%) agencies. The research also found that identifying people and locations; discovering criminal activity and locations; and gathering evidence are the top activities, while Facebook and YouTube are the most widely used platforms.

LexisNexis also reported that among the law enforcement respondents:

- 67% believe social media helps solve crimes more quickly.

- 87% of the time, search warrants utilizing social media to establish probable cause hold up in court when challenged, according to respondents.

- Close to 50% of respondents use social media at least weekly.

- Only 10% of respondents learned how to use social media for investigations through formal training given at the agency.

- Lack of access and familiarity are primary reasons for nonuse—70% are either unable to access social media during work hours or do not have enough background to use it.

As the comfort level with the latest technology grows among practitioners, its utility should show similar progression. A review of the Steubenville, Ohio, juvenile rape case (see Box 4.1) provides a good illustration of how the mining of information from cellphones (e.g., photos and text messages) can be used by law enforcement in the investigation of an alleged crime and in the identification of suspects. The evidence in this case was "pieced together from an analysis of nearly 350,000 text messages, plus hundreds of thousands of pictures, videos, chats and other exchanges of ultra-connected teens" (Wetzel, 2013). The evidence not only led to the conviction of the two primary offenders in 2013, but is also being used to determine if any charges are warranted against other individuals for failing to report the crime.

Sherer (2011) reports that texts and social media posts are fast becoming standard evidence in criminal and civil proceedings (e.g., contested divorces). For example,

A series of text messages discussing what appears to be plans for an armed robbery are expected to be used as evidence against three capital murder suspects in an upcoming Lauderdale Circuit Court trial. In a preliminary hearing, Florence police investigator Brian Perry read some of the texts recovered from cellphones that were being used by the suspects charged with the July shooting death of a Florence teenager. (Sherer, 2011)

Despite the enthusiasm and its increasing functionality, the use of advancing technology in the identification, apprehension, and prosecution of criminal offenders is not without substantial hurdles. As Murphy and Fontecilla (2013, p. 11) explain, "Social media evidence is the new frontier of criminal proceedings and it raises unique legal challenges, including issues of admissibility and a defendant's constitutional rights in material that social media companies maintain."

The Stored Communications Act (1986) enables electronic service providers to release noncontent information (e.g., names, addresses) and communication contents (e.g., emails) to a law enforcement agency if the contents suggest child abuse or appear to pertain to the commission of a crime. In the interests of domestic security, Fourth Amendment protections against unreasonable search and seizure may or may not apply, depending on the specific circumstances of a given case. Murphy and Fontecilla (2013) explain that the Stored Communications Act (SCA) and related legislation have recently come under fire in the courts, as they have failed to keep pace with the rapid advancements in social media capabilities. They argue that privacy concerns, ethical issues, and a defendant's right to present exculpatory evidence are all factors relating to the authentication and admissibility of evidence, and that "such evidence will likely continue to be the subject of vigorous disputes between parties that may mean the difference between ultimate guilt or innocence" (p. 25).

Burshnic (2012, p. 1264) likewise notes that Congress has failed to update the SCA to "conform to modern day innovations related to e-mail and cellphones," while the issues presented by social networking sites only compound the problem, particularly as they pertain to civil litigation. In sum, keeping up with technology will remain a challenge to the courts and the criminal justice system, as well as all relevant branches of federal, state, and local government.

☐ Conclusion

Cellphones and the Internet have helped individuals connect and learn from each other in ways that most of us never imagined. Today's mobile phone is a pervasive tool. It has become such an important aspect of a user's daily life that it has moved from being a mere "technological object" to a key "social object" (Ishii, 2006; Srivastava, 2005). Individuals are increasingly utilizing this technology to build social networks via the device's contact list. While the use of a mobile phone has yielded numerous benefits for its users, such as increasing social inclusion and connectedness (Mathews, 2004; Wei & Lo, 2006), not to mention increased feelings of safety and security, we have only begun to explore the benefits that these, and future technologies, will bring to our lives. However, the ever-advancing world of mobile technology has also provided new opportunities for criminal and deviant activities to emerge.

Social networking criminality is evidenced from the use of cellphones by incarcerated offenders to engage in further criminal activity, to the proliferation of illegal spam messaging, sexting, and texting while driving. Understanding and managing these evolving forms of texting deviance presents challenges to all components of government and the criminal justice system. Determining the line between acceptable and deviant behavior is not a new hurdle—yet as is the case with so many other phenomena, keeping up with advancing technology and its subsequent criminal applications is likely to remain a social priority.

☐ Discussion Questions

1. Discuss the intended and unintended impact that mobile technology had on the Steubenville rape case. How might this case impact future criminal investigations?

2. Do you agree that cellphone use (of any kind) should be banned while someone is driving? Why or why not?

☐ Key Terms and Concepts

CAN-SPAM Act

Sexting

Short message service (SMS)

Smishing

Spam

Stored Communications Act (SCA)

Texting

TWD

□ References

Burshnic, R. J. (2012). Applying the Stored Communication Act to the civil discovery of social networking sites. *Washington and Lee Law Review, 69*, 1259–1293.

CAN-SPAM Act of 2003. *Controlling the assault of non-solicited pornography and marketing.* Retrieved May 5, 2013, from http://uscode.house.gov/download/pls/15C103.txt

Carroll, J., Howard, S., Peck, J., & Murphy, J. (2007). From adoption to use: The process of appropriating a mobile phone. *Australasian Journal of Information Systems, 10*(2).

CBS. (2013, January 3). 2 Westmoreland Co. teens charged under new law regulating sexting. Retrieved from http://pittsburgh.cbslocal.com/2013/01/03/2-westmoreland-co-teens-charged-under-new-law-regulating-sexting

Child Pornography Prevention Act of 1996. 18 U.S.C. 2241, 2243, 2251, 2252, and 2256, Chapter 110 42 U.S.C. 2000aa. Retrieved from http://www.gpo.gov/fdsys/search/pagedetails.action?st=Child+Pornography+Prevention+Act+of+1996&granuleId=&packageId=BILLS-104hr4123ih

Communications Act of 1934. 47 U.S.C. § 151. Retrieved from http://www.criminalgovernment.com/docs/61StatL101/ComAct34.html

CTIA. (2013). U.S. wireless quick facts. Retrieved on May 4, 2013, from http://www.ctia.org/advocacy/research/index.cfm/AID/10323

Fahlman, S. (2002). Selling interrupt rights: A way to control unwanted e-mail and telephone calls [Technical forum]. *IBM Systems Journal, 41*(4), 759–766.

Federal Bureau of Investigation. (2013, April 23). Press release: Thirteen correctional officers among 25 black guerilla family gang members and associates indicted on federal racketeering charges. Retrieved on April 28, 2013, from http://www.fbi.gov/baltimore/press-releases/2013/thirteen-correctional-officers-among-25-black-guerilla-family-gang-members-and-associates-indicted-on-federal-racketeering-charges

Federal Communications Commission. (2013). *Consumer guide: Cramming—unauthorized, misleading, or deceptive charges placed on your telephone bill guide.* Washington, DC: Consumer and Governmental Affairs Bureau. Retrieved on April 27, 2013.

Federal Trade Commission. (2011). Press release: FTC asks court to shut down text messaging spammer. Retrieved from http://www.ftc.gov/opa/2011/02/loan.shtm

Federal Trade Commission. (2013a). Consumer information: Text message spam. Retrieved on April 27, 2013, from http://www.consumer.ftc.gov/articles/0350-text-message-spam

Federal Trade Commission. (2013b). Press release: FTC cracks down on senders of spam text messages promoting "free" gift cards. Retrieved from http://www.ftc.gov/opa/2013/03/textmessages.shtm

Governors Highway Safety Association. (2011). Distracted driving: What research shows and what states can do. Washington, DC: GHSA.

Hampton, K. N., Goulet, L. S., Rainie, L., & Purcell, K. (2011, June 16). Social networking sites and our lives: How people's trust, personal relationships, and civic and political involvement are connected to their use of social networking sites and other technologies. *Pew Internet & American Life Project.*

Henry, K. (2011). The latest evolution in text messaging. Retrieved from http://www.heartlandconnection.com/news/story.aspx?id=585845#.Ugzz6ojD9dg

Herman, J. D. (2010). Sexting: It's no joke, it's a crime. *Illinois Bar Journal, 98,* 4, 192.

Insurance Institute for Highway Safety. (2013). *Cellphone and texting laws.* Retrieved on August 14, 2013, from http://www.iihs.org/laws/maptextingbans.aspx

International Association of Chiefs of Police. (2012). Social media and crime prevention fact sheet.

International Monetary Fund. (2013, March 31). *Factsheet: The IMF and the fight against money laundering and the financing of terrorism.* Retrieved from http://www.imf.org/external/np/exr/facts/aml.htm

Ishii, K. (2006). Implications of mobility: The uses of personal communication media in everyday life. *Journal of Communication, 56*(2), 346–365.

Lampe, J. R. (2013). A victimless sex crime: The case for decriminalizing consensual teen sexting. *University of Michigan Journal of Law Reform, 46,* 703–737.

Lee, M., Crofts, T., Salter, M., Milivojevic, S., & McGovern, A. (2013). "Let's get sexting": Risk, power, sex, and criminalization in the moral domain. *International Journal for Crime, Justice and Social Democracy, 2*(1), 35–49.

Lenhart, A. (2009). Teens and sexting: How and why minor teens are sending sexually suggestive nude or nearly nude images via text messaging. *Pew Internet & American Life Project.* Retrieved from http://www.pewinternet.org/Reports/2009/Teens-and-Sexting.aspx

Lenhart, A., Madden, M., Smith, A., Purcell, K., Zickuhr, K., & Rainie, L. (2011, November 9). Teens, kindness and cruelty on social networks. *Pew Internet & American Life Project.*

LexisNexis. (2013). Press release: Role of social media in law enforcement significant and growing. Retrieved May 5, 2013, from http://www.lexisnexis.com/media/press-release.aspx?id=1342623085481181

Lounsbury, K., Mitchell, K. J., & Finkelhor, D. (2011). The true prevalence of "sexting." Crimes Against Children Research Center (Sexting Fact Sheet, 4/29/11). Durham, NH: University of New Hampshire.

Mathews, R. (2004). The psychosocial aspects of mobile phone use amongst adolescents. *InPsych, 26*(6), 16–19.

McLaughlin, J. H. (2010) Crime and punishment: Teen sexting in context. *Penn State Law Review, 115,* 135.

Murphy, J. P., & Fontecilla, A. (2013). Social media evidence in government investigations and criminal proceedings: A frontier of new legal issues. *Richmond Journal of Law and Technology, 19*(3), 1–30.

nbc4i.com. (2013). *DeWine issues statement on Steubenville rape investigation.* Retrieved April 27, 2013, from http://www.nbc4i.com/story/21664769/dewine-issues-statement-on-steubenville-rape-investigation

National Highway Traffic Safety Administration. (2010, September). Distracted driving 2009, Traffic Safety Facts, research note. DOT HS 811 379. Washington, DC: U.S. Department of Transportation.

National Highway Traffic Safety Administration. (2012). Blueprint for ending distracted driving. DOT HS 811 629. Washington, DC: U.S. Department of Transportation.

O'Grady, M. (2012). SMS usage remains strong in the US: 6 billion SMS messages are sent each day. Retrieved from http://blogs.forrester.com/michael_ogrady/12-06-19-sms_usage_remains_strong_in_the_us_6_billion_sms_messages_are_sent_each_day

O'Keeffe, G. S., Clarke-Pearson, K., & Council on Communications and Media. (2011). The impact of social media on children, adolescents, and families. *Pediatrics, 127,* 800. [Originally published online; March 28, 2011: DOI: 10.1542/peds.2011-0054.]

Olsen, E. O., Shults, R. A., & Eaton, D. K. (2013). Texting while driving and other risky behaviors among US high school students. *Pediatrics, 131*(6); e1708-e1715.

Oremus, W. (2012). Hell phone: Is there any way to stop the scourge of text message spam? Retrieved from http://www.slate.com/articles/technology/technology/2012/04/how_to_stop_text_spam_why_cellphone_spam_is_on_the_rise_and_what_you_can_do_about_it_.html

Pew Research Center. (2013). Cell phone ownership hits 91% of adults. Retrieved August 14, 2013, from http://www.pewresearch.org/fact-tank/2013/06/06/cell-phone-ownership-hits-91-of-adults

Pyżalski, J. (2012). From cyberbullying to electronic aggression: Typology of the phenomenon. *Emotional and Behavioural Difficulties, 17*(3–4), 305–317.

Ranney, T. A. (2008). *Driver distraction: A review of the current state of knowledge.* Technical report DOT HS 810 787. Washington, DC: National Highway Traffic Safety Administration, U.S. Department of Transportation.

Schmidt, W. W. (2010). Online networking, texting and blogging by peace officers: Part one—Impeachment, policy & First Amendment issues. *Americans for Effective Law Enforcement (AELE) Monthly Law Journal,* 201. [ISSN 1935-0007.]

Sherer, D. (2011). Texting, social media more common in trials. *Times Daily.* Retrieved from http://timesdaily.com/stories/Texting-social-media-more-common-in-trials,184460

Smith, A., & Brenner, J. (2012, May 31). Twitter use 2012. *Pew Internet & American Life Project.*

Srivastava, L. (2005). Mobile phones and the evolution of social behaviour. *Behaviour & Information Technology, 24*(2), 111–129.

Stern, J. (2012). Happy 20th birthday, text message, but you're past your prime. Retrieved May 4, 2013, from ABC News: http://abcnews.go.com/Technology/happy-20th-birthday-text-message-now-past-prime/story?id=17864096#.UYVdeh7D-nA

Stonecypher, L. (2011). Definition of cybercrime. What is cybercrime? Different types of illegal Internet activities. Retrieved from http://www.brighthub.com/internet/security-privacy/articles/3435.aspx

Stored Communication Act. (1986). 18 U.S.C. §§ 2701-2712: Stored wire and electronic communications and transactional records access. Retrieved from http://www.gpo.gov/fdsys/pkg/USCODE-2010-title18/html/USCODE-2010-title18-partI-chap121.htm

Trombley, D. (2010, March). Understanding the distracted brain. Why driving while using hands-free cell phones is risky behavior. White Paper. *National Safety Council.*

Wei, R., & Lo, V. H. (2006). Staying connected while on the move: Cell phone use and social connectedness. *New Media & Society, 8*(1), 53–72.

Wilms, T. (2012, September 18). It is time for A "parental control, no texting while driving" phone. *Forbes Business.*

Wood, R. H. (2010). The failure of sexting criminalization: A plea for the exercise of prosecutorial restraint. *Michigan Telecommunications and Technology Law Review, 16,*151–178.

Wetzel, D. (2013). Steubenville suspect's text messages paint disturbing picture of night of alleged rape. *Yahoo! Sports.* Retrieved on March 23, 2013, from http://sports.yahoo.com/news/highschool--steubenville-suspects--text-messages-paint-disturbing-picture-of-night-of-alleged-rape--according-to-prosecutors-053236470.html

Williams, A. F., Tefft, B. C., & Grabowski, J. G. (2012.) Graduated driver licensing research, 2010–present. *Journal of Safety Research, 43*(3), 195–203.

Identity Theft and Social Networks

Jordana N. Navarro

Tennessee Technological University

Jana L. Jasinski

University of Central Florida

Contents

Attractive Targets: Why Identity Thieves Like Social Networks   72
Types of Identity Theft   73
    Financially Motivated Identity Theft   73
    Other Types of Identity Theft   74
Tactics Utilized by Identity Thieves Online   75
    Aggregating Publicly Available Data   75
    Malicious Software   76
    Phishing and Spear-Phishing   79
    Social Engineering, Evil Twin Attacks, and Profile Squatting   81
Selling Victims Out: Underground Identity Theft Market   83
Emerging Trends in Online Identity Theft   84
Conclusion   85
References   86

Identity theft is frequently referred to as one of the fastest growing crimes in the United States (Aïmeur & Schonfeld, 2011; Brody, Mulig, & Kimball, 2007; Hoofnagle, 2007; Lynch, 2005; Slosarik, 2002). In 2012, the U.S. Federal Trade Commission (FTC) received more than 2 million complaints, and approximately one in five of those complaints related to identity theft (Small, 2013). In addition, as of September 30, 2012, the U.S. Internal Revenue Service (IRS) had already identified more than 600,000 incidents of identity theft relating to tax administration alone (White, 2012). Prohibited by the Identity Theft and Assumption Deterrence Act, identity theft is defined as

> knowingly transferring or using, without lawful authority, a means of identification of another person with the intent to commit, or aid or abet, any unlawful activity that constitutes a violation of Federal law or that constitutes a felony under any applicable State or local law. (Federal Trade Commission, 1998)

Despite widespread recognition of identity theft as a serious social problem affecting consumers, businesses, and governments, there is a dearth of information on the actual scope of the problem (Allison, Schuck, & Lersch, 2005; Hoofnagle, 2007; May & Headley, 2004; Newman & McNally, 2005; Slosarik, 2002). Determining the prevalence of identity theft is difficult for the following reasons (Hoofnagle, 2007; May & Headley, 2004; Newman & McNally, 2005; Stana, 2002):

- Victims may not learn of thefts until months later.

- Victims may decline to report identity thefts to law enforcement.

- Victims may report thefts to other agencies instead of law enforcement (i.e., banks, credit card companies).

- Thefts may span multiple jurisdictions, resulting in confusion regarding investigation responsibility.

- Due to the complexity of these crimes, an identity theft may only be part of the possible countless other offenses a perpetrator engaged in.

Accounting for these barriers, the Bureau of Justice Statistics (BJS) reported that approximately 8.6 million households experienced an identity theft in 2010, representing an increase of 5.5% from 2005 data (Langton, 2011). Victim characteristics derived from 2005 and 2010 data indicate that individuals 65 years old or older were less likely to suffer identity theft than households headed by younger individuals (Langton, 2011). However, risk of identity theft to non-Hispanic Caucasian and Asian heads of household increased between the two years (Langton, 2011). Finally, risk of identity theft increased among households with an income of $75,000 or more and among households that did not disclose income (Langton, 2011). These data indicate victims of identity theft suffered a total financial loss of approximately $13.3 billion in 2010 (Langton, 2011). Monetary cost is only part of the damage, though; evidence suggests victims experience extensive nonmonetary damages as well (Hoofnagle, 2007; May & Headley, 2004; Newman & McNally, 2005; Lynch, 2005; Sharp, Shreve-Neiger, Fremouw, Kane, & Hutton, 2004; Slosarik, 2002).

According to May and Headley (2004), an identity theft victim spends an average of 200 hours trying to repair the damage caused by the violation. These hours are spent contacting banking institutions, credit bureaus, and other vendors; copying documents; obtaining legal assistance; and spending hours on the phone to all relevant parties (May & Headley, 2004). In addition, victims of identity theft may encounter additional barriers to obtaining employment in the forms of destroyed credit (Hoofnagle, 2007) or criminal histories for offenses the perpetrator engaged in using the stolen information (Lynch, 2005; Newman & McNally, 2005). Taking into account the extensiveness of these consequences, it is not surprising that research suggests victims also experience psychological and physical ramifications of identity theft.

One study found within two weeks of learning of an identity theft, victims felt angry and irritable, fearful and anxious, and frustrated (Sharp et al., 2004). At 26 weeks following the victimization, victims were angry, desperate, and distressed. Moreover, victims also experienced physical reactions such as anxiety, appetite problems, headaches, sleep problems, and weight changes (Sharp et al., 2004). Although this chapter is primarily concerned with identity thefts of individual victims, businesses and governments also bear direct costs (i.e., resulting from the actual fraud) and indirect costs (i.e., resulting from conducting investigations) for these offenses in excess of millions of dollars annually (Hoofnagle, 2007; Lynch, 2005; May & Headley, 2004; Newman & McNally, 2005; The President's Identity Theft Task Force, 2007).

Less is known about perpetrators of identity theft, and what information is known can be largely inconsistent across studies. For example, while some evidence suggests African American females comprise a large proportion of offenders (Allison et al., 2005), other research indicates perpetrators are from a variety of backgrounds (Aïmeur & Schonfeld, 2011). Research has shown that perpetrators also vary in age, typically operate independently, and often have no prior criminal background

(Aïmeur & Schonfeld, 2011; The President's Identity Theft Task Force, 2007). However, identity theft rings operated by formal organizations—such as the Hell's Angels—are also known to exist (May & Headley, 2004; Newman & McNally, 2005; The President's Identity Theft Task Force, 2007). Finally, although some research has found that victims may not know perpetrators (Allison et al., 2005), other evidence indicates that it is not uncommon for the victim and perpetrator to indeed be familiar with each other (Finn & Banach, 2000; Newman & McNally, 2005; The President's Identity Theft Task Force, 2007). According to Neman and McNally (2005), if the victim and perpetrator are known to each other, the most frequently reported relationship is through a familial association.

Far from a novel crime, some suggest the rapid advancement of technology, particularly the rise in popularity of social networks, has exacerbated the identity theft problem by providing a rich setting for criminals (Weir, Toolan, & Smeed, 2011). This chapter will explore the aforementioned topic in detail by first providing an overview of social network characteristics that make these cyberspace "hangouts" attractive targets for identity thieves. Discussion will then focus on different forms of identity theft, and how identity thieves exploit social networks to steal personal information. Finally, concluding discussion will provide information on emerging methods of identity theft within social networks.

☐ Attractive Targets: Why Identity Thieves Like Social Networks

Social networks are online social structures comprised of nodes representing people and organizations that are interconnected through business relationships, familial background, friendships, general interests, and shared values or visions (Bilge, Strufe, Balzarotti, & Kirda, 2009). Since bursting onto the technological scene, social networks have grown in popularity at an exceedingly rapid pace and now constitute some of the largest databases in the world (Aïmeur & Schonfeld, 2011; Bilge et al., 2009; Debatin, Lovejoy, Horn, & Hughes, 2009). For example, although social network giant Facebook was established in 2004, as of 2013 the site boasts more than a billion monthly active users (Facebook, 2013). This growth in popularity is likely due to the substantial benefits of social networks that are free to users: the ability to facilitate instantaneous access to long-lost friends, loved ones, and professional acquaintances regardless of geographic boundary (Bilge et al., 2009).

Private individuals are not the only ones increasingly utilizing social networks; companies also heavily utilize social networks for advertising purposes (Timm & Perez, 2010). For example, MySpace and Facebook generated more than $300 million in advertising revenue in 2006 alone (Timm & Perez, 2010). The popularity of social network sites among individuals and companies is one of the primary reasons why they are prone to security threats (Sood & Enbody, 2011). According to Timm and Perez (2010), social network sites provide access to millions of potential victims and plenty of tactics to evade detection. Moreover, because security and privacy controls are generally not a top priority for developers, safeguards against attacks are relatively weak (Aïmeur & Schonfeld, 2011; Al Hasib, 2009; Bilge et al., 2009).

While more attention has been placed on social network privacy controls as of late (see, for example, Arthur, 2012), ownership to protect oneself is still largely the responsibility of individual users. This burden of responsibility may be unduly placed, as research suggests that social network users are not fully aware of how their profile information is accessed or shared by others, including search engines, or knowledgeable about general security awareness (Al Hasib, 2009; Aïmeur & Schonfeld, 2011; Bilge et al., 2009). As a result, the convergence of these three factors—motivated offenders, suitable targets, and a general lack of safeguards—produces online environments where identity theft is relatively inexpensive to commit and the chances of arrest are significantly lower than for other types of crimes (Lynch, 2005).

☐ Types of Identity Theft

Although identity theft victims primarily suffer financial loss (Lynch, 2005), victims may be targeted in order to damage reputations or destroy brands (Aïmeur & Schonfeld, 2011; Al Hasib, 2009). Victims may also be targeted as a means to acquire access to health services, employment, or evade detection by law enforcement (May & Headley, 2004; Sterritt, 2011; The President's Identity Theft Task Force, 2007). Arguably, in some cases, motivations may be complex and multifaceted. For example, a perpetrator may target a particular victim to not only cause financial ruin, but also destroy the victim personally.

Financially Motivated Identity Theft

Two of the most common types of financially driven identity theft are the creation of new accounts and account takeovers (Hoofnagle, 2007; The President's Identity Theft Task Force, 2007; Vacca, 2003). The former type entails perpetrators utilizing stolen personal information to obtain access to a plethora of services, including but not limited to credit cards, mortgages, phone accounts, and utility accounts (Acquisti & Gross, 2009a; Hoofnagle, 2007; The President's Identity Theft Task Force, 2007; Vacca, 2003). In contrast, an account takeover entails perpetrators acquiring security credentials in order to assume control over their victims' financial accounts for the purposes of stealing funds and making illegal transactions (Hoofnagle, 2007; Sharp et al., 2004). Upon obtaining access, perpetrators also acquire the ability to change credentials in order to prevent victims from accessing their own accounts (Timm & Perez, 2010).

According to May and Headley (2004), financially driven identity theft has become a booming business coordinated by organized international networks of thieves targeting large numbers of victims in order to steal as much capital as possible. Some of these organizations identified include the Hell's Angels, Mara Salvatrucha (MS-13), and foreign groups based overseas (Newman & McNally, 2005; The President's Identity Theft Task Force, 2007). Particularly unsettling is the fact that most victims do not learn of the theft until potentially years later (Slosarik, 2002) or after they are denied credit (The President's Identity Theft Task Force, 2007). This lag in awareness is likely due to the common practice of changing victims' mailing addresses to prolong detection, among others (May & Headley, 2004).

Other Types of Identity Theft

Perpetrators may engage in identity theft for several other nefarious purposes (Aïmeur & Schonfeld, 2011). For example, one such purpose is to acquire access to services in order to assimilate into society (Acquisti & Gross, 2009a; Aïmeur & Schonfeld, 2011; The President's Identity Theft Task Force, 2007). Access to services could entail using stolen information to obtain medical services (or make false claims for medical care) and to obtain passports in order to secure employment (Aïmeur & Schonfeld, 2011; The President's Identity Theft Task Force, 2007). Perpetrators may also engage in identity theft in order to participate in crimes under the guise of another individual or to evade detection by law enforcement altogether by masquerading as someone else (Aïmeur & Schonfeld, 2011; Lynch, 2005; Newman & McNally, 2005). Finally, perpetrators may engage in identity theft in order to personally harm victims by destroying reputations (Timm & Perez, 2010). After providing a brief overview of the various types of identity theft, the following discussion focuses on how these crimes are conducted online and within social network sites—often with unsettling ease (Slosarik, 2002).

☐ Tactics Utilized by Identity Thieves Online

The advancement of technology—particularly the creation of online social networks—has created environments where identity theft is substantially easier to commit with significantly less risk (Lynch, 2005; Slosarik, 2002). In the following sections, several of the most common methods utilized today are discussed. These methods include relatively simple techniques (i.e., aggregation of publicly available data, evil twin attacks) and more complex high-tech procedures (i.e., malware, phishing attacks). Because perpetrators are increasingly using social networks to engage in identity theft, the following discussion will also include examples of how the aforementioned methods occur within these online communities.

Aggregating Publicly Available Data

While researchers have identified several well-known high-tech and low-tech methods utilized by identity thieves, one mid-tech method also utilized simply involves the aggregation of publicly available online data using a computer and widely available search engines or social network databases (Aïmeur & Schonfeld, 2011; Allison et al., 2005; Lynch, 2005; The President's Identity Theft Task Force, 2007; Timm & Perez, 2010). According to Aïmeur and Schonfeld (2011), Internet users are largely unaware of the amount of personal information they disclose online, which is then accessed by search engines, social network sites, and other online services. Even fewer users are aware that these data can easily be aggregated and linked together in order to steal identities (Aïmeur & Schonfeld, 2011; Marshall & Tompsett, 2005).

One particularly infamous case of identity theft through aggregation of publicly available data occurred less than five years ago. In 2010, a 20-year-old college student successfully hacked into Sarah Palin's Yahoo email account by resetting her password using only publicly available online information (Aïmeur & Schonfeld, 2011; Lehrman, 2010). In another widely discussed case, Herbert Thompson (a professor and software developer) was able to successfully obtain access to an acquaintance's bank account in less than an hour by utilizing only publicly available online information (Aïmeur & Schonfeld, 2011; Thompson, 2008). Adding to this alarm, relatively recent research has uncovered that

Social Security numbers can be successfully predicted from information frequently posted online and on social network profiles.

The importance of safeguarding Social Security numbers cannot be understated, as identity thieves can completely decimate victims' personal and financial lives by merely knowing these authentication numbers (Acquisti & Gross, 2009a, 2009b; Slosarik, 2002). Therefore, given this importance, Acquisti and Gross (2009b) recently evaluated whether Social Security numbers could be predicted from publicly available information regarding date of birth and hometown—two pieces of information also included on social network profiles (Gross & Acquisti, 2005). After taking into account the standard formatting of Social Security numbers,* the scholars were able to successfully predict—on first attempt—the partial Social Security numbers for 7% of the individuals born nationwide from 1973 to 1988 whose information resided within the Death Master File (DMF) database maintained by the Social Security Administration. Moreover, the success rate increased to 44% for individuals born after 1988 (Acquisti & Gross, 2009b). Given the potential risks of overexposing one's personal information, Thompson (2008) cautions Internet users to "think first, post later." Thompson's advice is particularly important for social network users, as these sites are becoming frequent conduits to infect users with malicious software, otherwise referred to as malware (Hunter, 2008).

Malicious Software

The advancement of the Internet has led to identity thieves utilizing increasingly sophisticated methods to steal personal information, such as the creation and dissemination of malware (Aïmeur & Schonfeld, 2011; Bilge et al., 2009; Emigh, 2006; Jaishankar, 2008; Newman, 2006; Sood & Enbody, 2011). The term *malware* defines a malicious type of software that performs an undesirable function to the user (Emigh, 2006; Timm & Perez, 2010). Several of the most common categories of malware include crimeware, spyware, adware, browser hijackers, downloaders, toolbars, and dialers (Emigh, 2006; Timm & Perez, 2010). Although all

---

* According to Acquisti and Gross (2009b), the construction of Social Security numbers follows a relatively standard format. The first three numbers, referred to as the area number, correspond to the zip code of the mailing address included on the original application for the identifier (Acquisti & Gross, 2009b). The two next digits are referred to as the group number and follow a precise and nonconsecutive order between 01 and 99 (Acquisti & Gross, 2009b). Finally, the serial number is the last set of four digits that are assigned consecutively from 0001 to 9999 (Acquisti & Gross, 2009b).

types of malware are undesirable, crimeware and spyware are particularly important for the problem of identity theft (Emigh, 2006).

Crimeware broadly defines any type of malware designed to facilitate an illegal activity, such as stealing personal information (Emigh, 2006; Timm & Perez, 2010). Relatedly, spyware broadly defines any type of malware designed to secretly collect information about users, which then may also be used to engage in identity theft (Timm & Perez, 2010). Specific types of malware include the following: Trojan horses, backdoors, keyloggers, screen loggers, and worms (Aïmeur & Schonfeld, 2011; Emigh, 2006; Newman, 2006; The President's Identity Theft Task Force, 2007; Timm & Perez, 2010). Although the umbrella term *malware* is used to describe any type of malicious software, each particular program functions slightly differently.

A widely recognized form of malware is a Trojan horse. A Trojan horse conceals itself by appearing to be legitimate software, but actually provides unauthorized access to a computer (Newman, 2006; Timm & Perez, 2010). Similarly, backdoor malware facilitates access to a computer system by specifically bypassing normal authentication procedures (Timm & Perez, 2010). Keyloggers and screen loggers are types of malware designed to record either keystrokes or screen shots of confidential information—such as usernames and passwords—and send this information back to a storage location (Aïmeur & Schonfeld, 2011; Timm & Perez, 2010). Finally, worms are an infectious type of malware that can rapidly propagate—without assistance from users—to compromise the security of many other machines (Emigh, 2006; Lehrman, 2010; Newman, 2006; Sood & Enbody, 2011; Timm & Perez, 2010).

According to Emigh (2006), not only can malware be used to collect sensitive information about victims, but it can also be utilized to gather information about each victim's colleagues and acquaintances. Moreover, because malware software often appears to perform legitimate functions (e.g., appear as an update to Adobe Flash), victims may not realize their information has been stolen for some time. While all forms of malware pose dangers to users, worms are particularly vicious within social networks and are becoming a frequently utilized method by identity thieves to steal personal information (Bilge et al., 2009; Emigh, 2006; Jaishankar, 2008; Lehrman, 2010; Newman, 2006; The President's Identity Theft Task Force, 2007; Thomas & Nicol, 2010).

Evidence suggests that social network users place too much implicit trust in their online interactions, thereby exposing themselves to cybercriminals seeking to exploit that confidence (Bilge et al., 2009; Thomas & Nicol, 2010; Timm & Perez, 2010). One method of exploitation increasing in frequency is the utilization of social network sites to distribute destructive worms, such as the infamous Koobface program. First appearing in 2008, Koobface (an anagram for Facebook) used social network users' contact lists to replicate itself at a rapid pace, ultimately compromising victims' information (Lehrman, 2010; Thomas & Nicol, 2010; Timm & Perez, 2010).

The start of Koobface's infection began when unsuspecting social network users were sent a communication from seemingly trusted sources that contained a hyperlink to a third-party site (Thomas & Nicol, 2010). Although appearing as legitimate contacts, these communications may have come from other compromised accounts or forged accounts automatically created by Koobface (Thomas & Nicol, 2010). However, because the messages appeared to be from legitimate sources, naive users followed the provided navigations, received a prompt to update a legitimate piece of software (Adobe Flash in this case), and were duped into installing the Koobface worm on their own machines (Lehrman, 2010; Thomas & Nicol, 2010). As a result of installing the malicious software, victims unknowingly compromised their personal information as well as granted perpetrators unauthorized access to their social network accounts to further spread the Koobface worm (Lehrman, 2010; Thomas & Nicol, 2010).

In their relatively recent investigation of Koobface, Thomas and Nicol (2010) discovered the worm was sent to over 213,000 social network users, netting over 157,000 clicks (i.e., number of times the malicious link was accessed) for perpetrators. Moreover, while the Koobface worm targeted Facebook users, similarly constructed and equally destructive worms have also surfaced on other social network sites, like MySpace and Twitter (Sanzgiri, Joyce, & Upadhyaya, 2011; Sood & Enbody, 2011). Despite the infamy of these worms and risks of malware in general, evidence indicates that the average social network user still does not have a holistic understanding of how to protect himself or herself from attacks.

Relatively recent studies support the notion that social network users may be continuing to place themselves in vulnerable positions. For example, research conducted by Debatin et al. (2009) found that while half of the respondents noted they increased their social network account privacy settings, a relative majority also had over 300 friends with varying degrees of connection to the user. In addition, over 90% of respondents included their full real name, gender, date of birth, and hometown on their profiles; a comparable percentage also included information relating to friends, family members, and pets as well (Debatin et al., 2009). Taking into account that security questions may reference the aforementioned information (i.e., a pet's name), the availability of this information in an online forum can easily be used to compromise users' identities. Related to the problem of malware, another method that identity thieves utilize to acquire victims' personal information is through conducting phishing frauds (Brody et al., 2007).

Phishing and Spear-Phishing

The term *phishing* stems from the word *fishing* because it involves a process of casting many emails—or messages within a social network site—in an attempt to lure and hook unwary victims (Brody et al., 2007; Jagatic, Johnson, Jakobsson, Menczer, 2007; Jaishankar, 2008; Lynch, 2005; Newman & McNally, 2005). In contrast to the previous section, phishing scams are essentially online cons meant to dupe victims into *voluntarily disclosing* personal information (Aïmeur & Schonfeld, 2011; Brody et al., 2007; Hoofnagle, 2007; Hunter, 2008; Jagatic et al., 2007; Jaishankar, 2008; Lynch, 2005; Timm & Perez, 2010). In addition to indiscriminate phishing scams, a more lethal form of this con—referred to as spear-phishing—is gaining increasing attention from cybersecurity guardians (Brody et al., 2007). Considered a hybrid form of phishing, spear-phishing targets specific victims instead of a broad audience (Brody et al., 2007). As a result, spear-phishing is more difficult to detect, because the communication appears to legitimate (Brody et al., 2007).

Although phishing scams continue to evolve with technology, research has established a fairly predictable pattern associated with these assaults. The process begins with phishers sending a message to victims luring them to a seemingly legitimate website; however, the website provided is actually spoofed or malicious (Aïmeur & Schonfeld, 2011; Brody et al., 2007; Hoofnagle, 2007; Hunter, 2008; Jagatic et al., 2007; Lynch, 2005; Timm & Perez, 2010). In order to encourage users to navigate to the spoofed site, phishing messages typically employ a scare tactic and stress an immediate action is necessary from the target (Lynch, 2005; Timm & Perez, 2010). For example, a phisher may send an email notifying targets that their PayPal accounts have been compromised and requesting they reset their security credentials immediately (Newman, 2006). However, instead of linking to the legitimate PayPal site, a malicious website address is noted instead (Newman, 2006). An example of this trick is the difference between the legitimate website address for PayPal (www.paypal.com) and a potential spoofed website address (www.paypa1.com) that has the number one noted in place of the lowercase *l* (Newman, 2006). Targets that fall for the deception and click the malicious link are then navigated to the bogus website created by the phisher, which is usually indistinguishable from its legitimate counterpart (Brody et al., 2007; Lynch, 2005). Although targets may believe they are logging in to the legitimate site, they are actually disclosing their login credentials to the phisher to enact further damage (Lynch, 2005; Timm & Perez, 2010).

Given the enormity and general lack of safeguards on social network sites, phishing attacks have become more sophisticated and can now easily exploit contacts in these online databases (Jagatic et al., 2007;

Timm & Perez, 2010). Indeed, according to Timm and Perez (2010), phishing attacks on social network sites have increased by 240%, including Facebook, MySpace, and Twitter. In order to illustrate how phishing scams occur within these online communities, information regarding several actual attacks targeting three major social networks is discussed in the following section.

In early 2009, Twitter users received phishing messages from followers enticing them to click a malicious link (Timm & Perez, 2010). Targets that clicked the link were directed to a spoofed site that appeared to be Twitter's main page and prompted them to log back in (Timm & Perez, 2010). The Twitter accounts of the users that fell for the scam and entered their credentials were then compromised and used as conduits to send additional phishing messages (Timm & Perez, 2010). Similar attacks also occurred on Facebook and MySpace. In these attacks, phishing messages were sent to users advertising opportunities to earn quick money (Timm & Perez, 2010). Users that followed the provided navigations were then prompted to reenter their security credentials; however, instead of accessing the social network, users only succeeded in compromising their own accounts (Timm & Perez, 2010). While some scams may only involve attempts to dupe targets into disclosing security credentials, other, more sophisticated deceptions include tricking targets into downloading malware to further compromise their information.

In an example provided by Timm and Perez (2010), the phisher sent the target a message through a social network enticing the "phish" to watch a funny video. After clicking on the link, the target was taken out of the social network to a seemingly legitimate video-hosting site (Timm & Perez, 2010). As noted by Timm and Perez (2010), the target then received a notice to update his or her software in order to view the video. However, the supposed update was actually malware that assumed control of the target's browser upon installation (Timm & Perez, 2010).

Although the example provided by Timm and Perez (2010) illustrates how phishing and malware were used to ultimately conduct a browser hijack, the same method of attack is increasingly being utilized to disseminate all types of malicious software (i.e., keyloggers, screen loggers, worms, etc.). Indeed, according to Jaishankar (2008), malware is the main method utilized by phishers to engage in cybercrime, such as identity theft. Although malware and phishing pose serious threats of identity theft, evidence repeatedly suggests that the weakest link to safeguarding information is the social network user and the implicit trust placed in online interactions (Thomas & Nicol, 2010). The aforementioned is exactly why relatively simple forms of social engineering can be as dangerous to users as the high-tech methods previously discussed.

Social Engineering, Evil Twin Attacks, and Profile Squatting

In contrast to the high-tech methods (i.e., malware and phishing) previously discussed, conducting identity theft through relatively simple forms of social engineering—such as in evil twin attacks or profile squatting—requires minimal technological knowledge. Social engineering broadly defines attempts to manipulate victims in order to extract some information from them or to encourage them to engage in malicious activities on behalf of the attacker (Aïmeur & Schonfeld, 2011; Huber, Kowalski, Nohlberg, and Tjoa, 2009; Lehrman, 2010; Newman, 2006; The President's Identity Theft Task Force, 2007; Timm & Perez, 2010). For example, the process of spreading malware is considered a form of social engineering, because perpetrators manipulate victims into installing the malicious software that then potentially facilitates illegal activities (Emigh, 2006; The President's Identity Theft Task Force, 2007). Similarly, phishing is also a form of social engineering, because it involves manipulating victims into disclosing confidential information under false pretenses (The President's Identity Theft Task Force, 2007). Likewise, conducting an evil twin attack or profile squatting is a form of social engineering, because the actions are ultimately deceptions by the perpetrator in order to achieve an overall objective.

An evil twin attack simply involves perpetrators pretending to be legitimate users in order to gain something they are not entitled too (Timm & Perez, 2010). Similarly, profile squatting involves perpetrators creating bogus profiles of renowned individuals or brands for the same purposes (Al Hasib, 2009). Evil twin attacks and profile squatting may occur on social networks for any of the following reasons: to trick friends into giving money to the perpetrator, to post inflammatory comments in the victim's name in order to damage that individual's reputation, and to post inaccurate comments regarding a company's performance under the guise of a high-level executive in order to influence stock prices (Timm & Perez, 2010). Accounting for the largely unrestricted registration process utilized among social networks and the lack of identity verification conducted by administrators, establishing false profiles entails minimal effort from identity thieves (Aïmeur & Schonfeld, 2011; Timm & Perez, 2010). Indeed, according to Timm and Perez (2010), the only information actually required in order to engage in an evil twin attack is the name of the person to impersonate. Any additional information to ensure the profile is believable can often easily be found online, although it is not necessary (Timm & Perez, 2010). Again, while motivations may vary, the two primary reasons perpetrators engage in these forms of identity theft are to harm victims financially or to harm victims personally (Al Hasib, 2009; Marshall & Tompsett, 2005; Timm & Perez, 2010).

A common method of stealing funds from victims via an evil twin attack is by impersonating friends who are in detrimental situations (Timm & Perez, 2010; Weir et al., 2011). For example, in a scenario provided by Weir et al. (2011), a social network user (the actual victim) receives a frantic message from a friend supposedly traveling abroad (actually, the message is from the identity thief who has assumed control of the friend's account). According to the message, the victim's friend was mugged and lost all his or her resources (i.e., money, passport, etc.) (Weir et al., 2011). As a result, the victim's friend is in desperate need of money and pleas for funds to be sent to a specified account (Weir et al., 2011). However, in reality, the identity thief is the actual owner of the account and subsequently defrauds the victim (Weir et al., 2011). Although victims in this case suffer financial repercussions, damage caused by these types of attacks may also be personally shattering.

The motivation of an evil twin attack may be nonmonetary and purely driven to enact personal damage on a victim, as the case of James Lasdun illustrates. According to Lasdun (2013), after rejecting the advances of a former student, the student began engaging in a variety of behaviors online meant to destroy his professional and personal reputation. One method of attack entailed masquerading either as the victim himself or as his professional associates (i.e., a program director) and posting defamatory comments (Lasdun, 2013). For example, due to the lack of restrictions and identity verification conducted online, the former student was able to post comments masquerading as Lasdun that openly claimed he plagiarized others (Lasdun, 2013). Although Lasdun's case is not specific to a social network, similar methods of identity theft occur in these venues as well.

In a case of profile squatting, a former executive created a forged profile pretending to be Sarah Palin (Rosman, 2009). Rosman (2009) reports that almost immediately after creating the fictitious profile, the imitator acquired approximately 100 friends. Moreover, as news regarding Palin fluctuated, the imitator received additional friendship requests from upwards of 500 users (Rosman, 2009). Although some followers of the fictitious profile were doubtful of its authenticity, Rosman notes the vast majority seemed unperturbed. In fact, the charade went on for some time until system administrators eventually closed the profile after the legitimate Sarah Palin (through her representatives) contacted the social network company (Rosman, 2009). While the individual behind the forged Sarah Palin account likely only represented a nuisance to the politician, Lasdun's case represents the other end of the extreme. Indeed, as noted by Lasdun (2013, p. 4), "You are what the Web says you are, and if it misrepresents you, the feeling of having been violated is crushing."

☐ Selling Victims Out: Underground Identity Theft Market

Identity theft is typically discussed in terms of three stages: acquisition or the acquiring or personal information, the use of the information or distribution of information to others, and the resulting fraud itself (Aïmeur & Schonfeld, 2011). In a rare investigation into the underground economy, scholars examined the financial windfall for identity thieves that trade in stolen information. As part of their inquiry, scholars were able to harvest stolen credential information in dropzones* maintained by identity thieves that stemmed from more than 173,000 compromised machines (Holz, Engelberth, & Freiling, 2008). In total, Holz et al. (2008) found 10,775 unique bank account credentials comprising the following locations (in order of highest to lowest amount of credentials stolen): PayPal, Commonwealth Bank, HSBC Holding, Bank of America, and Lloyds Bank. Credit card credentials were also recovered and represented several of the major credit grantors (in order of highest to lowest amount of credentials stolen): Visa, MasterCard, American Express, Diners Club, and other types (Holz et al., 2008). Through their analysis, Holz et al. (2008) estimated these credential data potentially netted identity thieves millions of dollars. Aside from financial information, social network accounts were also represented and commoditized.

Holz et al. (2008) found more than 78,000 social network credentials existed within identity thieves' dropzones consisting of the following providers (in order of highest to lowest amount of credentials stolen): Facebook, hi5, nasza-klasa.pl, odnoklassniki.ru, Bebo, YouTube, and other types. Moreover, slightly more than 7,000 credentials from online retailers were also recovered (Holz et al., 2008). According to Holz et al. (2008), the majority of these credentials belonged to eBay users, but a small minority belonged to Amazon and Overstock.com. As with bank account information, these data ranged in price from $1 to $15 for credentials to social network accounts and from $1 to $8 dollars for credentials to online retailers (Holz et al., 2008). Not only can these data be sold to engage in additional forms of identity theft, but they can also be used to strengthen attacks against others (Holz et al., 2008). For example, by accessing a specific social network account, identity thieves can attempt to spear-phish the original victim's friends and associates (Holz et al., 2008).

---

* According to Holz et al. (2008), a dropzone is a public directory on an online server that functions as an exchange site for data retrieved from keyloggers.

☐ Emerging Trends in Online Identity Theft

As the technology continues to advance, undoubtedly so will the methods utilized by identity thieves. In fact, one such advancement becoming increasingly popular in attacks on social networks is the distribution of malware through cross-site scripting (Timm & Perez, 2010). In contrast to identity theft largely by deception, in cross-site scripting, thieves exploit website vulnerabilities to distribute malware (Timm & Perez, 2010). In a persistent attack of this type, the only action required from the victim to become infected is to visit the compromised site (Timm & Perez, 2010). As soon as the compromised site is visited, the malware infects the victim's machine and enacts its damage (Timm & Perez, 2010).

Another evolution in malware distribution increasing in frequency is what is commonly referred to as a drive-by download. According to Sood and Enbody (2011), a drive-by download occurs when perpetrators exploit vulnerabilities in web browsers. Through these tactics, perpetrators facilitate the transfer of malware to machines without the victims' knowledge (Sood & Enbody, 2011). In a recent example of this type of attack, television network giant NBC was hacked by identity thieves who utilized a drive-by download to force malware onto potentially thousands of visitors to the NBC.com website (Infosecurity, 2013). The attack was so devastating that security experts took several hours to remove the malware from the site, which was suspected to have been in an infectious state for at least 24 hours before intervention (Infosecurity, 2013). After further investigation, the malware was determined to be the Citadel Trojan, known for engaging in banking fraud and cyber-espionage (Smith, 2013). NBC is not alone, however; as of this writing, several other high-profile companies had also been subjected to this type of attack (Apple, Facebook, the *Wall Street Journal*, and the *Washington Post*) (Infosecurity, 2013). A final trend warranting concern is the increasing utilization of botnets and puppetnets to act as proxies for perpetrator activities (Bailey, Cooke, Jahanian, Xu, & Karir, 2009; Huber et al., 2009; Timm & Perez, 2010).

Botnets surfaced in the early 2000s and have since been utilized to engage in a variety of criminal activities, including identity theft (Timm & Perez, 2010). According to Timm and Perez (2010), *bot* is an abbreviated term for *robot*, which refers to a machine compromised by malware that is under the control of the perpetrator (otherwise referred to as a herder). The dissemination of the malware to create the botnet (or group of compromised machines) may occur through deceptive methods previously discussed or through direct infection of operating systems (Timm & Perez, 2010). After infection, perpetrators then utilize the botnet as a proxy to engage in cybercrime, such as automated phishing attacks or identity theft scams (Bailey et al., 2009; Huber et al., 2009; Timm & Perez, 2010). Frighteningly, victims may not even be aware their systems have been compromised or their machines are being utilized to carry out such attacks on behalf of the perpetrator (Timm & Perez, 2010). Perhaps what is more alarming is that botnets have evolved and can now be launched within social networks.

A puppetnet is arguably the next evolutionary step in the botnet. A puppetnet is similar to a botnet in that a perpetrator has assumed remote control over victims' machines; however, in contrast to a botnet, puppets do not have to install any malware to become part of the puppetnet (Timm & Perez, 2010). Instead, victims merely have to access a malicious page—such as a social network application—to become part of the puppetnet (Timm & Perez, 2010). Subsequently, every time victims log in to the malicious application, their machines come under the control of the perpetrator to engage in a variety of activities (i.e., phishing scams, identity thefts). However, unlike their bot counterparts, puppets terminate the perpetrator's control whenever they exit the malicious site or application (Timm & Perez, 2010). Yet, in an environment where potentially millions of users could be accessing applications with malicious code throughout the day, the danger associated with puppetnets is readily apparent.

☐ Conclusion

This chapter began by discussing the problem of identity theft and copious gaps of information that persist regarding this type of crime—particularly related to identity theft on social networks. Although identity theft is not a new type of crime, the advancement of technology has provided a plethora of new methods to steal the personal information of others (Aïmeur & Schonfeld, 2011; Allison et al., 2005; Bilge et al., 2009; Debatin et al., 2009; Ho, Maiga, & Aïmeur; 2009; Lynch, 2005; Marshall & Tompsett, 2005; Slosarik, 2002; Timm & Perez, 2010). For example, instead of monitoring the incoming mail of a few victims, perpetrators have the ability to potentially steal the personal information of thousands of victims at once (Lynch, 2005). Indeed, the widespread congregation of millions of users on social network sites appears to have exacerbated this problem, especially given the relatively weak security and authentication procedures administrators utilize to police sites (Al Hasib, 2009). In addition, research suggests users may not fully understand the risks associated with overdisclosing personal information (Al Hasib, 2009; Bilge et al., 2009; Gross & Acquisti, 2005; Huber et al., 2009; Lehrman, 2010) or the potentiality to use this disclosed information to predict highly confidential data like social security numbers (Acquisti & Gross, 2009a). Therefore, awareness campaigns empowering social network users with knowledge regarding relatively low-tech methods of identity theft (i.e., aggregation of publicly available data, social engineering) as well as high-tech methods (i.e., malware attacks, phishing scams) is vital to combat this social problem. The necessity of this information is stressed in light of increasingly sophisticated tactics used by perpetrators to engage in identity theft within these forums, such as cross-site scripting, drive-by downloads, botnets, and puppetnets (Bailey et al., 2009; Huber et al., 2009; Timm & Perez, 2010). Given the enormous consequences identity theft has on victims, businesses (including social networks), and governments, empowering victims to be especially vigilant while online will assist in combating the efforts of these motivated offenders.

☐ References

Acquisti, A., & Gross, R. (2009a). Social insecurity: The unintended consequences of identity fraud prevention policies. In *Workshop on the Economics of Information Security* (pp. 24–25). Retrieved from http://www.heinz.cmu. edu/~acquisti/papers/acquisti-MISQ.pdf

Acquisti, A., & Gross, R. (2009b). Predicting Social Security numbers from public data. *Proceedings of the National Academy of Sciences, 106*(27), 10975–10980.

Aïmeur, E., & Schonfeld, D. (2011). The ultimate invasion of privacy: Identity theft. In *2011 Ninth Annual International Conference on Privacy, Security and Trust (PST)* (pp. 24–31). Institute of Electrical and Electronics Engineers (IEEE). Retrieved from http://www.site.uottawa.ca/~ttran/teaching/csi5389/ papers/Aimeur_and_Schonfeld_PST2 011.pdf

Al Hasib, A. (2009). Threats of online social networks. *IJCSNS International Journal of Computer Science and Network Security, 9*(11), 288–293.

Allison, S. F., Schuck, A. M., & Lersch, K. M. (2005). Exploring the crime of identity theft: Prevalence, clearance rates, and victim/offender characteristics. *Journal of Criminal Justice, 33*(1), 19–29.

Arthur, C. (2012). Facebook to improve privacy controls over public visibility. *The Guardian.* Retrieved from http://www.guardian.co.uk/technology/2012/ dec/12/facebook-improve- privacy-controls-pictures-public

Bailey, M., Cooke, E., Jahanian, F., Xu, Y., & Karir, M. (2009, March). A survey of botnet technology and defenses. In *Conference for Homeland Security, 2009. CATCH'09. Cybersecurity Applications & Technology* (pp. 299–304). Institute of Electrical and Electronics Engineers (IEEE).

Bilge, L., Strufe, T., Balzarotti, D., & Kirda, E. (2009, April). All your contacts are belong to us: Automated identity theft attacks on social networks. In *Proceedings of the 18th International Conference on World Wide Web* (pp. 551–560). Association for Computing Machinery (ACM). Retrieved from http:// dl.acm.org/citation.cfm?id=1526784

Brody, R. G., Mulig, E., & Kimball, V. (2007). Phishing, pharming and identity theft. *Academy of Accounting and Financial Studies Journal, 11*(3), 43–56.

Debatin, B., Lovejoy, J. P., Horn, A. K., & Hughes, B. N. (2009). Facebook and online privacy: Attitudes, behaviors, and unintended consequences. *Journal of Computer-Mediated Communication, 15*(1), 83–108.

Emigh, A. (2006). The crimeware landscape: Malware, phishing, identity theft and beyond. *Journal of Digital Forensic Practice, 1*(3), 245–260.

Facebook. (2013). *Key facts.* Retrieved from http://newsroom.fb.com/Key-Facts

Federal Trade Commission. (1998). *Identity theft and assumption deterrence act.* Retrieved from http://www.ftc.gov/os/statutes/itada/itadact.htm

Finn, J., & Banach, M. (2000). Victimization online: The down side of seeking human services for women on the Internet. *Cyberpsychology and Behavior, 3*(2), 243–254.

Gross, R., & Acquisti, A. (2005). Information revelation and privacy in online social networks. In *Proceedings of the 2005 ACM Workshop on Privacy in the Electronic Society* (pp. 71–80). ACM.

Ho, A., Maiga, A., & Aïmeur, E. (2009, May). Privacy protection issues in social networking sites. In *IEEE/ACS International Conference on Computer Systems and Applications, 2009. AICCSA 2009* (pp. 271–278). Institute of Electrical and Electronics Engineers (IEEE). Retrieved from http://ieeexplore.ieee.org/xpl/login.jsp?tp=&arnumber=5069336&url=http%3A%2F%2Fi eeexplore.ieee.org%2Fxpls%2Fabs_all.jsp%3Farnumber%3D5069336

Holz, T., Engelberth, M., & Freiling, F. (2009). Learning more about the underground economy: A case-study of keyloggers and dropzones. *Computer Security—ESORICS 2009*, 1–18.

Hoofnagle, C. J. (2007). Identity theft: Making the known unknowns known. *Harvard Journal of Law and Technology, 21*, 98–122. Retrieved from http://scholarship.law.berkeley.edu/facpubs/470

Huber, M., Kowalski, S., Nohlberg, M., & Tjoa, S. (2009, August). Towards automating social engineering using social networking sites. In *International Conference on Computational Science and Engineering, 2009. CSE'09* (Vol. 3, pp. 117–124). Institute of Electrical and Electronics Engineers (IEEE).

Hunter, P. (2008). Social networking: The focus for new threats—and old ones. *Computer Fraud & Security, 2008*(7), 17–18.

Infosecurity. (2013). *NBC hack serves Citadel malware to visitors.* Retrieved from http://www.infosecurity-magazine.com/view/30905/nbc-hack-serves-citadel-malware-to-visitors/

Jagatic, T. N., Johnson, N. A., Jakobsson, M., & Menczer, F. (2007). Social phishing. *Communications of the ACM, 50*(10), 94–100.

Jaishankar, K. (2008). Identity related crime in the cyberspace: Examining phishing and its impact. *International Journal of Cyber Criminology, 2*(1), 10–15.

Langton, L. (2011). *Identity theft reported by households, 2005–2010.* U.S. Department of Justice, Office of Justice Programs, Bureau of Justice Statistics.

Lasdun, J. (2013). I will ruin him. *The Chronicle of Higher Education.* Retrieved from http://chronicle.com/article/I-Will-Ruin-Him/136693/

Lehrman, Y. (2010). The weakest link: The risks associated with social networking websites. *Journal of Strategic Security, 3*(2), 63–72.

Lynch, J. (2005). Identity theft in cyberspace: Crime control methods and their effectiveness in combating phishing attacks. *Berkeley Technology Law Journal, 20*, 259–300.

Marshall, A. M., & Tompsett, B. C. (2005). Identity theft in an online world. *Computer Law & Security Review, 21*(2), 128–137.

May, D. A., & Headley, J. E. (2004). *Identity theft* (p. 1). Memphis, TN: P. Lang.

Newman, G. R., & McNally, M. M. (2005). *Identity theft literature review.* U.S. Department of Justice, National Institute of Justice.

Newman, R. C. (2006). Cybercrime, identity theft, and fraud: Practicing safe Internet-network security threats and vulnerabilities. In *Proceedings of the 3rd Annual Conference on Information Security Curriculum Development* (pp. 68–78). Kennesaw, GA: ACM.

The President's Identity Theft Task Force. (2007). *Combatting identity theft: A strategic plan.* Retrieved from http://www.identitytheft.gov/reports/StrategicPlan.pdf

Rosman, K. (2009). Sarah Palin's Facebook alter-ego gets found out. *The Wall Street Journal.* Retrieved from http://blogs.wsj.com/speakeasy/2009/08/13/sarah-palins-facebook-alter-ego-gets-found-out/

Sanzgiri, A., Joyce, J., & Upadhyaya, S. (2012). The early (tweet-ing) bird spreads the worm: An assessment of Twitter for malware propagation. *Procedia Computer Science, 10*, 705–712.

Sharp, T., Shreve-Neiger, A., Fremouw, W., Kane, J., & Hutton, S. (2004). Exploring the psychological and somatic impact of identity theft. *Journal of Forensic Sciences, 49*(1), 131–136.

Slosarik, K. (2002). Identity theft: An overview of the problem. *The Justice Professional, 15*(4), 329–343.

Small, B. (2013). *Top complaint to the FTC? ID theft, again.* U.S. Federal Trade Commission. Retrieved from http://www.consumer.ftc.gov/blog/top-complaint-ftc-id-theft-again

Smith, G. (2013). NBC.com hacked, experts say website may have spread malware. *The Huffington Post.* Retrieved from http://www.huffingtonpost.com/2013/02/21/nbccom-hacked-experts-war_n_2735545.html

Sood, A. K., & Enbody, R. (2011). Chain exploitation—Social networks malware. *ISACA Journal, 1*, 31.

Stana, R. M. (2002). *Identity theft: Prevalence and cost appear to be growing.* U.S. General Accounting Office. Retrieved from http://www.gao.gov/assets/240/233900.pdf

Sterritt, S. N. (2011). Applying the common-law cause of action negligent enablement of imposter fraud to social networking sites. *Seton Hall Law Review, 41*, 1695.

Thomas, K., & Nicol, D. M. (2010, October). The Koobface botnet and the rise of social malware. In *2010 5th International Conference on Malicious and Unwanted Software (MALWARE)* (pp. 63–70). Institute of Electrical and Electronics Engineers (IEEE).

Thompson, H. H. (2008). How I stole someone's identity. *Scientific American.* Retrieved from http://www.scientificamerican.com/article.cfm?id=anatomy-of-a-social-hack

Timm, C., & Perez, R. (2010). *Seven deadliest social network attacks.* Burlington, MA: Syngress.

Vacca, J. R. (2003). *Identity theft.* Upper Saddle River, NJ: Prentice Hall.

Weir, G. R., Toolan, F., & Smeed, D. (2011). The threats of social networking: Old wine in new bottles? *Information Security Technical Report, 16*(2), 38–43.

White, J. (2012). *Identity theft: Total extent of refund fraud using stolen identities is unknown.* U.S. Government Accountability Office. Retrieved from http://www.gao.gov/assets/660/650365.pdf

6
CHAPTER

Wall Posts and Tweets and Blogs, Oh My! A Look at Cyberbullying via Social Media

Robin M. Kowalski

Clemson University

Gary W. Giumetti

Quinnipiac University

Contents

Trends in Social Media Usage	93
How Might Social Media Be Changing the Way We Communicate?	94
Outcomes of Social Media Usage	95
Cyberbullying	97
Defining Cyberbullying	97
Traditional Bullying Versus Cyberbullying	99
Prevalence Rates of Cyberbullying	100
Cyberbullying via Social Media	101
Effects of Cyberbullying via Social Media	103
Prevention and Intervention	103
References	105

"Teen Rape Case Shines Light on Social Media, Cyberbullying." "Steubenville Rape Case Brings Lessons in Social Media, Sexting, and Cyber-Bullying." These are just two headlines of news stories surrounding the recent conviction, in Steubenville, Ohio, of two teens, Trent Mays and Ma'lik Richmond, convicted of raping a 16-year-old West Virginia high school student at a party during the summer of 2012 (*The Australian*, 2013). Of relevance to the headline is that hundreds of texts, videos, and posts about the event from fellow partygoers as well as pictures of the victim, referred to as the "dead" drunk girl, were circulated via social media long before the case played out in the courtroom. In one report, Ohio Attorney General DeWine "said investigators analyzed 13 cellphones, and from those, reviewed: 396,270 text messages, 308,586 photos, 940 video clips, 3,188 phone calls, 6,422 contacts" (Cunningham, 2013). Following the conviction, additional charges were levied against two girls, ages 15 and 16, who made death threats via Twitter and Facebook against the victim. As stated by one journalist, "The case has raised awareness of the power and danger of social media and cyber bullying, as sexually explicit or other humiliating pictures and videos spread like wildfire with a click of a mouse or a tap on a smartphone" (*The Australian*, 2013).

In another well-publicized story, Rebecca Marino, a 22-year-old Canadian tennis professional who rose as high as 38th in the World Tennis Association rankings, recently withdrew from the professional circuit citing depression and cyberbullying as the reasons (Beattie, 2013). Marino indicated in press releases that she had suffered from depression for years, but that following her loss at Wimbledon last year, the cyberbullying she experienced via social media had reached levels that forced her to withdraw from professional tennis. In writing about Marino's decision, sport's writer Damien Cox (2013) stated, "But in the social media world, one that permits cowards to attack others under the cover of anonymity, we are more and more encountering an environment in which those who have a talent or an opinion or are simply different are exposed to a vicious tsunami of abuse that once didn't exist."

Situations such as those described above are an unfortunate reminder of how easy it has become for perpetrators of bullying to enact their aggressive behavior through social media. While bullying has been around for hundreds of years, the situations described would not have played out as they did even 15 years ago when social media was just coming onto the scene. In the current chapter, we highlight trends in social media usage in the past decade, point out ways in which communication patterns may have changed in part due to social media, and review some recent research findings illustrating the prevalence and impact of cyberbullying via social media, including a discussion of what cyberbullying is and how similar to and different from traditional bullying it is.

☐ Trends in Social Media Usage

Before examining cyberbullying as it occurs through social network-ing, it is important to understand the infusion of social media within our culture. Social media has been defined as "any Web site that allows social interaction" (O'Keeffe & Clarke-Pearson, 2011). Defined in this way, social media includes social networking sites (e.g., Facebook, MySpace, LinkedIn), video sites (e.g., YouTube), gaming sites and vir-tual worlds (e.g., Second Life), and blogs (O-Keeffe & Clarke-Pearson, 2011). The use of social media has increased markedly in recent years among people of all demographics. In 2010, Lenhart and her colleagues (Lenhart, Purcell, Smith, & Zickuhr, 2010) released a report detailing the prevalence of use of a variety of social media along with changes in that use over time. Among the findings were that blogging had decreased among young people, and that Facebook had emerged as the premier social networking site. Specifically, among users of social net-working sites, 73% have a profile on Facebook and 14% subscribe to LinkedIn. Currently, there are over 1 billion active users of Facebook (Fowler, 2012) and over 500 million users on Google+ or Twitter (Lunden, 2012; Weber, 2012), where an active user is defined as some-one who has logged on to the site at least once in the previous month. Users spend over 700 billion minutes a month on Facebook. A survey by Commonsense Media (2009) of teens' use of social media found that 22% of those surveyed indicated that they checked their profile more than 10 times a day, with another 51% checking more than once a day. YouTube currently has over 1 billion visitors to the site each month (YouTube, 2013).

Duggan and Brenner (2013) found that 16% of adults use Twitter, with 8% using Twitter on a typical day, doubling the number in two years. Part of this increase they attribute to the increase in availability and use of smartphones. Additionally, they reported that 67% of Internet users have a profile on a social networking site, and 13% use Instagram. Recent polls of Internet users in the United States indicate that 83% of individuals between the ages of 18 and 29 are using a social networking site of some kind (Duggan & Brenner, 2013). Across all social media types surveyed, a higher percentage of women than men used each respective venue, and younger individuals were more likely to use all types of social media than older individuals. Smith and Brenner (2012) found that 44% of cellphone users have slept with their phones next to them at night for the sole purpose of ensuring that they don't miss important messages or updates. It is fairly clear that social media have become a prominent part of the lives of many individuals, but for what purposes do individuals use social media?

Social networking sites are used for a number of different purposes, with perhaps the two most common being interacting with friends/ acquaintances and sharing news and personal events with one's social network. While some have wondered whether individuals use social media as a way of branching out and meeting new people, recent research suggests that adolescent users of Facebook and MySpace tend to use it to maintain or strengthen preexisting offline relationships (Reich, Subrahmanyam, & Espinoza, 2012), rather than interacting with unknown others. The major way in which these connections are maintained is through status updates or comments posted on the status updates or photos of others. Such posts on Facebook are visible to friends in an automatically updating feed of information (Walther, Van Der Heide, Kim, Westerman, & Tong, 2008), and users tend to spend more time reading through posts of others than creating their own posts (Pempek, Yermolayeva, & Calvert, 2009).

Beyond interacting with friends on these websites, individuals also share reactions to local and world news stories. This has become quite easy to do, as many external websites now have Facebook-enabled hyperlinks that allow users to quickly and easily post a comment and a link to a news story to their profile page. Additionally, with the rise in smartphones with built-in cameras, individuals can now take a snapshot of a personal event and quickly post it to Facebook for others to see. Recent research findings indicate that these features make Facebook a richer medium for communicating with one's social network (as compared to email or text messaging) (Park, Chung, & Lee, 2012).

☐ How Might Social Media Be Changing the Way We Communicate?

As a means of communicating with others, social networking sites appear to be changing the way that we communicate with one another (Sugarman & Willoughby, 2013). One major way in which communication differs when delivered via social media is that it is much more likely to be brief, occur more rapidly, be text based, and be visible to many individuals (Park et al., 2012). For example, Twitter is a microblogging site that allows users to share brief 140-character tweets with fellow users. As of December 2012, Twitter had over 200 million active users who post over 340 million tweets a day (Fiegerman, 2012). Following large national or international events, the number of tweets per second reaches into the tens of thousands.

Additionally, the potential size of one's social network is now much larger, as the average number of Facebook "friends" in a college student sample was 768 (Giumetti & Williams, 2013), leading one group of researchers to ask how the infusion of Facebook into one's life may be changing communication patterns (Manago, Taylor, & Greenfield, 2012). In their study, Manago and colleagues asked a sample of college students at UCLA to report on their patterns of use on Facebook and the contents of their social network. Results indicated that the majority of contacts in a given individual's friend list can be categorized as superficial acquaintances, rather than close relationships, and the most common form of communication on Facebook involved emotional self-disclosure, suggesting that individuals today more frequently engage in public forms of expression that were once more private.

Since larger online social networks are now more common, communications sent over these media now have a greater reach. That is, one can now get a message out to thousands (or millions) of people through Facebook or Twitter, without much filtering or censoring. Previously we might have sent a news story to the newspaper or tried to get some time on TV, but someone might have prevented us from sharing our message if they did not like it (E-Guillotine, 2013). Features such as these have led scholars to wonder whether social media sites might be having a positive or negative impact on individuals.

☐ Outcomes of Social Media Usage

Starting with the possible positive outcomes, a recent study by Manago et al. (2012) found that individuals with larger numbers of friends on Facebook tended to report higher levels of life satisfaction and also higher levels of perceived social support. Another recent study found that social networking sites might be beneficial for individuals with low self-esteem, as they can help them to develop social capital in a way that might not be possible for such individuals in offline environments (Steinfield, Ellison, & Lampe, 2008). One other positive outcome of social networking sites is that they can make for more fluid social interactions for youth and adults with disabilities such as Asperger's and other autism spectrum disorders (Kowalski & Fedina, 2011; Mazurek, 2013).

While there might be several positive outcomes associated with social media usage, there are also several possible negative outcomes. Anecdotal evidence suggests that interacting over social media may be negatively impacting social skills. Because so many adolescents and young adults connect to Facebook using a smartphone, and because they can bring this device with them anywhere, any downtime they have might be spent browsing the site or interacting with others online, rather than interacting with others around them in a face-to-face manner.

Indeed, research by Jenkins-Guarnieri, Wright, and Hudiburgh (2012) indicates that the intensity of Facebook use is negatively related to perceived competence at initiating interpersonal relationships (after controlling for several personality variables). The development (or lack thereof) of interpersonal skills needed for fluid face-to-face interactions is particularly important given the young ages with which children are being exposed to social media. According to *Consumer Reports*, 5.6 million active users of Facebook do not meet the required minimum age of 13. Only a small percentage of parents of children this age (18%) friend them, believing that they are not at risk online for at least another couple of years (Mangis, 2012).

Facebook usage might also be linked with changes in personality. Meta-analytic research suggests that people have become more narcissistic over time (Twenge, Konrath, Foster, Campbell, & Bushman, 2008), and one reason for this may be that sites like Facebook allow users to perform for a greater audience and inflate their self-esteem. A recent study supports a link between higher levels of social activity on Facebook and levels of narcissism as reported through self-report surveys and other reports based on viewing a user's online profile (Buffardi & Campbell, 2008). Increased levels of narcissism have been linked with other negative behaviors, including impulsivity, self-defeating behaviors, and aggression (Miller et al., 2009).

Another possible negative outcome of social media usage is a feeling of disconnectedness. Specifically, a study by Stepanikova, Nie, and He (2010) found that individuals who used Facebook excessively reported greater feelings of disconnection. Other research indicates that use of social media sites may be simultaneously associated with feelings of being connected with others while also feeling disconnected. In a study by Sheldon, Abad, and Hinsch (2011), the researchers found that among frequent users of Facebook, feelings of disconnectedness motivate users to access Facebook, and greater usage is linked with higher feelings of connectedness. If we take Facebook use to the extreme, researchers have also found that excessive use of the site might be akin to an addiction (Kuss & Griffiths, 2011) and be disruptive to daily functioning.

One final negative outcome is an increased potential for miscommunication. The majority of communication sent over social networking sites is text based, and as a communication medium, text is a fairly lean or impoverished channel (Park et al., 2012). Text-based communications lack other important information that a message recipient might use to decode the meaning of a message, including such features as vocal inflection, gestures, and immediate feedback. For these reasons, ambiguous messages sent over social networking sites may be more likely to be misunderstood. Additionally, many features of social media may make it an attractive place to engage in misbehaviors such as cyberbullying

(Patchin & Hinduja, 2006; Kowalski, Limber, & Agatston, 2012a; Ybarra & Mitchell, 2004). These features include reproducibility, lack of emotional reactivity, perceived uncontrollability, relative permanence, and 24/7 accessibility (Kiesler, Seigel, & McGuire, 1984; Pearson, Andersson, & Porath, 2005). In an online context, communicators do not frequently get instant feedback with regard to emotional reactions from recipients, thus making it easier to offend others. Additionally, online communications can be accessed 24 hours a day, 7 days a week, which allows individuals to transmit and receive hurtful messages at all hours of the day, making an individual feel that the situation is inescapable (Kowalski et al., 2012a). Combined, these features may help us to understand why cyberbullying is becoming more problematic via social media today.

☐ Cyberbullying

Recent years have witnessed a flurry of attention devoted to the topic of cyberbullying. A significant amount of attention in the popular press has catered to the topic of electronic bullying, driven unfortunately by a number of suicides that appear to be linked, in part, to cyberbullying. In academic circles, the number of publications in the PsychINFO database devoted to the topic increased from 1 in 2005 to 387 in 2013. Similarly, an increasing amount of legislation has been passed. In 2007, only five states had some type of legislation that covered cyberbullying or electronic bullying. Currently, there are 45 states with this type of legislation. Although a federal law is not currently on the books, such a law is now under consideration.

A rapid increase in attention to the topic of cyberbullying on so many different fronts begs the question of why. Why is this topic garnering so much attention? Is this enough attention? And, what is cyberbullying anyway? How does cyberbullying differ from traditional bullying? What are the primary venues by which cyberbullying occurs?

Defining Cyberbullying

In spite of the surge of research attention devoted to the topic of cyberbullying in recent years, researchers have yet to reach a consensus on the best way to define cyberbullying (Olweus, 2013; Ybarra, Boyd, Korchmaros, & Oppenheim, 2012). Whereas some conceptualizations of cyberbullying are general (e.g., bullying that occurs via the Internet or mobile phones), other definitions are much more specific, defining cyberbullying as bullying that occurs through specific venues (e.g., email, instant messaging). Additionally, whereas some have defined cyberbullying as part of a "general pattern of bullying" (Olweus, 2013), others draw more clear distinctions between cyberbullying and traditional bullying (Runions, Shapka, Dooley, & Modecki, 2013), a point we will return to below. This issue of defining cyberbullying is confounded by the fact that cyberbullying can occur through any of a number of different venues (e.g., chat rooms, websites, instant messaging, online gaming, social network sites, etc.).

In this chapter, cyberbullying will be defined as aggression that is repeatedly and intentionally carried out through electronic media (e.g., email, instant messages, social networking sites, text messages) (Kowalski et al., 2012a). Which of these electronic media is the venue used for cyberbullying depends on the particular study read, the age of the participants sampled, and the most popular type of technology at the time the study is conducted. For example, in an investigation of cyberbullying among over 3,700 middle school children, Kowalski and Limber (2007) found that instant messaging was the most common venue by which American participants were both victims and perpetrators of cyberbullying. Katzer, Fetchenhauer, and Belschak (2009), in their examination of cyberbullying among 1,700 5th through 11th grade German students, observed chat rooms to be the most common venue by which participants reported being both victims and perpetrators of cyberbullying. Given the time in which these articles were published, however, were these exact investigations to be conducted today, our guess is that, with the rise in the use of social media, social networking sites, such as Facebook, would likely emerge as the most common venue by which cyberbullying occurs.

Recent research studies looking at patterns of online activity among youth have suggested that such an increase in cyberbullying via social media is indeed occurring. The Youth Internet Safety Surveys, for example, which examined online activities of youth ages 10 to 17, found that the percentage of youth who reported being harassed online nearly doubled from 2000, the time of the first survey (6%), to 2010, the time of the third survey (11%) (Jones, Mitchell, & Finkelhor, 2013). Administrators of the surveys attribute the increase to an increasing presence of the Internet among young people, and specifically, an increasing number of youth using smartphones and social networking sites (Jones et al., 2013). Additionally, Jones et al. (2013) asked participants to indicate the location on the Internet where cyberbullying first occurred (email, chat, instant messaging, social networking, texting, or other). In the 2000 and 2004 instances of the survey, instant messaging was the most common venue through which cyberbullying first occurred (34% and 47%, respectively), but this changed in 2010. The number one venue in 2010 was social networking sites, with 82% of the sample indicating that this was the location where they had first experienced cyberbullying.

Traditional Bullying Versus Cyberbullying

A cursory look at definitions of traditional bullying and cyberbullying would show that they share certain features in common. They are both acts of aggression that are typically repeated over time and that occur between individuals whose relationship is defined by a power imbalance (Kowalski et al., 2012a; Olweus, 1993, 2013). Importantly, this power imbalance can take any of a number of different forms, including physical stature, social status, and technological expertise (Dooley, Pyzalski, & Cross, 2009; Pyzalski, 2011). In spite of the features that they share in common, however, traditional bullying and cyberbullying differ along several key dimensions. First, whereas the identities of perpetrators of traditional bullying are known, perpetrators of cyberbullying can often remain anonymous. Kowalski and Limber (2007) found that just under 50% of the middle school victims of cyberbullying in their study did not know the identity of the individual who cyberbullied them. Perceived anonymity opens up the pool of individuals who might be willing to perpetrate cyberbullying relative to traditional bullying. Deindividuation that results from anonymity leads people to say and do things anonymously that they would be unwilling to say or do in face-to-face encounters, such as those that characterize traditional bullying (Diener, 1980; Postmes & Spears, 1998).

Second, most traditional bullying occurs at school during the school day (Nansel et al., 2001). Cyberbullying, on the other hand, can occur at any time of the day or night. Even if the individuals targeted on websites, social network sites, or via Twitter, for example, decide not to view the negative information being posted about them, that does not mean that the information is not being posted and read by others. This also highlights the public nature of cyberbullying relative to traditional bullying. Whereas only a few individuals may witness an individual being traditionally bullied, hundreds, if not thousands, may witness someone be cyberbullied.

A third difference between the two types of bullying stems from a similarity: Youth who are bullied typically do not report their bullying. Where the two types of bullying diverge is in the reasons that youth report for not telling. Targets of traditional bullying often do not report their bullying to others because they fear retribution by their perpetrators. Targets of cyberbullying often do not report because they fear that parents or other adults will remove the technology by which they have been cyberbullied, as a means of protecting them in the future (Kowalski et al., 2012a). Given the pervasive use of technology and social media noted earlier in this chapter, to remove the technology revictimizes the victim.

To validate these conceptual differences and similarities between traditional bullying and cyberbullying, researchers have empirically examined the relationship between the two types of bullying. The overall consensus that emerges from the literature is that while the two types of bullying are related, they are not two forms of the same thing. The strongest relationships that have been observed have been between perpetrators of cyberbullying and perpetrators of traditional bullying, as well as between victims of cyberbullying and victims of traditional bullying (Gradinger, Strohmeier, & Spiel, 2009; Hinduja & Patchin, 2008; Kowalski, Morgan, & Limber, 2012b; Smith et al., 2008). Additionally, a meta-analysis conducted to examine this relationship across studies found strong relationships between being a perpetrator of traditional bullying and a perpetrator of cyberbullying ($r = .45$) and between being a victim of cyberbullying and a perpetrator of cyberbullying ($r = .51$) (Kowalski, Giumetti, Schroeder, & Lattanner, 2013). A slightly weaker relationship was observed between being a victim of traditional bullying and a victim of cyberbullying ($r = .40$).

Prevalence Rates of Cyberbullying

The frequency with which cyberbullying occurs is highly variable across studies, varying with the definition provided (or not) to participants, the time parameter used to assess cyberbullying (e.g., two months, six months, one year, lifetime), the stringency of the criteria used to determine whether cyberbullying occurred (e.g., at least once versus two to three times a month or more), and the age of the participants sampled, to name just a few variables. Additional debate has surrounded the issue of whether rates of cyberbullying are remaining relatively constant (Olweus, 2013) or whether they are increasing with time and new technologies (Slonje & Smith, 2008). Across studies, prevalence rates for cyberbullying victimization range between approximately 10% and 40% (Lenhart et al., 2010; Tokunaga, 2010).

Regardless of the absolute level of cyberbullying that is reported across studies, recent research seems clear that the venue by which the cyberbullying is occurring is changing, with social media becoming an increasingly popular method for perpetrators to use to cyberbully others. The expanse of social media, the ease of accessing social media via smartphones, and the real-time nature of social media make it a valuable communication tool whether used for good or ill.

Cyberbullying via Social Media

In a story that made international headlines, Amanda Todd committed suicide at the age of 15, five weeks after posting a nine-minute video on YouTube in which she silently used note cards to detail the bullying that she experienced online. When Amanda was only 12, she went into an online chat room where another individual asked her to flash her breasts and took a screenshot when she did. He used that image to blackmail Amanda for three years, threatening to share the image with her friends and family if she did not "put a show on for him." Once the image was disseminated online, Amanda was cyberbullied relentlessly by her classmates and friends via social media. She changed schools three times and attempted suicide twice before she was successful the third time. Sadly, the cyberbullying over social media did not stop with Amanda's death, but continues today as students and others continue to revile the young girl (Baur, 2012). In an interesting twist, just a couple of weeks following Amanda's death, over 17 million people had viewed her video. Thus, the social media outlet by which she had been so cruelly bullied may also be the means by which people are educated about bullying.

Dr. Nancy Willard (2007) has created a taxonomy of cyberbullying that includes flaming (i.e., an online fight), harassment (i.e., repeatedly sending offensive messages via technology), denigration (i.e., using technology to disseminate false information about others), impersonation (i.e., posing as the victim and electronically disseminating negative and offensive information as if it were coming from the victim himself or herself), outing and trickery (e.g., getting others to disclose very personal information and then electronically sharing that information with others), exclusion (i.e., blocking people from chat rooms and buddy lists), cyberstalking (i.e., repeatedly sending harassing and threatening electronic communications), and sexting (i.e., sending nude or seminude pictures or videos electronically). Cyberbullying via social media can take any of the forms listed in Willard's taxonomy. For example, although flaming could take place via more private correspondences such as email, it typically occurs in more public forums, such as chat rooms found in social media sites (Willard, 2007). Importantly, although some critics argue that flaming is not a type of cyberbullying because there is no imbalance of power, we would disagree. The power in a flame war (i.e., a series of insulting messages) lies in the hands of the individual who initiates the online fight against an unsuspecting target.

Similarly, Twitter and Facebook can be used to share personal information about others that they would choose not to have shared. For example, a recent case of cyberbullying among middle school students has emerged, focusing on a Facebook page called "Let's Start Drama"

(Bazelon, 2013). On this profile page, a middle school girl posts rumors about other students, and frequently pits photos of two girls against one another, asking "Who's Prettier?" a practice that has reportedly led to much conflict and even fist fights among students at school.

Other sites like Instagram can be used for the purposes of sexting. In a new twist, photos shared via Instagram or other social media venues, such as YouTube, have been used for shaming, sometimes called slut shaming. In one variation of shaming, nude or seminude pictures or videos, most often of females, will be posted on social media sites in an attempt to shame the target for her sexual behavior (Fagbenle, 2013). As noted by Fagbenle, in many instances the target does not know that pictures or videos were even taken at the time that the sexual encounter occurred. She goes on to say "this is the new scarlet letter," albeit on a much grander scale. In another variation, photos that are knowingly posted on a social network site by the target are then altered by others along with comments designed to teach the target a lesson about her appearance, behavior, etc. A Facebook page called "Hey Girls, Did You Know" is used expressly for this purpose (Miller, 2013). Many college campuses are all too familiar with shaming sites, such as Juicycampus.com or CollegeACB, where students can post a feed "Top Ten Sluts at [college name]," to which people will then respond with the names of those they think fit the bill.

Other social networking sites, such as Ask.fm, allow users to ask questions of one another. Whereas some of the questions are completely innocuous, such as "What do you enjoy doing?" others are much more damaging and fall within the rubric of cyberbullying, such as "Why doesn't anyone like you?" As with some other types of social media, question askers can remain completely anonymous. Cyberbullying that has occurred on Ask.fm is believed to have been one factor involved in several suicides perpetrated by members of the site (Beckford, 2013). Young people gravitate toward social media, in part, as a way of trying on identities that they may not be able to assume in real life (Sivashanker, 2013). However, the barrage of negative comments and bullying that may follow can clearly produce a host of negative consequences (Kowalski & Limber, 2013).

Given the diversity of ways in which people can use social media to cyberbully others, it is hardly surprising that researchers are finding relationships between involvement in social media and involvement in cyberbullying, as victim or perpetrator. In one study, for example, Kwan and Skoric (2013) examined the extent to which Singaporean youth who were users of Facebook had experienced cyberbullying as victims and perpetrators on the social network site. Just under 60% of the 13- to 17-year-olds indicated that they had been targets of cyberbullying on Facebook, most often by receiving nasty messages, being insulted, or threatened. Fifty-seven percent indicated that they had cyberbullied others on Facebook, most commonly by blocking others or by sending nasty messages. Cyberbullying victimization was correlated with the intensity of Facebook use (i.e., number of Facebook friends, time spent on Facebook) and perpetration with performance of risky behaviors on Facebook, such as revealing very personal information or friending strangers (Kwan & Skoric, 2013; see also Staksrud, Ólafsson, & Livingstone, 2013). Consistent with published research, cyber victimization and perpetration on Facebook were significantly correlated with involvement in traditional bullying.

Effects of Cyberbullying via Social Media

The 24/7 accessibility associated with cyberbullying mentioned earlier suggests that targets of cyberbullying can rarely escape the bullying. As noted earlier, even when victims are not logging on to their Facebook accounts or checking their Twitter feed, derogatory messages about them are still being seen by others. Victims of cyberbullying have been shown to have higher levels of depressive symptomology (Wang, Nansel, & Iannotti, 2011) and suicidal ideation (Hinduja & Patchin, 2010; Kowalski & Limber, 2013) than those not involved with cyberbullying. Kowalski and Limber (2013) found that children who were cyberbully victims had the highest rates of anxiety, depression, and school absences. Children *not* involved in cyberbullying had the highest self-esteem and grades and the fewest symptoms of health problems. Staude-Müller, Hansen, and Voss (2012) observed that personality influences the effects of cyber victimization, with individuals higher in neuroticism and with a prior history of victimization having a more adverse reaction to their victimization.

Still other research, however, shows that the modality by which the cyberbullying occurs is a critical factor affecting perceptions of the seriousness of the bullying. College students in one study (Slonje & Smith, 2008) perceived cyberbullying via the distribution on social media of undesired pictures and video clips to be more upsetting than other types of cyber victimization.

☐ Prevention and Intervention

As anyone can attest who has had to live without email for a day, few of us would desire to be without all of our technological toys. However, it is important that we understand the dark side of technology and identify ways in which we can try to shield our youth from the negative effects. Figuring out how best to work with youth as they navigate the ever-changing world of social media with its pros and cons has been a subject of discussion among law and policy makers, parents, educators, law enforcement, and researchers (Palfrey, Gasser, & Boyd, 2010). Educators, not surprisingly, emphasize educating young people on the potential hazards, such as cyberbullying, associated with social media use. Many parents, on the other hand, want to limit their children's access to social media as a way of protecting them from potential bullying.

Unfortunately, communication between adults, namely, parents, and children about social media and the safest ways to navigate it is hampered by the digital divide. Parents, who did not grow up with the technology, are digital immigrants and, as such, are often woefully unfamiliar with both the dangers posed by social media and the extent to which social media permeates youth culture today. Young people, on the other hand, are digital natives. Their comfort level with technology, and their developmental inability to fully anticipate consequences, often leads them to make poor choices when using social media.

For starters, parents need to attend to warning signs that their child may be involved with cyberbullying, as either victim or perpetrator or bystander. These warning signs include depression, anxiety, poor performance in school, a reduced desire to attend school, and feelings of dismay after using technology (Kowalski et al., 2012a). Additionally, parents, in particular, need to set up rules for Internet and cellular phone use, along with the consequences for violation of those rules. For example, if a 13-year-old wants to have a profile on a social network site, then the parent may stipulate that the child has to friend the parent.

The burden, however, does not rest entirely on parents. Schools need to do schoolwide assessments to determine the prevalence of cyberbullying and the venue through which cyberbullying is occurring. Armed with this information, schools can look at trends in technology use among their students over time, as well as target their prevention and intervention efforts toward the groups and venues most involved with cyberbullying.

For individuals who are cyberbullied via social media, there are steps they can take. First, they can block the perpetrator and make sure that their own privacy settings are set up. Second, they can report the individual to the Internet service provider. Every social media site has terms of use associated with it that are violated in the case of many instances of cyberbullying. It is up to the target to report these violations. If a user of Facebook reports being bullied or harassed on the site, the Facebook User Operations team removes the post in question from the site (Bazelon, 2013). But with so many reports of bullying and harassment appearing on the site, complaints often fall through the cracks.

Third, if there are direct threats involved, then law enforcement should be contacted (Kowalski et al., 2012a).

Importantly, the medium through which negative messages are being sent can also be the conduit through which positive social change can be brought (Alhabash et al., 2013). Limber, Kowalski, and Agatston (2009a, 2009b) recommend that schools encourage youth to create "positive social sites." In this way, the youth can see the benefits that follow from social media and ways in which social media can be used to disseminate information about cyberbullying and how to reduce its frequency.

☐ References

Alhabash, S., McAlister, A. R., Hagerstrom, A., Quilliam, E., Rifon, N. J., & Richards, J. I. (2013). Between likes and shares: Effects of emotional appeal and virality on the persuasiveness of anticyberbullying messages on Facebook. *Cyberpsychology, Behavior & Social Networking, 16*(3), 175–182. doi: 10.1089/cyber.2012.0265

The Australian. (2013, March 18). Teen rape case sheds light on social media, cyberbullying. Retrieved from http://www.theaustralian.com.au/news/world/teen-rape-case-shines-light-on-social-media-cyber-bullying/story-e6frg6so-1226599850801

Baur, B. (2012, October 24). *Bullied teen Amanda Todd's video passes 17M views*. ABC News. Retrieved from http://abcnews.go.com/

Bazelon, E. (2013, February 20). How to stop the bullies. *The Atlantic*. Retrieved from http://www.theatlantic.com/

Beattie, J. (2013, February 21). *Rebecca Marino, 22, quits professional tennis due to depression, cyberbullying*. New England Sports Network. Retrieved from http://nesn.com/

Beckford, M. (2013, January 12). Pupils and parents warned over social networking website linked to teen abuse. *The Daily Mail*. Retrieved from http://www.dailymail.co.uk/

Buffardi, L. E., & Campbell, W. (2008). Narcissism and social networking web sites. *Personality and Social Psychology Bulletin, 34*(10), 1303–1314. doi: 10.1177/0146167208320061

Commonsense Media. (2009, August 10). *Is social networking changing childhood?* Retrieved from http://www.commonsensemedia.org/teen-social-media

Cox, D. (2013, February 21). *Canadian Rebecca Marino battles depression, cyber-bullies*. Retrieved from http://nesn.com/2013/02/rebecca-marino-22-quits-professional-tennis-due-to-depression-cyberbullying/Cox

Cunningham, L. (2013, March 20). *Steubenville rape case brings lessons in social media, sexting, and cyberbullying*. Retrieved from http://www.newsnet5.com/dpp/news/local_news/steubenville-rape-case-brings-lessons-in-social-media-sexting-and-cyber-bullying#ixzz2O54PEkbG

Diener, E. (1980). *The psychology of group influence*. New York: Erlbaum.

Dooley, J. J., Pyzalski, J., & Cross, D. (2009). Cyberbullying versus face-to-face bullying: A theoretical and conceptual review. *Zeitschrift für Psychologie/Journal of Psychology, 217,* 182–188. doi: 10.1027/0044-3409.217.4.182

Duggan, M., & Brenner, J. (2013, February 14). *The demographics of social media users—2012.* Retrieved from http://www.pewinternet.org/Reports/2013/Social-media-users.aspx

E-Guillotine. (2013). *How social media changed the way we interact with the world.* Retrieved from http://www.e-guillotine.com/how-social-media-changed-the-way-we-interact-with-the-world.php

Fagbenle, T. (2013, January 7*). Online 'shaming': A new level of cyberbullying for girls.* [Audio podcast]. Retrieved http://www.npr.org/

Fiegerman, S. (2012, December 18). *Twitter now has more than 200 million monthly active users.* Retrieved from http://mashable.com/2012/12/18/twitter-200-million-active-users/

Fowler, G. A. (2012, October 4). Facebook: One billion and counting. *The Wall Street Journal.* Retrieved from http://online.wsj.com

Giumetti, G. W., & Williams, M. (2013). [Spring 2013 student survey]. Unpublished raw data.

Gradinger, P., Strohmeier, D., & Spiel, C. (2009). Traditional bullying and cyberbullying: Identification of risk groups for adjustment problems. *Zeitschrift für Psychologie/Journal of Psychology, 217*(4), 205–213. doi: 10.1027/0044-3409.217.4.205

Hinduja, S., & Patchin, J. W. (2008). Cyberbullying: An exploratory analysis of factors related to offending and victimization. *Deviant Behavior, 29,* 129–156. doi: 10.1080/01639620701457816

Hinduja, S., & Patchin, J. W. (2010). Bullying, cyberbullying, and suicide. *Archives of Suicide Research, 14*(3), 206–221. doi: 10.1080/13811118.2010.494133

Jenkins-Guarnieri, M. A., Wright, S. L., & Hudiburgh, L. M. (2012). The relationships among attachment style, personality traits, interpersonal competency, and Facebook use. *Journal of Applied Developmental Psychology, 33*(6), 294–301. doi: 10.1016/j.appdev.2012.08.001

Jones, L. M., Mitchell, K. J., & Finkelhor, D. (2013). Online harassment in context: Trends from three youth Internet safety surveys (2000, 2005, 2010). *Psychology of Violence, 3,* 53–69. doi: 10.1037/a0030309

Katzer, C., Fetchenhauer, D., & Belschak, F. (2009). Cyberbullying: Who are the victims? A comparison of victimization in Internet chatrooms and victimization in school. *Journal of Media Psychology, 21,* 25–36. doi: 10.1027/1864-1105.21.1.25

Kiesler, S., Seigel, J., & McGuire, T. (1984). Social psychological aspects of computer-mediated communication. *American Psychologist, 39,* 1123–1134. doi: 10.1037/0003-066X.39.10.1123

Kowalski, R. M., & Fedina, C. (2011). Cyber bullying in ADHD and Asperger syndrome populations. *Research in Autism Spectrum Disorders, 5*(3), 1201–1208. doi: 10.1016/j.rasd.2011.01.007

Kowalski, R. M., Giumetti, G., Schroeder, A., & Lattanner, M. (2013). Bullying in the digital age: A critical review and meta-analysis of cyberbullying research among youth. *Psychological Bulletin,* in press.

Kowalski, R. M., & Limber, S. P. (2007). Electronic bullying among middle school students. *Journal of Adolescent Health*, *41*(6, Suppl), S22–S30. doi: 10.1016/j.jadohealth.2007.08.017

Kowalski, R. M., & Limber, S. (2013). Psychological, physical, and academic correlates of cyberbullying and traditional bullying. *Journal of Adolescent Health*, 53(1, Suppl), S13–S20. doi: 10.1016/j.jadohealth.2012.09.018

Kowalski, R. M., Limber, S. E., & Agatston, P. W. (2012a). *Cyberbullying: Bullying in the digital age* (2nd ed.). Malden, MA: Wiley-Blackwell.

Kowalski, R. M., Morgan, C. A., & Limber, S. E. (2012b). Traditional bullying as a potential warning sign of cyberbullying. *School Psychology International*, *33*, 505–519. doi: 10.1177/0143034312445244

Kuss, D. J., & Griffiths, M. D. (2011). Online social networking and addiction: A review of the psychological literature. *International Journal of Environmental Research and Public Health*, *8*(9), 3528–3552.

Kwan, G. C. E., & Skoric, M. M. (2013). Facebook bullying: An extension of battles in school. *Computers in Human Behavior, 29*, 16–25. doi: 10.1016/j.chb.2012.07.014

Lenhart, A., Purcell, K., Smith, A., & Zickuhr, K. (2010). Social media and mobile Internet use among teens and young adults. Retrieved from http://www.pewinternet.org/~media//Files/Reports/1010/PIP_Social_Media_and_Young_Adults_Report_Final_with_toplines.pdf

Limber, S., Kowalski, R. M., & Agatston, P. (2009a). *Cyber bullying: A prevention curriculum for grades 6–12*. Center City, MN: Hazelton.

Limber, S., Kowalski, R. M., & Agatston, P. (2009b). *Cyber bullying: A prevention curriculum for grades 3–5*. Center City, MN: Hazelton.

Lunden, I. (2012, July 30). Twitter passed 500M users in June 2012, 140M of them in US. *Tech Crunch*. Retrieved from http://techcrunch.com

Manago, A. M., Taylor, T., & Greenfield, P. M. (2012). Me and my 400 friends: The anatomy of college students' Facebook networks, their communication patterns, and well-being. *Developmental Psychology*, *48*(2), 369–380. doi: 10.1037/a0026338

Mangis, C. (2012, June 4). Facebook may let children under age 13 use the site. *Consumer News*. Retrieved from http://news.consumerreports.org/

Mazurek, M. O. (2013). Social media use among adults with autism spectrum disorder. *Computers in Human Behavior, 29*, 1709–1714. doi: 10.1016/j.chb.2013.02.004

Miller, J. (2013, January 8). New form of cyber bullying concerns local police departments. Retrieved from http://fox59.com

Miller, J. D., Campbell, W., Young, D. L., Lakey, C. E., Reidy, D. E., Zeichner, A., & Goodie, A. S. (2009). Examining the relations among narcissism, impulsivity, and self-defeating behaviors. *Journal of Personality*, *77*, 761–794. doi: 10.1111/j.1467-6494.2009.00564.x

Nansel, T., Overpeck, M., Pilla, R., Ruan, W., Simons-Morton, B., & Scheidt, P. (2001). Bullying behaviors among US youth: Prevalence and association with psychosocial adjustment. *Journal of the American Medical Association*, *285*, 2094–2100. doi: 10.1001/jama.285.16.2094

O'Keeffe, G. S., & Clarke-Pearson, K. (2011). The impact of social media on children, adolescents, and families. *Pediatrics*, *127*, 800–804. doi: 10.1542/peds.2011-0054

Olweus, D. (1993). *Bullying at school: What we know and what we can do*. New York: Blackwell.

Olweus, D. (2013). School bullying: Development and some important challenges. *Annual Review of Clinical Psychology, 9,* 1–14. doi: 10.1146/annurev-clinpsy-050212-185516

Palfrey, J., Gasser, U., & Boyd, D. (2010, February 24). *Response to FCC notice of inquiry 09-94 "Empowering parents and protecting children in an evolving media landscape."* Youth and Media Policy Working Group Initiative. Berkman Center for Internet & Society, Harvard University. Retrieved from http://cyber.law.harvard.edu/sites/cyber.law.harvard.edu/files/Palfrey_Gasser_boyd_response_to_FCC_NOI_09-94_Feb2010.pdf

Park, N., Chung, J., & Lee, S. (2012). Explaining the use of text-based communication media: An examination of three theories of media use. *Cyberpsychology, Behavior & Social Networking, 15*(7), 357–363. doi: 10.1089/cyber.2012.0121

Patchin, J., & Hinduja, S. (2006). Bullies move beyond the schoolyard: A preliminary look at cyberbullying. *Youth Violence and Juvenile Justice, 4,* 148–169. doi: 10.1177/1541204006286288

Pearson, C. M., Andersson, L. M., & Porath, C. L. (2005). Workplace incivility. In S. Fox & P. E. Spector (Eds.), *Counterproductive work behavior: Investigations of actors and targets* (pp. 256–309). Washington, DC: APA.

Pempek, T. A., Yermolayeva, Y. A., & Calvert, S. L. (2009). College students' social networking experiences on Facebook. *Journal of Applied Developmental Psychology, 30*(3), 227–238. doi: 10.1016/j.appdev.2008.12.010

Postmes, T., & Spears, R. (1998). Deindividuation and antinormative behavior: A meta-analysis. *Psychological Bulletin, 123,* 238–259. doi: 10.1037/0033-2909.123.3.238

Pyzalski, J. (2011). Electronic aggression among adolescents: An old house with a new façade (or even a number of houses). In C. Halligan, E. Dunkels, & G-M. Franberg (Eds.), *Youth culture and net culture: Online social practices* (pp. 278–295). Hershey, PA: IGI Global.

Reich, S. M., Subrahmanyam, K., & Espinoza, G. (2012). Friending, IMing, and hanging out face-to-face: Overlap in adolescents' online and offline social networks. *Developmental Psychology, 48*(2), 356–368. doi: 10.1037/a0026980

Runions, K., Shapka, J. D., Dooley, J., & Modecki, K. (2013). Cyber-aggression and victimization and social information processing: Integrating the medium and the message. *Psychology of Violence, 3,* 9–26. doi: 10.1037/a0030511

Sheldon, K. M., Abad, N., & Hinsch, C. (2011). A two-process view of Facebook use and relatedness need-satisfaction: Disconnection drives use, and connection rewards it. *Journal of Personality and Social Psychology, 100*(4), 766–775. doi: 10.1037/a0022407

Sivashanker, K. (2013). Cyberbullying and the digital self. *Journal of the American Academy of Child & Adolescent Psychiatry, 52*(2), 113–115. doi: 10.1016/j.jaac.2012.11.008

Slonje, R., & Smith, P. K. (2008). Cyberbullying: Another main type of bullying? *Scandanavian Journal of Psychology, 49,* 147–154. doi: 10.1111/j.1467-9450.2007.00611.x

Smith, A., & Brenner, J. (2012). *Twitter use 2012.* Retrieved from http://www.pewinternet.org/~/media//Files/Reports/2012/PIP_Twitter_Use_2012.pdf

Smith, P. K., Mahdavi, J., Carvalho, M., Fisher, S., Russell, S., & Tippett, N. (2008). Cyberbullying: Its nature and impact in secondary school pupils. *Journal of Child Psychology and Psychiatry, 49*(4), 376–385. doi: 10.1111/j.1469-7610.2007.01846.x

Staksrud, E., Ólafsson, K., & Livingstone, S. (2013). Does the use of social net-working sites increase children's risk of harm? *Computers in Human Behavior, 29*, 40–50. doi: 10.1016/j.chb.2012.05.026

Staude-Müller, F., Hansen, B., & Voss, M. (2012). How stressful is online victimization? Effects of victim's personality and properties of the incident. *European Journal of Developmental Psychology, 9*(2), 260–274. doi: 10.1080/17405629.2011.643170

Steinfield, C., Ellison, N. B., & Lampe, C. (2008). Social capital, self-esteem, and use of online social network sites: A longitudinal analysis. *Journal of Applied Developmental Psychology, 29*(6), 434–445. doi: 10.1016/j.appdev.2008.07.002

Stepanikova, I., Nie, N. H., & He, X. (2010). Time on the Internet at home, loneliness, and life satisfaction: Evidence from panel time-diary data. *Computers in Human Behavior, 26*(3), 329–338. doi: 10.1016/j.chb.2009.11.002

Sugarman, D. B., & Willoughby, T. (2013). Technology and violence: Conceptual issues raised by the rapidly changing social environment. *Psychology of Violence, 3*, 1–8. doi: 10.1037/a0031010

Tokunaga, R. S. (2010). Following you home from school: A critical review and synthesis of research on cyber bullying victimization. *Computers in Human Behavior, 26*, 277–287. doi: 10.1016/j.chb.2009.11.014

Twenge, J. M., Konrath, S., Foster, J. D., Campbell, W., & Bushman, B. J. (2008). Egos inflating over time: A cross-temporal meta-analysis of the Narcissistic Personality Inventory. *Journal of Personality, 76*(4), 875–902. doi: 10.1111/j.1467-6494.2008.00507.x

Walther, J. B., Van Der Heide, B., Kim, S., Westerman, D., & Tong, S. (2008). The role of friends' appearance and behavior on evaluations of individuals on Facebook: Are we known by the company we keep? *Human Communication Research, 34*(1), 28–49. doi: 10.1111/j.1468-2958.2007.00312.x

Wang, J., Nansel, T. R., & Iannotti, R. J. (2011). Cyber and traditional bullying: Differential association with depression. *Journal of Adolescent Health, 48*, 415–417. doi: 10.1016/j.jadohealth.2010.07.012

Weber, H. (2012, December 6). Google+ by the numbers: 500m+ users, 235m of them active and 135m using the stream. *The Next Web*. Retrieved from http://thenextweb.com/

Willard, N. E. (2007). *Cyberbullying and cyberthreats: Responding to the challenge of online social aggression, threats, and distress*. Champaign, IL: Research Press.

Ybarra, M. L., Boyd, D., Korchmaros, J. D., & Oppenheim, J. (2012). Defining and measuring cyberbullying within the larger context of bullying victimization. *Journal of Adolescent Health, 51*, 53–58. doi: 10.1016/j.jadohealth.2011.12.031

Ybarra, M. L., & Mitchell, K. J. (2004). Online aggressor/target, aggressors, and targets: A comparison of associated youth characteristics. *Journal of Child Psychology and Psychiatry, 45*, 1308–1316. doi: 10.1111/j.1469-7610.2004.00328x

YouTube. (2013, March 21). YouTube hits 1 billion monthly users. *Deadline News*. Retrieved from http://www.deadline.com

CHAPTER 7

Understanding Digital Piracy Using Social Networks
An Integrated Theory Approach

George E. Higgins

University of Louisville

Contents

Occurrences of Digital Piracy   113
Explanations of Digital Piracy   116
Integrated Theory of Digital Piracy   118
Policy Implications   121
Conclusion   122
References   122

The development of the Internet has had important influences on society. New industries have developed (i.e., computer hardware and software, engineering, sales, etc.). One industry, crime, has found a new venue for production. Adler and Adler (2006) argue that cybercrime, the type of criminal activity that takes place using a computer, is one of the fastest growing types of behaviors. The number of criminal behaviors and the scope of criminal behaviors are vast and have attracted research attention in the criminological literature since the 1970s (Higgins & Marcum, 2011; Hinduja & Patchin, 2010; Holt & Lampke, 2009; Holt & Bossler, 2009).

While some argue that the behaviors that take place using the computer are the same non-computer-based behaviors, the Internet has some attractive qualities for criminal activity. For instance, the Internet provides the individual with a sense of anonymity and confidentiality in the performance of his or her criminal behavior. To clarify, the cybercriminal, an individual that performs criminal behavior using the Internet, usually has a sense that his or her activities are going undetected because no one is overtly monitoring his or her behavior. Further, the cybercriminal may be able to perform his or her actions in confidence because the use of pseudonames is a normal action on the Internet. In addition, the Internet is user-friendly. This means that most actions using the Internet do not require a substantial amount of computer savvy to perform criminal activities.

Social networks provide an additional environment that individuals may use to perform criminal activity. Social networks are environments where individuals may share personal information about themselves with others. A nonexhaustive list of examples of social networks includes Facebook, MySpace, Instagram, and Twitter. In general, social networks operate using the Internet, which means that many of the attributes above will apply here. However, it is important to note that the popularity of social networks has changed access to the Internet. In the late 20th and early 21st centuries, Internet access came primarily through computers. As the 21st century matures, access to the Internet increasingly comes through the use of mobile telephones. Thus, the further development of the mobile telephone provides additional "on ramps" to the Internet and social networks that may provide opportunities for criminal behavior.

The primary goal of this chapter is examine and understand pirates of digital media (i.e., digital piracy) who use social networks to perform their actions. The understanding of digital piracy begins by examining the occurrences of the behavior. In addition, this chapter will cover a number of explanations of this behavior from multiple disciplines. Specifically, the chapter will cover information that comes from the sociological, economic, information/technology/computer science, and criminological theories. This provides the most salient risk factors for digital piracy. The chapter moves to a presentation of an integrated theory of digital piracy—that is likely to explain other criminal behavior as well—using the risk factors. The chapter ends with potential policy implications for reducing instances of digital piracy using social networks.

☐ Occurrences of Digital Piracy

Understanding occurrences of digital piracy requires a cogent definition of the behavior. In the empirical literature, a formal definition of digital piracy is elusive. An early definition of piracy is the illegal duplication of copyrighted computer software (Koen & Im, 1997; Straub & Collins, 1990). The issue with this definition is that it leaves out other forms of digital piracy. A broader definition of digital piracy is the illegal copying of digital goods, software, digital documents, digital audio (including music and voice), and digital video for any reason other than to create a backup without the explicit permission of or compensation to the copyright holder (Gopal, Sanders, Bhattacharjee, Agrawal, & Wagner, 2004; Higgins & Marcum, 2011). This definition has import because it encapsulates the different forms of digital piracy and it takes many of the legal issues into account.

Digital piracy is not only a social or behavioral science phenomenon. Since the federal Copyright Act of 1976, as amended in the Computer Software Act of 1980, digital piracy has been an illegal behavior. Under these acts, the copyright owner has the right to reproduce, copy, prepare derivative works, share copies, perform, and display copyrighted material for life plus 50 years (for individuals) or life plus 75 years (for corporations) (Higgins & Marcum, 2011). Under these acts, penalties for violating these conditions include prison and hefty fines. It is instructive to understand that organizations (e.g., corporations or schools) and individuals may be prosecuted and convicted for digital piracy whether the actions are intentional or unintentional.

While these acts only covered software, the Copyright Felony Act of 1992 amended them to include recorded sound, movies, or software. Another advance of this particular act is that it delineates the qualifications of felony digital piracy. Specifically, the individual or organization only has to pirate 10 copies within a 180-day period, but the pieces have to contain a retail value of $250,000. In addition, the government has to show intent and that copyright infringement has occurred. These qualifications move piracy into a felony that may result in 10 years of prison with several thousand dollars in fines.

The Copyright Felony Act of 1992 advanced the legal issues in fighting digital piracy. The No Electronic Theft (NET) Act advanced the legal issues again. The NET Act reduced the number of pirated pieces and the monetary value of the digital piracy. Specifically, the piracy has to only include one piece for a value of $1,000. This type of piracy may result in prison and hefty fines.

When felonies occur, information is necessary to understand them so that they may be reduced. Digital piracy is not any different, so to delve into this topic, it is important to review the main sources of crime data. One source is the Uniform Crime Reports (UCR). The UCR, maintained by the FBI, provides the most cited information about crime in the United States. The UCR is a collection of crime data from local law enforcement. Local law enforcement provides information about known crimes, arrests, and crimes cleared by arrest. The information that comes from these data is helpful in describing offenders and changes in offending. While this information is helpful, an issue with these data should be apparent—not all law enforcement will report. Other issues with these data include: (1) The police must know that the crime has taken place, and (2) sometimes criminal behaviors get combined when reporting occurs (e.g., a robbery and a homicide may be reported as a homicide, which means that the robbery information is lost).

These problems with the UCR suggest that other forms of data are necessary. Another form of data that is often used in criminology to understand the occurrence of crime is the National Crime Victimization Survey (NCVS). The NCVS is a nationally representative survey of households that has been used to compare statistics on crime from other data sources such as the UCR. The use of surveys is important because it allows individuals to anonymously and confidentially self-report being a victim of criminal behavior. The NCVS overcomes one of the issues with the UCR by capturing crime information that the police may not know about. However, the NCVS does not alleviate all of the problems that come from the UCR.

In an attempt to address the remaining problems of the UCR, the U.S. government has instituted that National Incident-Based Reporting System (NIBRS). The NIBRS system relies on law enforcement to report all aspects of a crime. In other words, when a robbery and a homicide occur in the same incident, the robbery and the homicide are reported—not just the homicide. The issue with NIBRS is that the offense has to be known to the police. While this is an improvement, the effort does not overcome all of the issues with the UCR.

The problems for the UCR, NCVS, and NIBRS do not end with the issues outlined. The problem with these major sources of crime data is that they do not provide any information about digital piracy, with the exception of child pornography cases, and many other cybercrimes. In the context of the UCR, the data come in an aggregate form that may not be precise enough to provide information about digital piracy. A plausible situation may occur where a cybercriminal is pirating digital media while committing another crime, and the reporting of the digital piracy is not recorded in the UCR. In this situation, if the recording were to take place, no category exists in the UCR for digital piracy. The same issues plague NIBRS in reporting digital piracy.

The NCVS does not offer any additional help. The survey is designed to address victimization issues. Digital piracy may not be a victimization issue for many individuals. Digital piracy is primarily a behavior that is perpetrated against entities—musical groups, software, including gaming—companies, or movie production companies. These groups do not usually take part in the NCVS. Further, the NCVS utilizes self-reports. While self-reports have been a mainstay in criminology for many years, some suggest that there are problems with self-report data (Hindelang, Hirschi, & Weiss, 1981; Junger-Tas & Marshall, 1999).

Given that the official sources for information are not able to provide information about digital piracy, the data for understanding digital piracy come from for-profit and nonprofit organizations (e.g., Business Software Alliance, BitTorrent, Motion Picture Association, and the International Phonographic Federation). These organizations provide information about the piracy that takes place in the areas of software, games, movies, and music. While they have an interest in this type of behavior and may provide a skewed view of the behavior, these organizations seem to provide the most cogent information about digital piracy. This is not to say that other forms of data on digital piracy do not exist, but to date, they have not been found by this author.

Because of these issues, the trends of digital piracy are difficult to track, but the for-profit and nonprofit organizations provide some indications about the occurrence of the behavior. Regardless of the issues that arise from these organizations, they show some interesting trends in digital piracy. One area for focusing on digital piracy is in the collegiate environment. College students and faculty rely on expensive and powerful forms of software to learn and disseminate vast amounts of knowledge. From 2003 to 2007, the Business Software Alliance (BSA) showed that students' software piracy seemed to be declining. This can be misleading when considering that the drop is from 68% in 2003 to 55% in 2007. Fifty-five percent of all college students in the United States pirating software is still a large number. This is consistent with others that show that piracy is relevant among college students (Hinduja, 2003; Morris & Higgins, 2010). During the same period, the BSA showed that digital piracy among faculty increased from 29% to 33%. This information suggests that digital piracy is occurring on college campuses and requires some explanation.

The trends do not seem to stop with software piracy, and continue with music piracy. Among college students, the BSA found that from 2003 to 2005 music piracy remained relatively stable. This is consistent with a growing body of academic literature that has taken smaller samples (Holt & Bossler, 2009; Morris & Higgins, 2010). Pirating games and movies seem to have similar fates—they remain stable or are slightly increasing.

The trends of the college students are consistent with other age groups. For instance, teenagers have similar trends. For-profit and non-profit groups show that trends with digital piracy are decreasing when it comes to software, but increasing when it comes to movies, music, and games (Higgins & Marcum, 2011; Malin & Fowers, 2009). While these trends may contain some bias, they provide an overall conclusion that digital piracy is occurring.

The occurrence of digital piracy may have undesirable influences on society. As mentioned above, digital piracy is an illegal behavior that may be punishable by law. In addition, the promulgation of digital piracy may reduce the appeal for others to produce creative activity. In other words, some may take a fatalistic stance toward developing creative works because of a perception that their works will be pirated. This does not allow society to advance as rapidly. Further, digital piracy has important economic influences. Specifically, it has the ability to reduce taxes, wages, and potential for jobs (Hinduja, 2003; Higgins, 2005; Higgins & Marcum, 2011).

☐ Explanations of Digital Piracy

The stimulus for the behavior comes from humans. Digital piracy may be performed by individuals, groups, or programmed machines. Regardless of the entity that is performing digital piracy, a human had to set the process into motion. Because this is a human issue, theory is necessary to provide a cogent explanation of why the behavior is occurring. For this chapter, theory is a set of interrelated or intercorrelated concepts and propositions that are designed to explain a behavior (Higgins, 2005), concepts are abstractions from reality (e.g., self-control), and propositions are the equivalent to a hypothesis (i.e., a testable statement). Several theories from different disciplines (i.e., business, information technology/computer science, criminological, and economics) have been used to explain digital piracy.

Before moving into a brief summary of the theories that have been used in these different disciplines, it is instructive to understand that all of these theories share the same foundation. Specifically, the foundation is that individuals are rational beings. Rationality in this context is that individuals, whether consciously or unconsciously, will weigh the potential benefits against the potential consequences. When the benefits outweigh the consequences, the individual is likely to perform the behavior. Some disciplines will use different language to discuss this issue. For instance, sociology, business, or information technology may suggest that individuals operate under a condition of volitional control. Volitional control is essentially the same process explained above.

With this in mind, the business and information technology literature seems to be blended with similar explanations of digital piracy. The majority of the literature (Straub & Collins, 1990) seems to use at least some derivative of the theory of planned behavior (TPB). The TPB is a motivational theory that has similarities to different forms of learning theories. The TPB operates as a full theory. This means that anything not explicitly mentioned in the TPB is likely to be mediated by the TPB. Ajzen (1991) relies on a number of concepts to arrive at the complete theory.

In the TPB the most proximal concept to behavior is an individual's intentions to perform the behavior. Ajzen (1991) argues that intentions are an individual's readiness to perform a behavior. The intentions are influenced by three other concepts. The first concept is attitudes. Ajzen (1991) argues that attitudes are an individual's positive or negative perception of a behavior. Intentions are influenced by subjective norms. Ajzen (1991) argues that subjective norms are an individual's perceptions of the pressure to perform a behavior. Intentions and behavior are influenced by the individual's perceived behavioral control. Ajzen (1991) argues that perceived behavioral control is the individual's perception of performing the behavior. This theoretical premise shows promise in understanding digital piracy.

From the economics literature, the central focus tends to be on demand. For instance, Besen and Kirby (1989) (BK) argue that the demands of copies depend on the demands for the original and actual prices. Using the BK model, the value a person places on the original or copy is a predictor of which one is purchased. In addition, the economics literature indicates that digital piracy is a moral issue. Those individuals that have lower morality are more likely to perform digital piracy.

In the criminological literature, researchers use a number of theories to understand digital piracy. Some researchers have used deterrence theory to understand digital piracy. The central thesis of deterrence theory is that threats of punishment keep individuals from performing criminal behavior. The threats may come in two forms: specific or general. Specific deterrence is intent on keeping one individual from committing crime, whereas general deterrence is designed to keep a group from committing crime. Wolfe, Higgins, and Marcum (2008) show that general deterrence has relevance for digital piracy.

Another criminological theory that has importance for understanding digital piracy is social learning theory (SLT). Akers (1998) purports that individuals learn criminal behavior just like any other behavior. The learning process occurs through differential association (association with peers), definitions (positive attitudes for performing a behavior), imitation (seeing someone perform the behavior), and reinforcement (being rewarded for performing the behavior). A number of studies show support for this version of social learning theory (Morris & Higgins, 2010). It is important to keep in mind that this version of social learning theory is similar to the TPB from the business, information, and technology literature.

Gottfredson and Hirschi's (1990) self-control is another theory that criminologists use to examine digital piracy. They suggest that individuals who are subjected to poor or ineffective parenting are likely to have lower levels of self-control. Individuals with lower levels of self-control are likely to produce criminal activity when given an opportunity. In 2004, Hirschi respecified self-control theory. The respecification suggests that individuals with higher levels of self-control are less likely to commit crime. Both versions of self-control theory show promise in understanding digital piracy (Higgins, Wolfe, & Marcum, 2008).

Overall, understanding digital piracy from a theoretical perspective is complex. Multiple theories may provide equally as well understandings of the behavior. To review, the most salient risk factors for digital piracy seem to come from self-control theory or some form of social learning theory. Given that self-control and social learning theory seem to explain digital piracy, it seems important to determine if a theoretical integration is possible.

☐ Integrated Theory of Digital Piracy

Higgins and Marcum (2011) propose that the complexities of digital piracy may be best understood using an integrated theoretical approach. They argue that integrating theories brings together multiple risk factors in a cogent and coherent way. Further, Higgins and Marcum (2011) argue that integrated theory provides the most promise in developing policy to prevent or intervene in instances of digital piracy.

The integrated theory that we propose is one that encapsulates self-control, social learning, and theory of planned behavior. These theories are integrated to provide a developmental perspective of digital piracy. Specifically, some of the measures from each of the theories are organized to precede other measures. Figure 7.1 shows the integrated model.

Before describing the entire model, it is instructive to understand how the integrated theoretical premise views human beings. Higgins and Marcum (2011) see humans as rational individuals that are capable of making decisions. To explicate, individuals will use the amount of information that they have at the time to make a decision. In other words, the individual will operate from a bounded rational perspective. This means that the individual is not expected to have all information about a specific behavior or situation. The only information that is necessary for

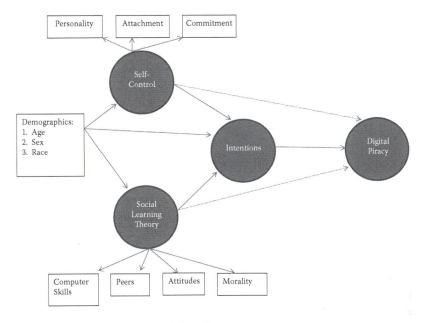

FIGURE 7.1 Integrated theory of digital piracy.

a decision is the information that is in the present. When this information indicates that the pleasure of a behavior will outweigh the pain of a
behavior, the individual is likely to perform the behavior.

From this point of view, the first theory that is encountered in the
model is the individual's level of self-control. Higgins and Marcum (2011)
do not attempt to redefine self-control. Rather, they use Gottfredson and
Hirschi's (1990) and recent reformulations (Hirschi, 2004; Gottfredson,
2006) as the basis. In other words, individuals that endure poor or ineffective child rearing are not likely to have the ability to foresee the consequences of their actions.

Higgins and Marcum (2011) see promise in intentions. They see
intentions, similar to Ajzen (1991), as a mechanism that prepares the
individual for action. The preparation is one that provides the motivation
for criminal behavior. Some may argue that the use of motivation is not
congruent with Gottfredson and Hirschi's (1990) view of self-control.
While not explicitly stated, Higgins and Marcum (2011) seem to be following Agnew's (1995) suggestion that the motivational components of
the general crime theories—including self-control theory—need to be
explicitly stated. Agnew (1995) argues that freedom is the proper motivational component for self-control theory, and Higgins and Ricketts (2004)
show support for this view. However, Higgins and Marcum (2011) take a
different tact using intentions. The role of intentions pays homage to the
perspective that intent is a necessity for a crime. In other words, intent

prepares the individual to commit a crime; thus, it is a motivational component that cannot be discounted in criminal activity, especially in digital piracy. Others in the criminological literature seem to provide similar conclusions about the importance of intentions (Higgins et al., 2008), but this is done through the rational choice literature.

Higgins and Marcum (2011) also make use of social learning theory. They seem to balance the parts of learning from TPB and Akers's (1998) version of social learning theory. In particular, they seem to make use of computer-related skills. Their view seems to be that if individuals are to perform digital piracy, they need to have the requisite skills to do so. In other words, the individual needs basic computer skills to reach or use social network outlets. A basic understanding of these outlets will allow piracy to occur. The remaining pieces of social learning theory are similar to the TPB. In other words, Higgins and Marcum (2011) focus on three parts of the theory (i.e., peer association, attitudes, and morality). These make up the remaining parts of their use of social learning theory.

Higgins and Marcum (2011) deliver several different hypotheses using these components that are the essence of their integrated theory. One hypothesis suggests that individuals that have lower levels of self-control are unable to fully see the consequences of their actions; thus, they are likely to develop intentions to perform digital piracy easier than individuals with higher levels of self-control. In the context of social networks, individuals are likely to use the social networks, without forethought, and perform digital piracy.

Another hypothesis is that individuals with low self-control are likely to seek the basic skills necessary to perform digital piracy. These individuals do not lack tenacity, but they are deficient in delay in gratification. Without the delay in gratification, individuals are much more likely to learn digital piracy is all right to perform and the skill set to perform the behavior. In the context of social networks, peer association may be relevant in the learning process. Peers may provide not only an avenue, but also additional skills and locations on other social networks to perform digital piracy.

The next hypothesis is that individuals that socially learn that digital piracy is a proper behavior are likely to do it. These individuals are likely to perform the behavior because they believe they have the requisite skills, their peers participate in the behavior and will reinforce or praise the behavior, and they see the behavior as being consistent with their moral code. Therefore, individuals who socially learn that digital piracy is a proper behavior are likely to do it using social networks. The social networks may provide the peers an opportunity to locate the media to pirate. In addition, the social networks may provide the information about the techniques to perform the behavior.

The next hypothesis is that individuals that are high on intentions are likely to perform digital piracy. These individuals have the motivation to perform the behavior. Specifically, these individuals feel as though they are ready to perform the behavior. This means that the individual feels that he or she has acquired the skills and support, and does not see the negative consequences of performing the behavior.

Finally, demographics seem to have an influence on digital piracy, and should have an influence on digital piracy using social networks. Following Hinduja (2003), males are more likely than females to digitally pirate. Wolfe, Higgins, and Marcum (2008) show that younger individuals are more likely to digitally pirate than older individuals. Higgins and Marcum (2011) seem to suggest that demographics influence digital piracy through their integrated theory. This means that the theoretical constructs of their theory serve as mediators of the influence of demographics.

To date, Higgins and Marcum's (2011) integrated theory for digital piracy has not undergone empirical scrutiny. However, some have examined pieces of this integrated theory that suggest that it has merit (Higgins, Fell, & Wilson, 2006). Cogent tests of the theory would consider not only cross-sectional data, but also longitudinal data. The theory lends itself to multiple forms of data collection and empirical study. Higgins and Marcum (2011) take the same stance as Tittle (1995) that empirical testing will provide the evidence for respecification. This model is ripe for testing in the context of criminal behavior using social networks, especially digital piracy.

☐ Policy Implications

The potential policy implications from this theoretical premise are vast, and require some organizing principles. One method to organize the potential policy implications is the occurrence of the implication. Higgins and Marcum (2011) take the position that the implications can occur proactively or reactively. Proactively, they argue that education is best. Their position is that teaching individuals about the problems that occur with digital piracy early on will assist in reducing instances of the behavior later. In the context of intentions, social network sites should make sure that it is difficult for individuals to upload or download pirated media. From a self-control perspective, social networking sites should limit access to the ability to upload and download information. Proactively and from a social learning theory perspective, social network organizations may be able to raise the awareness of the consequences of the actions.

Reactively, to thwart intentions for digital piracy, social networking sites may be able to remove the individual from the site. From a self-control perspective, a reactive policy needs to be a swift reaction. With the speed of technology, the detection of digital piracy through social networks means that an individual may be blocked immediately. The speed is important because it allows the to individual feel the consequences immediately. From a social learning perspective, the individual should feel swift positive punishment.

☐ Conclusion

Digital piracy is an emerging criminal behavior. This type of criminal behavior does not have any real boundaries. Digital piracy may take place at home or through social networking sites. The development of social networking sites provides an opportunity for digital piracy to go undetected. As mentioned above, the depth and breadth of digital piracy are unknown. The different locations where the behavior may take place make it nearly impossible for the behavior to be tracked. One way to fully understand digital piracy is by examining the behavior academically and through organizations. To assist in understanding why the behavior occurs, an integrated theory to explain digital piracy is a reasonable option.

☐ References

Adler, P., & Adler, P. A. (2006). The deviance society. *Deviant Behavior, 27,* 129–147.

Agnew, R. (1995). Testing the leading crime theories: An alternative strategy focusing on motivational processes. *Journal of Research in Crime and Delinquency, 32,* 363–398.

Ajzen, I. (1991). The theory of planned behavior. *Organizational Behavior and Human Decisions Processes, 50,* 179–211.

Akers, R. (1998). *Social learning and social structure: A general theory of crime and deviance.* Boston, MA: Northeastern University Press.

Besen, S. M., & Kirby, S. N. (1989). Private copying, appropriability, and optimal copying royalties. *Journal of Law and Economics, 32,* 255–280.

Gopal, R., Sanders, G., Bhattacharjee, S., Agrawal, M., & Wagner, S. (2004). A behavioral model of digital music piracy. *Journal of Organizational Computing and Electronic Commerce, 14,* 89–105.

Gottfredson, M. (2006). The empirical status of control theory in criminology. In F. T. Cullen, J. P. Wright, and K. Blevins, *Taking stock: The empirical status of criminological theory* (pp. 77–101). New Brunswick, NJ: Transaction Publishers.

Gottfredson, M., & Hirschi, T. (1990). *A general theory of crime.* Stanford, CA: Stanford University Press.

Higgins, G. E. (2005). Can low self-control help with the understanding of the software piracy problem? *Deviant Behavior, 26,* 1–24.

Higgins, G. E., Fell, B. D., & Wilson, A. L. (2006). Digital piracy: Assessing the contributions of an integrated self-control theory and social learning theory. *Criminal Justice Studies: A Critical Journal of Crime, Law and Society, 19*(1), 3–22.

Higgins, G. E., & Marcum, C. D. (2011). *Digital piracy: An integrated theoretical approach.* Durham, NC: Carolina Academic Press.

Higgins, G. E., & Ricketts, M. L. (2004). Motivation or opportunity: Which serves as the best mediator in self-control theory? *Western Criminology Review, 5*(2), 77–96.

Higgins, G. E., Wolfe, S. E., & Marcum, C. D. (2008). Digital piracy: An examination of multiple conceptualizations and operationalizations of self-control. *Deviant Behavior, 29,* 440–460.

Hindelang, M. J., Hirschi, T., & Weiss, J. G. (1981). *Measuring delinquency.* Beverly Hills, CA: Sage Publications.

Hinduja, S. (2003). Trends and patterns among online software pirates. *Ethics and Information Technology, 5,* 49–61.

Hinduja, S., & Patchin, J. (2010). Bullying, cyberbullying, and suicide. *Archives of Suicide Research, 14,* 206–221.

Hirschi, T. (2004). Self-control and crime. In R. F. Baumeister and K. D. Vohs (Eds.), *Handbook of self-regulation: Research, theory, and applications* (pp. 537–552). New York, NY: Guilford Press.

Holt, T., & Bossler, A. M. (2009). Examining the applicability of lifestyle-routine activities theory for cybercrime victimization. *Deviant Behavior, 30,* 1–25.

Holt, T., & Lampke, E. (2010). Exploring stolen data markets online: Products and market forces. *Criminal Justice Studies, 23,* 33–50.

Junger-Tas, J., & Marshall, I. H. (1999). The self-report methodology in crime research. In M. Tonry (Ed.), *Crime and justice: A review of research* (Vol. 25, pp. 291–367). Chicago, IL: University of Chicago Press.

Koen, C., Jr., & Im, J. H. (1997). Software piracy and its legal implications. *Information & Management, 31,* 265–272.

Malin, J., & Fowers, B. (2009). Adolescent self-control and music and movie piracy. *Computers in Human Behavior, 25,* 718–722.

Morris, R., & Higgins, G. E. (2010). Criminological theory in the digital age: The case of social learning theory and digital piracy. *Journal of Criminal Justice, 38,* 470–480.

Straub, D. W., & Collins, R. W. (1990). Key information liability issues facing managers: Software piracy, proprietary databases, and individual rights to privacy. *MIS Quarterly, 14,* 143–156.

Tittle, C. (1995). *Control balance: Toward a general theory of deviance.* Boulder, CO: Westview Press.

Wolfe, S., Higgins, G. E., & Marcum, C. D. (2008). Deterrence and digital piracy: A preliminary examination of the role of viruses. *Social Science Computer Review, 26,* 317–333.

Patterns of Sexual Victimization of Children and Women in the Multipurpose Social Networking Sites

Debarati Halder

Centre for Cyber Victim Counseling

K. Jaishankar

Manonmaniam Sundaranar University

Contents

Patterns of Sexual Victimization in the MPSNSs   129
    Sexual Victimization of Children   129
    Sexual Victimization of Women   134
Reasons for Growth of Sexual Crimes in the MPSNSs   138
    Growing Popularity of the MPSNSs for Forming Relationships   138
    Lack of Awareness of Female Users   139
Discussion and Conclusion   139
References   143

Social networking sites have become imminent components of modern-day communication channels. Boyd and Ellison (2007) defined social networking sites as "web based services that allow individuals to (i) construct a public or semi-public profile within a bounded system, (ii) articulate the list of others users with whom they share connection and (iii) view and traverse their list of connections and those made by others within the system." From the definition we can infer that social networking sites provide immense freedom to users to showcase themselves and also contact others and discuss with others in both a private and a public mode. The social networking sites can be either backed and financially supported by multipurpose web companies like Google, which besides being a major search engine* also hosts numbers of social networking sites like YouTube, Google+, Orkut, and so on, or created, hosted, and financially supported by web companies whose main aim is to provide an information network and get people connected with each other, like Twitter† or Facebook,‡ which provides a platform not only to interact with people but also to publicize products for profit through it.

However, it must be noted that apart from the above social networking sites, there are numerous categories of interactive networking sites catering to various needs of web users, for example, interactive networking sites used for professional updates, job marketing, as well as socializing and networking with people in similar or related professions, such as LinkedIn; interactive networking sites meant for music sharing or for sharing frustrated feelings (Halder & Jaishankar, 2009) which would also allow users to write about ex-partners; and adult dating sites and adult matrimonial sites that are specifically used for searching suitable matches or alliances for dating as well as for marriage. In the last category, some sites also offer opportunities to socialize with other members by creating forums and consequently attract the broad category of social networking site. Based on these said purposes, interactive social networking sites can be broadly divided into five groups:

1. *Professional social networking sites* (PSWs): The best example of such PSWs is LinkedIn. PSWs are business network oriented (Papacharissi, 2009). In PSWs, users get the opportunity to access and share employee-related information. These sites also serve as virtual platforms for recruiting. PSWs may also include interactive communication sites meant for academicians like Academia.edu, ResearchGate,

---

* See "what we do for you" at http://www.google.co.in/intl/en/about/company/products/.
† See https://twitter.com/about.
‡ See http://www.facebook.com/legal/terms.

Academic Room, and so on, where users can create profiles with personal as well as professional information and share their research works.

2. *Adult dating and matrimonial sites* (AD&MSs): These sites are particularly meant for adult interacting and also virtual dating. Users also have the opportunity to set up real-life dating. Some AD&MSs are particularly created for matrimonial alliance searches, which may also allow virtual interacting with the prospective partners. It may be noted that unlike the previous categories of social networking sites, such AD&MSs may restrict the age group to 18 and above and may allow the contribution of adult content as per their own policies.

3. *Interactive communication sites for venting frustration*: Apart from providing platforms for socializing through the above categories of sites, one can find in the World Wide Web specific forums for venting anger and frustration. Such forums such as Ventyouranger.com, angryforum.com, cad-forums.com, and so on, provide opportunity for the users to express their frustration and anger on specific issues. It needs to be noted that some of these forums in their terms and policies expressly state that defamatory and hate messages should be avoided by the users. It must also be noted that apart from specific forums meant exclusively for venting anger, blog sites hosted by Google or WordPress can also be used for the same purpose. Such blogging sites become forums for interactive communication when the blogger gives the opportunity for viewers to discuss their views and type their reaction.

4. *Interactive vlogging sites* (IVSs): YouTube, being a video-sharing site hosted by Google,[*] allows users to share not only videos, but also vlogs (Wesch, 2009). In the IVSs, users are encouraged to share original videos. In addition, users also share *mashed videos* besides film/music clips, news clips, and so forth, on YouTube. While vlogging through original videos, users may also talk about individuals who have not given any specific permission to be filmed or discussed. In vlogging, other viewers may also interact with the vlogger through messages posted in the message section of the vlog. Such messages may also be personal comments of the viewers and may not be interactive in nature.

5. *Multipurpose popular social networking sites* (MPSNSs): MPSNSs are Facebook, Google+, Twitter, and the like, and they attract huge numbers of users due to their social bonding promises (Ellison, Steinfield,

---

[*] See http://www.youtube.com/t/about_youtube.

& Lampe, 2007). MPSNSs are mostly used to share personal information with existing, newly acquired, or "lost and found" friends and relatives. These sites not only cater to the needs for popular socializing, but also provide opportunities for creating numerous forums and groups on the basis of religion, race, culture, hobbies, and academic interests by the members themselves, which further become sub-hubs for members. MPSNSs also include characteristics of the above four categories of sites when they provide platforms to discuss issues regarding higher studies, job opportunities, and so on. Profiles created in MPSNSs with such aims may become useful portfolios themselves. In this way, MPSNSs also become chosen platforms for employers to do a quick search about the potential candidates (Vinson, 2013).

In all these interactive social networking sites, users are instructed to create profiles with basic personal data such as name, educational and professional qualifications, residential location, which may include continent, country, or specific region, race, language, and so on. While in PSWs, AD&MSs, and interactive communication sites for sharing frustration, the age limit may be restricted to 18 and above[*]; ISVs and MPSNSs are open to all individuals' from the age of 13.[†] Some of the common characteristics of all these categories of interactive communication sites are as follows:

- The website administration may not *suo motu* monitor the data contributed by the users.[‡]

- Openness of the data depends much upon the users' choice for safety options.[§]

- Even though the majority of these websites are hosted in the United States, the platform provided by them helps to build virtual global villages where users can interact with each other and contribute data irrespective of their race, religion, language, or geographic location.

---

[*] For example, LinkedIn restricts the minimum age of the member to 18 (see the definition of minimum age in para. 2C of the user agreement at http://www.linkedin.com/legal/user-agreement). Similarly, sites like Ventyouranger.com do not allow prospective users to register unless they are over 18 (see http://www.ventyouranger.com/forum/register.php).

[†] Consider the minimum age limit of Facebook, which is 13 (see registration and account security column for Facebook at https://www.facebook.com/legal/terms).

[‡] This is evident from the terms and conditions of all of these websites.

[§] These websites give the users several privacy options. These options can be availed while posting personal/professional information, pictures, or status updates.

Each of these groups of interactive communication websites may have its own policy guidelines framing up codes of conduct for the users, privacy guidelines, grounds for complaint, and declaration of the responsibility of the website in regard to take-down notices. It is interesting to note that in all these categories of social networking sites data swelling of individuals may be inevitable. This can happen due to a number of reasons, including online bullying (especially for minor users of MPSNSs), trolling, or sharing of personal stories in the forums in creation of *fake avatars* (Halder, 2013) of ex-girlfriends, ex-wives, female colleagues, bosses, and so on, with whom the data contributor may be angry or against whom the data contributor wants to take revenge. In this process, sexual crimes in the social networking sites are brought in.

In this chapter an attempt is made to explore the patterns of sexual crimes done in MPSNSs targeting women and female children. In the course, this chapter also shows how sexual crimes created in the MPSNSs may affect the usage of other categories of networking sites and vice versa. This chapter also throws light on reasons for turning these useful sites into a platform for victimizing women and female children, *modus operandi* of the crimes and patterns of victimization. This chapter is divided into two parts. The first part explains the different patterns of sexual crimes in the MPSNSs. This part is further divided into two segments, the first for female children and the second for women. The second part analyzes the reasons for the growth of sexual crimes in the MPSNSs.

☐ Patterns of Sexual Victimization in the MPSNSs

Sexual Victimization of Children

The most researched sexual crime in the MPSNSs is undoubtedly pedophilia (Jaishankar, Halder, & Ramdoss, 2008). The uniqueness of the MPSNSs lies in the fact that persons from the age group of 13 can become members/users. This has given wide opportunity for teenagers to discover a completely new world through the MPSNSs. The teenage users not only get to show off their latest profile pictures, but also can choose their own friends. The platform is basically a home without any strong adult supervision for teenage users. Paradoxically, unsupervised teenagers tend to fall prey for a number of unsocial "games," and MPSNS teen habitats are no exception. In case of sexual crimes targeting children in the MPSNSs, two distinct types of contributors can be found: (1) child user himself or herself who posts his or her detailed personal information and personal pictures through his or her own profile pages or school groups, and (2) adult perpetrator who may create an alluring profile for trapping the target victim (Savarimuthu, 2012); he or she may also create child pornographic materials with the contents that he or she may have collected from the MPSNSs for wider consumption by other adults, as well as young adults either in the MPSNSs or in AD&MSs or IVSs. With these two types of contributors, MPSNSs may witness a number of forms of sexual crimes, which are listed below:

1. *Creation of fake profiles by the adult perpetrator for alluring the victim.* Even though perpetrators can carry on with the sexual victimization of children with their original profiles, professional contributors to pedophilia may do this through their fake identities created especially to befriend the children (Broadhurst & Jayawardena, 2011). Such fake identities can be that of a teenager or a young adult or a friendly adult male/female. These fake identities use fictitious names and personal information, and they may prefer to opt for "customs settings," which would make their privacy settings look like "open only to close friends" or "open only to friends." It may be noted that MPSNSs like Facebook or Twitter in their policy guidelines clearly mention that no individual can create an account with false information. But such rules are grossly violated. It can further be noted that even though these MPSNSs have special safety regulations for preventing child sexual victimization, due to less monitoring of the contents filled in by the users, such profiles continue to harass children.

2. *Grooming and trapping children.* Grooming and trapping children can be done by many ways, including simple chatting in the MPSNSs. The adult perpetrators, through either their original profiles or their fake profiles, approach profiles of the children who are open to strangers (Broadhurst & Jayawardena, 2011). If the victim accepts the groomer as "friend," it becomes easier for the groomer to acquire information about the maturity status of the victim. This is mainly acquired from the status messages that are shared by the victim, unclaimed pictures with messages embossed on them, which may be shared from other friend's collections, and so on. In case the child has an open profile, it becomes even easier for the perpetrator to trap him or her. The perpetrator groomer finds emotionally disturbed children as an easy catch.* The grooming session may begin with sympathetic chats or motivating chats whereby the groomer may show himself or herself as equally

---

* Ibid.

disturbed or someone who has already gone through a similar situation. The communication may progress on a period-to-period or hour-to-hour or even day-to-day basis, slowly introducing the victim to sexually erotic speeches. Mostly when the victim is a younger teen, he or she may be asked about the types of underwear he or she is wearing, and then the speeches slowly move on to removing the clothes and orally representing private body parts. In the case of older and matured teens, the groomer may directly ask him or her to show his or her private body parts using webcams.* In this process, the groomer may also transform the victim to a contributor to pedophilia, as well as also turn him or her into a consumer of the same.

3. *Data mining from the profiles of children.* In the process of grooming of the victims, the perpetrator also gathers data about the victim himself or herself, the friends and acquaintances, and the victim's potential to contribute toward the victimization. Such data may be revealed by the victim himself or herself in the course of a grooming session or in his or her own profile or in the status messages. The perpetrator may also accumulate data from the acquaintances' profiles. Such data can speak about the victim's day-to-day activities, his or her likes and dislikes, and also sexual orientation. Data mining also extends to still and audiovisual images that may be available in the friends' or acquaintances' albums. It has also been seen that such predators may target visual images of the victim, especially girls where they are seen bikini clad or in swimsuits or underwear or revealing dresses.†

4. *Converting children into contributors to and consumers of pedophilic materials.* The most deplorable issue is the conversion of children into contributors to and consumers of pedophilic materials in the MPSNS. In the first case, children may get involved without awareness. Some children who may be unaware of social networking dangers may reveal much information about their activities online, including their present and future geographic locations. Along with this, they may also post personal pictures in their albums that may not have sufficient safety settings to prevent outsiders from looking at them. Such activities testify to the routine activities theory, whereby such child users become chosen targets of the perpetrators (Choi, 2012). MPSNSs like Facebook also provide options to download pictures from friends' albums. This makes the situation more vulnerable, as the perpetra-

---

* This is derived from the personal experience of the first author as a cyber victim counselor.
† Ibid.

tor may access and acquire the pedophilic material without actually asking the victim to contribute the same.

Even though children as contributors may have attracted research-ers' interests lately, the present behavioral pattern of child users of the Internet definitely demands thorough research on the adolescent sexual fantasies of children. Such fantasies may be revealed by chil-dren's dress and preference to watch visual images of adult men and women showing much skin. In Facebook, Twitter, and YouTube such sexual fantasies can be exercised by posting pictures whereby adoles-cent teens dress up in revealing dresses like adults, or share unclaimed pictures that depict such visual images. YouTube, on the other hand, provides excellent opportunities to upload sexual fantasy videos. Such videos can be posted by the matured teens by way of sharing sexted images, playing adult games such as imitating adult sexual activities in the video or acting like pregnant women, and so forth.* Child con-tributors are further encouraged by Internet games such as The SIMs.† These games encourage subscribers to create live images through cartoon-like figures, and such images can be made to act as per the wishes of the users/subscribers.

Children turn into consumers of the pedophilic materials especially when the perpetrator starts satisfying their adolescent sexual fanta-sies. This can happen either through chatting and introducing the vic-tim to pedophilic materials, or through directly sharing the content with the victim. Directly sharing the content involves a number of related issues, including peer-to-peer file sharing, sending the mate-rial to the victim's email ID free of cost on a trial basis, forwarding the content through the victim's online acquaintances, and so on. If the victim is convinced to buy the material, it may further involve secret usage of adult net banking facilities or credit card facilities. However, it must also be noted that what generates in the MPSNSs as guid-ance for ways to consume the pedophilic material may end in the victim actually accessing the material at YouTube and related sites. At YouTube, varieties of videos may be available, including personal

---

* For instance, on YouTube one can find numerous funny "playing adult" videos, including playing pregnant videos, playing sex videos, and so on, uploaded by teens.
† SIMs3 is a computer game (for better understanding see http://www.thesims3. com/), and many of these game videos are uploaded to YouTube by the users. For instance, the lead author came across numerous SIMs videos, such as the one titled "How to make your teen sim pregnant (re-do) without inteenimater." These videos are uploaded to YouTube by teens as well as adults, and there is no age restriction for viewers for most of these videos.

amateur videos covering sexual activities and movie clips showing sex scenes. While in some such videos YouTube may ask users to verify their age or restrict the user based upon the preliminary information supplied to it through the account information, many videos are open to the public, including children. This broadens the risk of introducing the child victim to sexually explicit materials, and they gradually get addicted to view more real-life images of such nature.

5. *Children versus children.* In the MPSNSs, cyberbullying of children by children remains the most highlighted issue when it involves children as perpetrators victimizing children. But at the same time, children can also turn into perpetrators for sexual crimes against their classmates or schoolmates. The best example of such sexual crimes executed through MPSNSs is "revenge porn." Halder (under review) defines revenge porn as

> an act whereby the perpetrator satisfies his anger and frustration for a broken relationship through publicizing false, sexually provocative portrayal of his/her victim, by misusing the information that he may have known naturally and that he may have stored in his personal computer, or may have been conveyed to his electronic device by the victim herself, or may have been stored in the device with the consent of the victim herself; and which may have been done to publicly defame the victim essentially.

As the definition suggests, revenge porn can be created by the perpetrator with the information about the victim that may be known to the perpetrator naturally by way of prior acquaintance with the victim, or with the information that may have been conveyed to the perpetrator by the victim or may have been stored in the electronic device of the perpetrator with the victim's consent.

Many child perpetrators may take an MPSNS as a good platform for floating a revenge porn image of their victims. The lead author has shown that this can be done through "camouflage porn," which may be created by the perpetrator in the MPSNS through profiles made up with the information about the victim, doctored pictures, sexted messages that may have been supplied by the victim himself or herself, and so forth (Halder, under review). Mostly, the revenge porn is created by the child perpetrator to take revenge over trivial to serious altercations, including issues such as real-life bullying, adolescent love and rejection of the same by the victim, competition in schools, and so on (Halder, under review). In the majority of these cases, revenge porn may be motivated by the perpetrator's ulterior wish to get the victim defamed by showcasing him or her in the ugliest sexual avatar form (Halder, under review).

Sexual Victimization of Women

Women are equally vulnerable targets of sexual crimes in the MPSNSs as children. In the recent statistics released by Working to Halt Online Abuse (WHOA), it has been shown that 80% of the victims are women and only 20% of the victims are male. The statistics also showed that 16% of the harassments began on Facebook, 4% on Twitter, and 1% on YouTube. Among the 327 cases WHOA received in 2012, 83% escalated to various forms of harassment, including sexual victimization, and the major platform for such escalation had been Facebook (22%), while Twitter also played its part (3%) sufficiently.* Nonetheless, Facebook and Twitter have been used for a couple of years to sexually victimize women due to the vast, free, nonmonitored space provided by these MPSNSs and a large audience that attracts these platforms. The chronology of sexual crimes that can happen to women is elaborated below:

1. *Creation of fake avatar of women.* Sexual crimes against women in the MPSNSs may happen mostly through creation of fake avatars of the victims by the harassers. Halder (2013) defines *fake avatars* as

   a false representation of the victim which is created by the perpetrator through digital technology with or without the visual images of the victim and which carry verbal information about the victim which may or may not be fully true and it is created and floated in the internet to intentionally malign the character of the victim and to mislead the viewers about the victim's original identity.

   As the definition suggests, fake avatars can be created either by verbal description of the characteristics of the victim in group discussions in the MPSNSs, or by creating a different profile of the fake avatar with the images and information to malign the character of the victim.

---

* See 2012 WHOA statistics at http://www.haltabuse.org/resources/stats/2012 Statistics.pdf.

Halder (2013) has shown that trolling* can be one of the best possible ways to create a fake avatar of the victim through verbal description. In trolling, the perpetrator(s) may post extremely abusive words about the victim, which may also include a description of the victim as a slut. As the trolling posts continue, the offending comments may increase, painting the victim in darker shades. The perpetrators may encourage new participants to engage in further discussion, which may even infringe on the privacy of the victim (Halder, 2013).

Apart from trolling, the perpetrator can also create a fake avatar of the victim by creating profiles with morphed images, derogatory comments, and descriptions that may indicate the victim solicits sex. Such profiles can be either a public profile that may have detailed private information of the victim or a private profile, which may be open only to the people who are listed in the friends' category of such a profile (Halder, 2013). Such a fake avatar of the victim may also have audiovisual images that may either have been created on YouTube with the images of the victim, or have already existed on YouTube. It is interesting to note that the perpetrator may intentionally insert such YouTube clips in the fake avatars, which may be sexually explicit in nature, or which may have a tagline indicating that it was made especially for the victim. Such sexual victimization of adult women in the MPSNSs may occur due to a number of reasons, including professional rivalry, domestic violence, dating violence, emotional breakups, and even sibling rivalry (Halder & Jaishankar, 2011). The perpetrator can thus be an ex-colleague, a dating partner, an ex-husband, a jilted lover, or even a sibling who has formed opinions against the victim.

2. *Sending sexual messages.* While creation of a fake avatar can be one of the most used ways to sexually victimize women, the other sexual crime that can take place in the MPSNSs is sending sexual messages to the victim. This can take place by three distinct methods: (a) grooming the women for sexual crime purposes, (b) chatting in the MPSNSs, and (c) bullying. While grooming the children for sexual crime purposes has attracted the attention of researchers, grooming women for sexual victimization purposes remains understudied. Online grooming of women may take place in the MPSNSs by perpetrators who may be looking for short-term flirting, or by habitual sex offenders, or by

---

* Halder (2013) defines trolling as "an extreme usage of freedom of speech which is exercised to disrupt the community discussions in social networking sites and which is done to deliberately insult ideologies such as feminism, secularism etc of the topic starter or the supporters of the topic starter."

regular amateur pornography consumers, or by creators/distributors of the pornography industry.

MPSNS provides a wide opportunity to fish out the victim for grooming (Broadhurst & Jayawardena, 2011). This may be possible when the victim is a new user of the MPSNS, or when the victim herself wants to get connected with male strangers. In the first case, the victim may not know about the basic safety regulations of cyberspace, may not be aware of the safety options available in the MPSNSs, and may reveal her information to the world, which may attract the perpetrator. It may be noted that in this case, the victim may be naive regarding the dangers. Hence, when the perpetrator approaches the victim, she may easily give in for the grooming course. The grooming may begin in a fashion similar to that in the case of children. The perpetrator may slowly gain the confidence of the victim and may ask her either to come on a webcam chat or directly telephone chat. He may also direct the victim to upload her attractive pictures and may coerce her to get involved in sexting.[*]

In the second case, when the victim wants to get connected with strangers, it becomes easier for the perpetrator to groom her for pornography. This may occur when the victim is mentally disturbed due to work-related problems or a broken relationship, or when she is disturbed due to domestic harassment by her spouse or even by parents or siblings, in the case where she is a spinster. In both cases, the perpetrator may ultimately try to make the victim a contributor to pornography by making her provide her photos as well audiovisual images that portray her as a sexually aroused woman. He may also try to make the victim a consumer of the pornographic clips, and so forth.[†]

Sexual crimes can also take place through chatting in the forum or group or in the personal chatting rooms provided by the MPSNSs, especially Facebook. It may be seen that in the case of group chatting, offensive comments having sexual contents may be posted by way of either bullying[‡] or trolling. The bully may use extremely harsh words to offend the victim. Halder (2013) differentiates trolling from

---

[*] This observation is derived from the personal experiences of the first author as a cyber victim counselor.

[†] Ibid.

[‡] Jaishankar (2009) defines *cyberbullying* as "abuse/harassment by teasing or insulting victims' body shape, intellect, family back ground, dress sense, mother tongue, place of origin, attitude, race, caste, class, name calling, using modern telecommunication networks such as mobile phones (SMS/MMS) and Internet (chat rooms, emails, notice boards and groups."

bullying by stating that "trolling ... differs from bullying ... that the persons who are trolling may not be directly and personally affected by the speech of the victim" (p. 195). In both cases, the comments may be posted targeting the victim in open forums with an intention that the other group members can directly see the sexually abusive posts. In the case of personal chat rooms, the victim may receive unwanted messages containing sexual speeches from persons who may already exist in her friends' list (in case she has restricted outsiders from personally chatting with her), or from persons who may start communication to personally know her more (in case she has kept her profile open for the public, giving opportunity for everyone to chat with her). In such cases, the perpetrator may differ from the groomer in the sense that the perpetrator does not approach the victim for transforming her into a consumer or contributor to the pornography industry, but the perpetrator may post the sexual comments either for self sexual gratification (in the case of personal chat room conversation) or for taking revenge or making fun of the victim for trivial disagreements.*

3. *Cyber-aided sexual violence against women.* Halder and Jaishankar (2011) pointed out that MPSNSs like Facebook, Orkut, and others can also become platforms to create cyber-aided sexual violence against women (p. 34). This may particularly happen when the perpetrator gets to know the victim through the profile information, geolocation, and so on, and hatches plans for sexual crimes in real life, including rape, molestation, and so forth. In the MPSNSs like Facebook, there are two broad categories of friends: (a) close friends and (b) friends. Facebook also provides three different categories of intimation status for these three types of acquaintances. For example, close friends can see all the status messages, photo albums, geolocation, groups, and favorite pages of the profile owners; friends may be restricted to those status updates, photo albums, and other information that are indicated specifically for them. Further, Facebook also provides opportunity for friends as well as close friends to tag a user to any place, picture, or status message, and by this the user's information can be viewed by others who are not friends with the user. In Twitter, similarly, status updates and personal information can be limited to followers if the user wishes to keep the profile private and limited only to those followers. But if the user wishes to open her information to the World Wide Web, neither Facebook nor Twitter restricts any individual (whether or not a member to these MPSNSs) from accessing and viewing the primary information. Given these

---

* This observation is derived from the personal experiences of the first author as a cyber victim counselor.

facts, the user becomes susceptible to physical violence as well as online abuse with the cyber aid.

☐ Reasons for Growth of Sexual Crimes in the MPSNSs

Growing Popularity of the MPSNSs for Forming Relationships

Facebook, Twitter, and Google-hosted social networking sites Google+ and YouTube have become imperative to our lives. As has been stated above, MPSNSs provide a wide range of platforms for multitasking. This brings in dangers and puts unaware or insecure users in peril. The majority of users avail Facebook for forming relationships of various natures. Facebook, Twitter, and so on, have provided a utopia for many where one can act as per one's own wishes if he or she fulfills the basic necessities of the platform. The relationships thus formed may not abide by the settled rules and regulations restricting the human mind. Sharing real-life tragedies (how trivial they may be) through status messages may immediately attract a pool of supporters in the MPSNS, and these supporters and friends may also motivate the user to take action that they feel is absolutely right. In this way, the user may either become the victim of groomers if the user is a woman, or (in the case of males especially) generate sympathy by sharing details about the ex-partner, colleague, and so on, who may be further targeted by such supporters. Similarly, in the case of online relationships, trivial disagreements can be published, and if the disagreement arises against a woman, some users may mob attack the woman, leaving her literally stripped in public (Halder, 2013). In this way, when the fake avatars are created, the user may get another group of supporters who may start liking the fake avatar for the sexual contents and thus escalate the humiliation of the victim.

The monitoring process of the MPSNSs provides further grounds for increasing sexual crimes. Neither Facebook nor Twitter nor Google provides strict monitoring of the activities of the users unless it is in the nature of harming of the child and reported by the parents or the police.* MPSNSs like Facebook and Google turn deaf ears to the report abuse petitions provided by the victims in the name of the

---

* This is evident from the terms and conditions of all these websites.

First Amendment guarantee of free speech (Halder & Jaishankar, 2011). Profile pictures using sexually explicit images are rampant on Facebook, and fake avatars are created to attract such profile owners who would use such avatars for sexual gratification. Further, none of these MPSNSs have any methodology to ascertain the real identity of the user. Facebook itself has confessed that many of the user profiles are fake (Sweney, 2012). This boosts the perpetrator to continue with the wrongdoing.

Lack of Awareness of Female Users

One of the major reasons for the growth of sexual crimes in the MPSNSs is the lack of awareness of female users, who are the potential victims. As has been stated above, the majority of sexual crimes may happen when the victim herself allows the perpetrator to either access her private information or communicate with her. Many victims refuse to stop communication with the perpetrator or delete the profile information when attacked.[*] Further, once victimized, many women victims and parents of minor victims immediately sought to contact the hackers to remove the offending posts or wrote back to the offender threatening him with dire consequences. This irrational coping mechanism only leads to further victimization, as this helps the perpetrator to escalate the harassment.[†]

☐ Discussion and Conclusion

MPSNSs have become a huge platform for exercising right to speech and expression. Guided by the First Amendment guarantees, these web platforms often turn into vicious grounds for women and children. MPSNSs like Facebook and Twitter offer restrictive policy guidelines for child safety that are heavily influenced by the Children's Online Privacy Protection Act of 1998. However, adolescent sexual fantasies cannot be completely regulated by laws. Also, contacting the children for grooming

---

[*] This observation is derived from the personal experiences of the first author as a cyber victim counselor.

[†] This was observed by the lead author in her presentation "Cyber Crime and Victim Turned Offenders: An Analysis of Impact of Victimisation and Coping Mechanisms of Women Victims" (with K. Jaishankar), at the Stockholm Criminology Symposium, organized by the Swedish National Council for Crime Prevention (Brottsförebyggande rådet—Brå), held June 11–13, 2012, in Stockholm, Sweden (invited presentation).

for sexual victimization purposes through camouflaged profiles can not be regulated as long as the MPSNSs take up *suo motu* monitoring of profile activities and restrict creation of fake identities. Such suggestions, on the other hand, may further bring possible problems of privacy infringement of the users by the MPSNSs, which these web portals may never do due to their business ethics. However, while these MPSNSs shift the burden of identifying the sex offenders' profiles largely to the users, positive efforts have been taken by these websites to restrict registered sex offenders from using the sites and banning child sexual exploitation through these web portals.* This also indicates that the liability of the MPSNSs may begin only when the child has actually encountered victimization. As such, there is no such positive mechanism to restrict adult sexual victimization.

Perceptions of restricted speech, including obscenity and speech and expression targeting modesty of women, differ from country to country. The MPSNSs being regulated by the U.S. laws often become nonchalant to "social reporting" on such speeches offered by women victims from within the United States and from jurisdictions outside the United States.† Further, the present trends of online as well as offline socialization motivate men and women to share personal details and updates almost on a daily basis. As has been mentioned above, this contributes to data stealing, and no one can expect complete privacy. To regulate offenses against the government, many governments have taken up privacy surveillance policies.‡ This has theoretically strengthened possibilities of government surveillance for online crimes such as this chapter addresses. But unfortunately, such issues are often overlooked, and this may further pull out huge debates on privacy invasions by government on the issue of right to speech and expression. Given these facts, victims of sexual offenses, especially women, may become completely helpless. The ever-expanding meaning of free speech in the First Amendment guarantee has further contributed to the increased sexual victimization of women as well children in the MPSNSs. The lead author in her capacity as a cyber victim counselor has experienced that many individuals

---

* Consider the policy of Facebook at http://www.facebook.com/help/2100815 19032737/, or Twitter policies on child sexual exploitation at https://support. twitter.com/groups/56-policies-violations/topics/236-twitter-rules-policies/ articles/37370-child-sexual-exploitation-policy.

† Ibid.

‡ Consider the recent uproar over the federal government's Internet surveillance program after whistle-blower Edward Snowden's revelation. See Greenwald, G., Macaskill, E., & Potras, L. (2013, June 10). Edward Snowden: The whistle blower behind the NSA surveillance revelations. *The Guardian*. Retrieved on June 15, 2013, from http://www.guardian.co.uk/world/2013/jun/09/ edward-snowden-nsa-whistleblower-surveillance.

who may have sent racy messages to women or matured teens, who may have conveyed supposedly undignified messages to other teens as well as adults, defend their actions on the grounds of expanded meaning of First Amendment guarantees. All these factors contribute to the making of new trends of, as well as sustained growth of, traditional forms of sexual victimization on the multipurpose social networking sites.

It has been proved time and again that the creation of new legal provisions cannot restrict online misbehaviors, especially where individuals can camouflage their identity under anonymous or fake identities. Hence, the scope of existing laws meant for protection of women and children must be examined and broadened to regulate the issue. In doing this, the police, the nongovernmental organizations (NGOs), and the legal experts, along with cyber criminologists, must be called in to form functional analysis of the laws for positive treatment of the problem. Similarly, web companies like Facebook, Twitter, and Google must create more sensitive customer care teams to review each social reporting complaint from the light of the due diligence clause.*

Government surveillance of Internet users has been vehemently criticized on the grounds of privacy invasion and free speech debates.† Even though government surveillances were proposed for antiterror plans and are being executed for gagging largely the whistle-blowers, if the surveillance was directed to regulate problems including online child sexual victimization, it may have yielded positive results. While

---

* Halder (2013) observes that "the US provision Section 230 of the Communication Decency Act (codified at 47USC), which regulates the liability of the service providers, under clause (C) with the heading 'PROTECTION FOR "GOOD SAMARITAN" BLOCKING AND SCREENING OF OFFENSIVE MATERIAL' in sub clause (1) states that 'no provider or user of an interactive computer service shall be treated as the publisher or speaker of any information provided by another information content provider'. In sub clause (2); it states no provider or user of an interactive computer service shall be held liable on account of (A) any action voluntarily taken in good faith to restrict access to or availability of material that the provider or user considers to be obscene, lewd, lascivious, filthy, excessively violent, harassing, or otherwise objectionable, whether or not such material is constitutionally protected; or (B) any action taken to enable or make available to information content providers or others the technical means to restrict access to material described in paragraph (1). Section 512(c) of the Digital Millennium Copyright Act further provides about the 'due diligence' of the service providers regarding the immunity for infringement of materials which are hosted in their website. The provision lays down three basic conditions to avail the immunity, i.e., (i) the provider must not have the requisite level of knowledge of the infringing activity; (ii) if the provider has the right and ability to control the infringing activity, it must not receive a financial benefit directly attributable to the infringing activity; (iii) upon receiving proper notification of claimed infringement, the provider must expeditiously take down or block access to the material."

† Ibid.

it cannot be denied that the web companies do provide mechanisms for surveillance to regulate this particular problem, we argue that such surveillance is extremely low compared to recent surveillance programs that caused worldwide uproar. Further, government surveillance may have yielded positive results if directed to regulate online sexual violence against women. But the practical disability due to privacy infringement issues of the harassed, along with the harasser, becomes imperative here. This may further lengthen the debate over the safe speech category. One obvious way to avoid such debates while providing better space for women and children users of the MPSNSs is to increase the tortuous liability of the MPSNSs. If the surveillance of the web companies becomes effective to regulate the problems that this chapter addresses, then it can be expected that need for government surveillance will automatically decrease. Along with it, parental surveillance styles must be made more child-friendly to make children understand that such surveillance would not deter their privacy completely (Yardi & Bruckman, 2011), but would actually enhance their security.

Awareness of adult as well as minor users plays a key role in preventing sexual crimes in the MPSNSs. Women and children need to understand the limitations for floating data in their web portals. Adolescent and adult users must also restrict experimenting with choice of friends and exhibiting private bathing/beach/compromising photos through social networking sites. This may attract predators with an understanding that such photo sharing has been done by the victim as a "mating call."[*] Simultaneously, all users, irrespective of their gender, must also understand their responsibilities and duties toward their friends in the MPSNSs. Unauthorized tagging of photos and names, publishing private affairs of acquaintances without their permission, introducing unknown people to closed groups, and so on, may prove beneficial for harassers for numerous victimizations, including stalking, sexual victimization, and creation of fake avatars. Further, victims, especially women, and parents of child victims must resist from taking up irrational coping mechanisms such as contacting the hackers to remove the offending posts.

Creation of awareness among the potential victims is the need of the hour. One best way to spread such awareness would be to arrange for seminars and workshops in the educational institutions, public libraries, and so on. The government as well as web companies, along with NGOs, may come forward with proposals to jointly arrange such awareness meetings. This will enhance their responsibility to the public as well.

---

[*] This is from the personal experience of the first author in her designation as a cyber victim counselor.

☐ **References**

Boyd, D. M., & Ellison, N. B. (2007). Social network sites: Definition, history, and scholarship. *Journal of Computer-Mediated Communication*, 13(1), article 11. Retrieved June 15, 2013, from http://jcmc.indiana.edu/vol13/issue1/boyd. ellison.html

Broadhurst, R., & Jayawardena, K. (2011). Online social networking and paedophilia: An experimental research "sting." In K. Jaishankar (Ed.), *Cyber criminology: Exploring Internet crimes and criminal behavior* (pp. 79–103). Boca Raton, FL: CRC Press, Taylor & Francis Group.

Choi, K. (2012). Cyber-routine activities: Empirical examination of online lifestyle. Digital guardians and computer crime victimization. In K. Jaishankar (Ed.), *Cyber criminology: Exploring Internet crimes and criminal behavior* (pp. 229–252). Boca Raton, FL: CRC Press, Taylor & Francis Group.

Ellison, N. B., Steinfield, C., & Lampe, C. (2007). The benefits of Facebook "friends": Social capital and college students' use of online social network sites. *Journal of Computer-Mediated Communication*, 12, 1143–1168. Retrieved June 15, 2013, from http://jcmc.indiana.edu/vol12/issue4/ellison.html

Halder, D. (2013). Examining the scope of Indecent Representation of Women (Prevention) Act, 1986 in the light of cyber victimisation of women in India. *National Law School Journal*, 11, 188–218.

Halder, D. (Under review). *Revenge porn by teens: Problems and solutions from transnational legal perspective.*

Halder, D., & Jaishankar, K. (2009). Online social networking and women victims. In K. Jaishankar (Ed.), *Cyber criminology: Exploring Internet crimes and criminal behavior* (pp. 301–320). Boca Raton, FL: CRC Press, Taylor & Francis Group. (Reprint of Cyber socializing and victimization of women. *Temida— The Journal on Victimization, Human Rights and Gender*, September 2009, 12(3), 5–26.)

Halder D., & Jaishankar, K. (2011). Cyber gender harassment and secondary victimization: A comparative analysis of US, UK and India. *Victims and Offenders*, 6(4), 386–398.

Jaishankar, K., Halder, D., & Ramdoss, S. (2008). Pedophilia, pornography and stalking: Analyzing child victimization in the Internet. In F. Schmallager & M. Pittaro (Eds.), *Crimes of the Internet* (pp. 28–42). Upper Saddle River, NJ: Prentice Hall.

Papacharissi, Z. (2009). The virtual geographies of social networks: A comparative analysis of Facebook, LinkedIn and a SmallWorld. *New Media Society*, 11, 199. Retrieved June 15, 2013, from http://tigger.uic.edu/~zizi/Site/Research_files/VirtualGeographiesFacebook.pdf

Savarimuthu, J. (2012). *Online child safety: Law, technology and governance.* Basingstoke, Hampshire: Palgrave Macmillan.

Sweney, M. (2012, August 3). Facebook quarterly report reveals 83m profiles are fake. *The Guardian.* Retrieved on June 15, 2013, from http://www.guardian.co.uk/technology/2012/aug/02/facebook-83m-profiles-bogus-fake

Vinson, K. E. (2010). The blurred boundaries of social networking in the legal field: Just face it. *University of Memphis Law Review*, 41, 355.

Wesch, M. (2009). YouTube and you: Experiences of self-awareness in the context collapse of the recording webcam. *Explorations in Media Ecology, 8*(2), 19–34.

Yardi, S., & Bruckman, A. (2011). *Social and technical challenges in parenting teens' social media use.* Retrieved on June 15, 2013, from http://gacomputes. cc.gatech.edu/Members/yardi/Yardi_ParentsTechnology11.pdf

9

CHAPTER

Case Study
Advancing Research on Hackers Through Social Network Data

Thomas J. Holt
Michigan State University

Olga Smirnova
East Carolina University

Deborah Strumsky
University of North Carolina at Charlotte

Max Kilger
Michigan State University

Contents

Keywords	146
Utilizing and Contextualizing Online Data Sources	148
Data and Methods	151
Demographics	154
Findings	155

Discussion and Conclusions   159

References   161

Criminological research on computer hackers has increased dramatically over the last two decades, driven in large part by either quantitative samples of college students or attendees at conventions, or limited qualitative data sources. These methods provide insight into the theoretical drivers of hacking, though limited information on the practices of active malicious actors in the computer underground. This study argues for the adoption of mixed methods analyses using data generated from multiple online data sources using a social network analysis of multiple Russian hacker groups. Using data triangulation from social network profiles, forums, and other online sources, this study highlights the demographic background of actors, their demonstrated skills, and the structure of social relationships between actors. The unique value of such analysis strategies relative to the ethical and methodological challenges they pose will be discussed in depth.

☐ Keywords

Computer hackers

Cybercrime

Malicious software

Network analysis

Over the last 30 years, societies around the globe have come to depend on computers, cellular telephony, and the Internet for commerce, communication, and business generally (Brenner, 2008; Wall, 2007). As a consequence, the threat posed by computer hackers has increased dramatically because of their substantive interest in computers and technology and capacity to compromise and harm systems (Bachmann, 2010; Holt, 2007; Holt & Graves, 2007; Newman & Clarke, 2003; Schell & Dodge, 2002; Wall, 2001, 2007). The constant changes in technology engender constant shifts in the tactics of hackers, such as the use of unique attack tools like botnet malware, which can be used to infect systems worldwide and remotely control them to send out spam, steal sensitive information, and attack other systems (Cooke, Jahanian, & McPherson, 2005; Ianelli & Hackworth, 2005; Rajab, Zarfoss, Monrose, & Terzis, 2006). The number of potential targets for attackers have also increased, including financial service providers like PayPal, where information for millions of customer is maintained (Chu, Holt, & Ahn, 2010; Newman & Clarke, 2003; Peretti, 2009).

Criminological research has increased in response to the increasing prominence of hackers and cybercrime generally. The corpus of studies explore the attitudinal and behavioral correlates of simple forms of hacking among juvenile (Holt, Bossler, & May, 2012) and college (Bossler & Burruss, 2011; Holt, Burruss, & Bossler, 2010; Holt & Kilger, 2008; Morris, 2011; Rogers, Smoak, & Liu, 2006; Skinner & Fream, 1997) samples. Several qualitative studies have developed small samples of active or incarcerated hackers to understand their attitudes toward hacking, social relationships, and the norms and values of this subculture (Holt, 2007, 2009; Meyer, 1989; Taylor, 1999; Thomas, 2002; Turgeman-Goldschmidt, 2008). A small number of studies utilizing populations of attendees at computer security conferences have given exposition on the attitudes of pro-social hackers and small populations of malicious hackers generally (Bachmann, 2010; Holt and Kilger, 2008; Schell and Dodge, 2002).

Though the existing body of research has helped to inform our knowledge of the hacker community, their findings may not be generalizable to the larger population of active malicious hackers, particularly in international contexts (Chu et al., 2010; Decary-Hetu & Dupont, 2012; Turgeman-Goldschmidt, 2008). For instance, most quantitative studies utilize surveys of U.S. college students and youth populations and find that the rates of participation in the creation and use of malicious software (Rogers et al., 2006; Skinner & Fream, 1997) and even minor forms of hacking (Bossler & Burruss, 2011; Holt et al., 2010; Morris, 2011) are generally less than 15% overall. Most qualitative studies also focus primarily on hackers in the United States and UK, and garner limited participation from highly active malicious actors (Jordan & Taylor, 1998; Holt, 2007, 2009; Taylor, 1999; Thomas, 2002). This is due to the substantive suspicions of participants in the computer underground who do not wish to report involvement in highly illegal acts of computer abuse (Gilboa, 1996; Taylor, 1999).

As a consequence, there is a need to improve our knowledge of the composition, activities, relationships, and capabilities of malicious hackers and malware writers around the world (Chu et al., 2010; Decary-Hetu & Dupont, 2012; Holt & Kilger, 2012). One way to move beyond the limitations of previous research is through the use of online data sources, such as posts from web forums, blogs, and other forms of computer-mediated communications (CMCs) where active malicious hackers and actors converge to discuss their interests (Chu et al., 2010; Franklin, Paxon, Perrig, & Savage, 2007; Decary-Hetu & Dupont, 2012; Holt &

Lampke, 2010; Mann & Sutton, 1998; Motoyama, McCoy, Levchenko, Savage, & Voelker, 2011; Thomas & Martin, 2006). These qualitative data sources can be used to develop data on the prevalence and costs of stolen data and malware services (Chu et al., 2010; Franklin et al., 2007; Holt & Lampke, 2010; Thomas & Martin, 2006), the flow of information between participants in online communities (Decary-Hetu & Dupont, 2012; Decary-Hetu, Morselli, & Leman-Langlois, 2012; Holt, 2012; Holt et al., 2008; Motoyama et al., 2011), and the factors that affect individual reputation and social status within large-scale communities (Holt, 2009; Holt & Lampke, 2010; Mann & Sutton, 1998; Motoyama et al., 2011).

This study attempts to demonstrate the value of online data to examine the malicious hacker community through an analysis of the network structure of multiple Russian hacker and malware writing groups. The demographic background of participants and their overall skill level are determined through the triangulation of data from social networking profiles, forums, and other online sources. In addition, the role of skill in structuring social relationships between participants is explored in order to better understand the composition and organization of a population of Russian actors. The value of online data will be discussed in depth, along with methodological concerns that arise in order to advance our knowledge of the hacker and malware community globally.

☐ Utilizing and Contextualizing Online Data Sources

Over the last two decades, criminologists have increasingly utilized online data to examine cybercrime and real-world offenses through the use of virtual data sources and CMCs (for review see Hine, 2005; Holt, 2010; Silvermann, 2011). These studies often utilize posts from web forums and bulletin board systems that are asynchronous systems, in that they allow individuals to discuss topics and interact in real time, or revisit them later for comment. The post and response structure of these systems provides direct insight into the social exchanges between participants online (Mann & Sutton, 1998; Miller & Slater, 2000; Silvermann, 2011).

Individuals have also increasingly adopted the use of social networking sites to express their thoughts and beliefs through text, images, and video, and provide links to others who share their interests (Garcia, Standlee, Bechkoff, & Cui, 2009; Hine, 2005; Silvermann, 2011). These sites can also be indexed or examined as a web log, or blog, where users post information in reverse chronological order on a single page that can be updated and tracked over time (Hookway, 2008). For instance,

Holt, Soles, and Leslie (2008) utilized data provided in a small sample of blogs from malicious software writers in Russia and China to assess their motivations for action and relationships to multiple hacker groups and forums.

The inherent value in these forms of computer-mediated communication is that they can be treated as longitudinal data that enable the exploration of changes in group dynamics and behavior over time while significantly reducing the costs of data collection (Garcia et al., 2009; Hine, 2005; Holt, 2010). Additionally, the volume of information provided is invaluable, as it can be used in conjunction with other online sources to validate claims made by hackers, such as their role in the creation of malicious software or attack tools (Decary-Hetu & Dupont, 2012; Holt et al., 2008). Identity profiles can also be created by triangulating small pieces of information provided in forum and blog posts. For instance, an email address provided in a social networking site can be used as a piece of information to develop search strings to capture and connect larger profiles of actors and their relationships (Holt, 2010).

To that end, there are a substantial number of web forums, Internet relay chat (IRC) channels, blogs, and other online resources that facilitate information sharing between hackers across the world (Chu et al., 2010; Franklin et al., 2007; Decary-Hetu & Dupont, 2012; Holt & Lampke, 2010; Mann & Sutton, 1998; Motoyama et al., 2011). These resources range from legitimate, ethical discussions of hacking to serious forums where individuals buy, sell, and trade malware and stolen data to facilitate attacks and identity theft (Holt & Kilger, 2012). More malicious forums and websites are, however, more difficult to access, as the operators may utilize registration-only forums that require usernames and passwords in order to observe the content (Chu et al., 2012; Decary-Hetu & Dupont, 2012; Holt, 2012; Mann & Sutton, 1998). These sites may also not turn up in traditional web searches through Google in order to reduce the likelihood of detection from law enforcement and researchers (Franklin et al., 2007; Holt & Lampke, 2010). Thus, research generated from these data sets is invaluable to understand the dynamics affecting relationships between serious criminal hacking and malware writing groups (Chu et al., 2010; Decary-Hetu & Dupont, 2012; Decary-Hetu et al., 2012; Motoyama et al., 2011).

The scope of information available through online data sources could prove pivotal in expanding our understanding of fundamental aspects of the hacker community. For instance, there is generally little information on the composition of skilled hackers and their relationship to other hackers generally. There is evidence of substantive variations in the skill and ability of actors (Furnell, 2002; Holt, 2007; Jordan & Taylor, 1998; Taylor, 1999). The top tier of hackers have the complex skills needed to create software and tools to facilitate complex automated attacks against a variety of systems (Holt, 2007; Holt & Kilger, 2012; Jordan & Taylor, 1998). Below this group lie a larger proportion of hackers with less technical skill, but who can apply tools and techniques to engage in attacks with or without authorization from system owners (Furnell, 2002; Holt & Kilger, 2012). Finally, the largest proportion of the hacker community have limited knowledge of computers, but learn techniques and acquire resources from the two groups above to expand their knowledge further (Furnell, 2002; Holt, 2007; Jordan & Taylor, 1998; Taylor, 1999).

There is generally little research validating the composition of the hacker subculture or the way in which information flows within these communities. Qualitative and limited quantitative evidence suggest hackers operate in loose social networks on and offline, but largely engage in attacks alone (Holt, 2007, 2009; Meyer, 1989; Schell & Dodge, 2002). This dynamic is changing due to the growth of forums and IRC channels where highly skilled hackers sell their resources to those less skilled actors in the community for a profit (Chu et al., 2010; Franklin et al., 2007; Holt & Lampke, 2010; Motoyama et al., 2011; Thomas and Martin, 2006). Many of the services offered depend on botnets and other platform-based malware, like iFrames, to send out spam, compromise systems, or sell financial credentials obtained from around the world (Chu et al., 2010; Franklin et al., 2007; Ianelli & Hackworth, 2005). The individuals who create and manage this infrastructure recognize that they can garner profit by leasing their tools to hackers with less skill but an interest in engaging in attacks. In turn, this is changing the value of skill within the hacker subculture, as actors can pay for services rather than take the time and resources needed to develop their own attack capabilities (Chu et al., 2010; Holt & Kilger, 2012; Holt & Lampke, 2010; Mann & Sutton, 1998).

The existing literature suggests that sophisticated hackers with the ability to create or leverage existing tools may be more centrally located within larger social networks and serve as a source of imitation for others. Few researchers have, however, attempted to model these relationships or assess the distribution of active participants in the hacker subculture within larger social networks or group structures generally. Data generated from online sources could provide the information needed to visualize social networks of participants, and address this critical and fundamental question. This study demonstrates the value in applying online data through the use of a mixed methods analysis of social network profiles and posts from multiple web forums to understand the composition of a population of Russian and Eastern European hackers and Internet users generally.

☐ Data and Methods

To assess the utility of social networking data to examine hackers and malware writers, this study began with the identification of seven group profiles of well-known hacker forums operating in Russia and Eastern Europe in a key social networking website for the Russian community. The researchers chose to focus on Russian groups since recent studies suggest that some of the most active stolen data and malware markets currently operate through web forums and CMCs in Russian language websites (see Chu et al., 2010; Dunn, 2012; Symantec, 2012). An additional group (RU Hack), operating only on this social networking website, was included to assess the relationship between active groups in the computer underground with a forum and large user population and a smaller group operating only in the blogosphere. In this way, we can understand how hacker groups operating in different spaces may relate to one another. Exploring the information provided on these group-specific profiles gave information on the number of individual usernames or profiles who self-identified as members within each group. This provided a sample of 336 distinct user profiles with no duplicates in the larger social networking site (see Table 9.1 for sample detail). The user profiles were differentially distributed across the various hacker groups, as

TABLE 9.1 User Populations by Group

Community	Members	Members in Multiple Groups	Percentage of Group
BH Crew (BH)	104	15	14.4
CUP (CU)	16	7	4.37
Damage Lab (DL)	27	5	18.5
Hell Knights Crew (HN)	2	2	100
HackZona (HZ)	117	23	19.7
Mazafaka (MF)	14	3	21.5
RU Hack (RU)	9	5	55.6
Zloy (ZL)	75	6	8

25 individuals belonged to multiple groups. In addition, these groups ranged in membership from 2 users in the Hell Knights Crew to 117 members in HackZona.

The information users posted in their blogs was also assessed to create social network data and generate basic descriptive information about that person. Blogs provide detailed information on individuals, including their relationships, behaviors, interests, attitudes, beliefs, education, and location (Hine, 2005; Holt, 2010; Holt et al., 2008). At the same time, the information provided by bloggers is self-reported, making it difficult to determine the legitimacy of these claims. Of most value are the reported friendship connections between participants. The term *friend* does not necessarily reflect the nature of relationships between the people, but rather demonstrates they are connected in some way, especially if they belong to the same group. The general network of relationships can be structured through three terms: *mutual friends*, in that two people have added connections to one another; *friends*, where a user has added another without a reciprocal tie, and *also friend of*, where a user has been added by another user without adding him or her in return. Using this information, we then create social networking structures of the hacker groups sampled.

Additionally, each username and its contact information were used to conduct Google search queries to determine the user's involvement in the hacker community. The results were then developed to create a risk index for each user based on his or her involvement in the creation, distribution, and use of malicious software and hacking techniques. Specifically, a four-frame risk typology was created, where those whose network information could be found through open-source searches were categorized as zero. Those whose searches indicated that they posted in or ran computer security blogs or participated in online discussions about security issues were given a rank of 1. These individuals were thought to pose a generally low risk to the larger community of computer users because of their neutral status.

Individuals whose profile searches indicated that they participated in hacking and malicious software forums, including posting tutorials or other information to engage in attacks, were ranked at 2. Users in this group posed a prospective risk to other computer users because they may engage in attacks against various targets. Finally, those whose searches indicated that they created and sold malicious software or hacking tools or served as hacker forum moderators or managers were given a score of 3. These individuals pose the highest risk because of the preponderance of information that supports their participation in the facilitation of attacks or malicious activity online.

These searches revealed that 70% of the user population posed no potential risk based on open-source data. The remaining proportion of

TABLE 9.2 Average Risk Level by Group

Network	N	Mean	Standard Deviation
BH Crew	104	0.5	0.9
CUP	16	0.5	1.0
Damage Lab	27	0.9	1.2
Hell Knights	2	3.0	0.0
HackZona	117	0.4	0.8
Mazafaka	14	1.0	1.2
RU Hack	9	1.1	1.4
Zloy	75	0.8	1.1

the population was in either the second risk category (19%) or the high-risk category (6.3%). These results support the general evidence that the hacker community is tiered in nature, with a very small proportion of high-skilled actors overall (Holt, 2010; Holt & Kilger, 2012). In addition, the distribution of risk is not even across all groups, as the Hell Knights Crew and RU Hack had the highest overall risk across all groups (see Table 9.2). The high-risk level in RU Hack is noteworthy given that it is the only group with a presence only on this social networking site. As a consequence, it may be that this group would otherwise be hidden by simply focusing on forums and other forms of CMC. Thus, the public profiles of well-known hacker groups may be diluted by those with minimal investment in the malware and hacking community, diminishing their perceived risk to the larger population of computer users.

The majority of high-risk actors (23) belonged to two groups, and only 2 individuals belonged to more than two groups. To clarify the relationship between risk and multiple group affiliation, a t-test with unequal variances was conducted. The results indicate that those with multiple group memberships had the highest overall risk levels. For instance, more than half of the members of the group RU Hack had overlapping memberships with other groups, as did 46% of the members of the group CUP. It is also important to note that the groups with high levels of overlap had the smallest number of members overall. This was supported through analysis of variance (ANOVA) analyses that find significant differences between groups based on risk levels. Thus, group membership is related to the overall level of actor risks.

☐ Demographics

In constructing the demographic content of users within these groups, it appears that the majority of respondents lived within the Russian Federation (see Table 9.3) and former Soviet republics. For instance, nine individuals self-identified living in Moscow, Chelyabinsk, Novosibirsk, and Murmansk. Their posts also suggest they genuinely live in these cities, which goes against the larger emphasis on secrecy within the hacker community (Jordan & Taylor, 1998; Taylor, 1999). There may, however, be value in revealing one's location in the blogosphere in order to connect with people from the same location who operate outside of the

TABLE 9.3 Location of Blog User

Country	Members	Percent[a]
Belarus	3	2.8
China	1	0.9
Estonia	1	0.9
Germany	3	2.8
Jamaica	1	0.9
Kyrgyzstan	1	0.9
Laos	2	1.9
Moldova	1	0.9
Puerto Rico	1	0.9
Russian Federation	78	73.6
United States	1	0.9
Ukraine	13	12.3

[a] Percentage excludes those respondents with no country location information included (n = 235).

hacker subculture. A small proportion also lived in parts of Europe and the United States, though a substantive proportion either did not include physical location information in their profiles or listed locations that do not exist, such as Hogwarts School of Magic.

Individual users were, however, less likely to indicate their former or current educational institution. Overall, 20% of the population listed they attended university, with 9% being current students. About 8% of users study in technical universities. A total of 16 users in the data indicated that they attended prestigious institutions in Moscow. For instance, two users stated they attend Lomonosov Moscow State University, one of whom is a level 3 threat. The other schools mentioned in the sample are mostly very well known schools throughout the region, such as Moscow Engineering-Physics Institute (National Research Nuclear University), with four total users studying there, or Moscow State Technical University n.a. N.E. Bauman (MSTU). An additional threat level 3 user indicated he attended South Ural State University.

This could be due to the fact that many of the users are students, and revealing their hacking skills and university information could lead to the identification of their real identity. It may also be that those with higher skill do not necessarily have a two- or four-year degree, but rather honed their skills on their own in keeping with the importance of self-learning within the hacker subculture (Bachmann, 2010; Holt, 2007; Jordan & Taylor, 1998; Schell & Dodge, 2002). Taking information from the profiles about education, it appears that a small proportion of the respondents are currently students attending formal universities within Russia.

In terms of age, the majority of respondents were between the ages of 21 and 29, in keeping with the general age distribution of the hacker community (Jordan & Taylor, 1998; Schell & Dodge, 2002). Furthermore, the language used by posters suggests that only seven individual profiles were females, again conforming to the general evidence on gender in the hacker community (Bachmann, 2010; Gilboa, 1996; Holt & Kilger, 2008; Jordan & Taylor, 1998; Schell & Dodge, 2002).

☐ Findings

Social network analyses were conducted in order to identify and model the prospectively hidden relationships between users on the basis of user centrality, group affiliation, and threat level. Social network modeling techniques allow for the visualization of large networks through multiple data points, which is ideal given the information provided on friendship networks in these data. Individual user profiles become network vertices, while their connections for membership and friendship

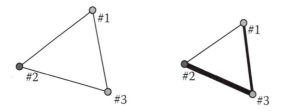

FIGURE 9.1 Example of network relationships.

ties determine the relationships between different vertices. Each user (U) has relationships with others through membership in the same group. Relationships are then connected through users who belong to multiple networks. The relationship (R) or set of arcs, or connections between users (U), serves to identify a given network (N = (U, R)). This structure is presented in Figure 9.1 to demonstrate hypothetical network relationships between three different actors. The shading of the nodes identifies their threat levels, while the weight of the lines shows the frequency of their communication.

In order to explore these networks, we created a global view of the network on the basis of group membership to understand the connections between groups (see Figure 9.2). The width of the line, or weight, indicates the strength of ties between each group. This representation demonstrates that the strongest connects are between the groups RU Hack, HackZona,

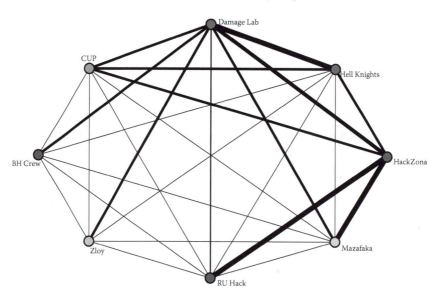

FIGURE 9.2 Visualizing group connectivity.

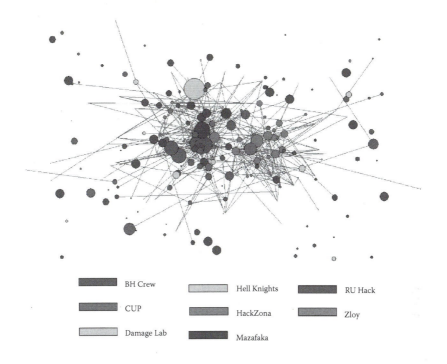

FIGURE 9.3 Popularity of Russian hackers by group membership.

and Mazafaka. In addition, HackZona is also closely connected to the Hell Knights Crew and Damage Lab. This global view highlights the overlapping memberships evident in the hacker community, which may create redundant networks for the flow of information and ideas through the hacker subculture (Decary-Hetu & Dupont, 2012; Decary-Hetu et al., 2012).

An additional sociograph was created measuring popularity based on the number of mutual friends partitioned by group membership (see Figure 9.3). The size of a node represents the number of mutual friends for each member of the group, while the edges represent the ties between two users who are mutual friends. This sociograph demonstrates that the members of RU Hack, Mazafaka, and Zloy are in the center of this network, which may be a function of the higher mean risk levels of this group. As a consequence, risk appears to be a key factor in relationships within the hacker community.

To further explore the relationship between risk and position within the network, a sociograph was created to explore connectivity and centrality partitioned by risk level (see Figure 9.4). The results demonstrate that high-risk nodes are centrally located within the network relative to the larger population of medium- and low-risk nodes that are more evenly

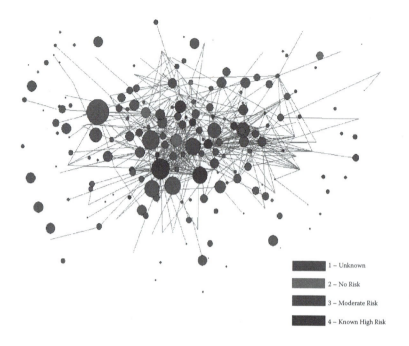

▮	1 – Unknown
▮	2 – No Risk
▮	3 – Moderate Risk
▮	4 – Known High Risk

FIGURE 9.4. Popularity of Russian hackers by risk level.

distributed throughout. The high-risk actors in this network are also con-nected to each other within two degrees of separation. Thus, high-risk actors either know one another or are tangentially connected through mutual associates. This is sensible given the limited number of high-threat actors in the total network. In fact, this sociograph demonstrates that there are fewer skilled hackers in the larger population of the hacker community overall, in keeping with general estimates of the composition of the hacker community generally (Holt & Kilger, 2012; Schell & Dodge, 2002).

The density of this network is 0.275, based on the number of actual connections divided by the number of total possible connections. This suggests that nodes within the network are not optimally connected, which may hinder the flow of information through participants. Since high-threat actors are centrally located, this supports the concept that they serve as key sources of innovation and hubs for the distribution for ideas (Holt, 2009; Holt & Kilger, 2008, 2012). Their generally small population size may, however, account for the constant and repeated use of older malware and attack mechanisms by the larger population of semiskilled actors, as they do not have the means to generate new tools on their own (Holt & Kilger, 2008, 2012).

☐ Discussion and Conclusions

As the world increasingly depends on computers and the Internet for all facets of life, the risks posed by hackers has concurrently grown. Criminological research has expanded our knowledge of the social aspects of hacking, though there are substantive issues that must be explored, most notably the composition of skill and ability, as well as the social relationships between actors (see Chu et al., 2010; Decary-Hetu & Dupont, 2012; Decary-Hetu et al., 2012). These issues may not be fully explored using small quantitative data sets or large-scale youth populations due in part to limited generalizability and the hidden nature of hacking generally (Bossler & Burruss, 2011; Holt et al., 2010, 2012; Morris, 2011; Rogers et al., 2006; Skinner & Fream, 1997). Thus, this study attempted to address these issues using social network analyses with data generated from multiple online sources.

The findings demonstrate the substantive value in alternative data sources and mixed methods analysis (see also Decary-Hetu & Dupont, 2012; Decary-Hetu et al., 2012). Specifically, the findings illustrate that a small proportion of actors are skilled computer hackers or malware writers, relative to a much larger population of semiskilled or nonskilled actors overall (Holt & Kilger, 2012; Jordan & Taylor, 1998). In addition, high-skilled hackers are centrally located in the larger social networks, suggesting they are the key source for innovation and development within this sample of actors (Decary-Hetu & Dupont, 2012; Holt & Kilger, 2012). At the same time, the low density of network connectivity may account for the repeated use and recycling of established malware and attack techniques from skilled to unskilled hackers (Chu et al., 2010; Decary-Hetu et al., 2012). Taken as a whole, these findings support the assertion that the hacker subculture is collegial in nature and tiered based on the ability of actors to apply their knowledge to create and utilize new tools (Holt, 2009; Holt & Kilger, 2008; Jordan & Taylor, 1998; Meyer, 1989; Schell & Dodge, 2002; Taylor, 1999).

These findings are not, however, generalizable to the entire Russian hacker community, but rather a proportion of the actors within this region. This sample may also overrepresent those individuals who are willing to divulge information that can be linked with their real-world identity. Thus, their actions may be different from other, more secretive hackers who actively minimize their public persona online. Future research is needed to replicate this study with samples from other social networking sites from populations of hackers in various countries across the world (Decary-Hetu & Dupont, 2012; Holt et al., 2008). This will help to clarify the validity of these findings and the structure of hacker social networks.

There are, however, substantive difficulties that arise in the investigation of online communities that must be carefully considered by researchers prior to data collection. Specifically, steps must be taken to diminish the overall online footprint of the researcher, whether as an academic or law enforcement practitioner. First and foremost, researchers must consider utilizing Internet connectivity separate from a university or agency in order to minimize their association to a specific institution. Not only will this help present a more innocuous presence online, but it will also reduce the likelihood of institutional resources being subject to compromise or attack (see Chu et al., 2010; Holt, 2010). Any sensitive information, such as personal financial data, student information, or institution-specific software, should also be removed to minimize harm in the event that a research computer is compromised. The research teams should also ensure that any computer used has up-to-date software with a full complement of antivirus and security software to serve as a prophylactic against infections.

Protocols must also be adopted to ensure that web-based content is retained locally in case website content is changed, removed, or completely deleted (Garcia et al., 2009; Mann & Sutton, 1998). Many forums and online resources within the hacker subculture are short-lived, or are not indexed by online archival websites, thereby increasing the likelihood of data attrition (see Chu et al., 2010; Holt, 2007). Thus, researchers should consider saving web content on local hard drives as html or in some text-based format so that the data remain in a consistent state for future analyses (Garcia et al., 2009; Holt, 2010).

This raises concerns about the ethics surrounding online data collection and information aggregation. The public nature of many forums, social networking profiles, and other CMCs enables almost anyone to access content, in much the same way as naturally occurring conversation in the real world (Hine, 2005; Miller & Slater, 2000; Silvermann, 2011). As a consequence, researchers have debated the need to notify participants in online communities that their activities are being observed (Garcia et al., 2009; Hine, 2005; Miller & Slater, 2000). Such a pronouncement may cause a contamination bias within criminal groups online due to fears over outsider involvement and law enforcement intervention (see Chu et al., 2010; Holt, 2010; Mann & Sutton, 1998). This sort of contamination bias is possible in virtual environments, and could lead some groups to disband entirely due to fear of detection by law enforcement. Surreptitious, covert data collection may be preferable for criminologists to cause minimal impact on participant behaviors (Holt, 2010; Silvermann, 2011). Thus, researchers must explore these issues with their local institutional review board to ensure their methods conform to ethical standards for research and participant protections.

A final concern lies in the impact that increased investigations with online data may have on the practices of hackers in general. Criminal behavior is adaptive, changing to reduce the likelihood of detection in response to differential investigative techniques (Newman & Clarke, 2003). For instance, stolen data markets in the United States became unreliable after law enforcement interventions in the mid-2000s (Symantec, 2012). Instead, users increasingly transitioned to registration-only forums and sites operating out of Russia and Eastern Europe, where there is a reduced risk of detection and infiltration by police agencies (Chu et al., 2010; Franklin et al., 2007; Holt & Lampke, 2010). Similar shifts may occur, particularly if research protocols are overly intrusive or well publicized, making it more difficult to identify the practices of hackers. Thus, researchers must carefully consider how their efforts will differentially impact the practices of the hacker subculture and hinder the efforts of research and law enforcement generally.

☐ References

Bachmann, M. (2010). The risk propensity and rationality of computer hackers. *International Journal of Cyber Criminology, 4*, 643–656.

Bossler, A. M., & Burruss, G. W. (2011). The general theory of crime and computer hacking: Low self-control hackers? In T. J. Holt & B. H. Schell (Eds.), *Corporate hacking and technology-driven crime: Social dynamics and implications* (pp. 38–67). Hershey, PA: IGI Global.

Brenner, S. W. (2008). *Cyberthreats: The emerging fault lines of the nation state*. New York: Oxford University Press.

Chu, B., Holt, T. J., & Ahn, G. J. (2010). *Examining the creation, distribution, and function of malware on-line*. Washington, DC: National Institute of Justice. Retrieved August 15, 2012, from www.ncjrs.gov./pdffiles1/nij/grants/230112.pdf

Cooke, E., Jahanian, F., & McPherson, D. (2005). The zombie roundup: Understanding, detecting, and disrupting botnets. In *SRUTI '05 Workshop Proceedings* (pp. 35–44). Berkeley CA: USENIX Association.

Decary-Hetu, D., & Dupont, B. (2012). The social network of hackers. *Global Crime, 13*, 160–175.

Decary-Hetu, D., Morselli, C., & Leman-Langlois, S. (2012). Welcome to the scene: A study of social organization and recognition among Warez Hackers. *Journal of Research in Crime and Delinquency, 49*, 350–382.

Dunn, J. E. (2012). Russia cybercrime market doubles in 2011, says report. *IT World Today*. Retrieved May 26, 2012, from http://www.itworld.com/security/272448/russia-cybercrime-market-doubles-2011-says-report

Franklin, J., Paxson, V., Perrig, A., & Savage, S. (2007). An inquiry into the nature and cause of the wealth of Internet miscreants. Presented at CCS07, October 29–November 2, 2007.

Furnell, S. (2002). *Cybercrime: Vandalizing the information society*. London: Addison-Wesley.

Garcia, A. C., Standlee, A. I., Bechkoff, J., & Cui, Y. (2009). Ethnographic approaches to the Internet and computer-mediated communication. *Journal of Contemporary Ethnography, 38*, 52–84.

Gilboa, N. (1996). Elites, lamers, narcs, and whores: Exploring the computer underground. In L. Cherny & E. R. Weise (Eds.), *Wired_Women* (pp. 98–113). Seattle: Seal Press.

Hine, C. (Ed.). (2005). *Virtual methods: Issues in social research on the Internet*. Oxford: Berg.

Holt, T. J. (2007). Subcultural evolution? Examining the influence of on- and off-line experiences on deviant subcultures. *Deviant Behavior, 28*, 171–198.

Holt, T. J. (2009). Lone hacks or group cracks: Examining the social organization of computer hackers. In F. Schmalleger & M. Pittaro (Eds.), *Crimes of the Internet* (pp. 336–355). Upper Saddle River, NJ: Pearson Prentice Hall.

Holt, T. J. (2010). Exploring strategies for qualitative criminological and criminal justice inquiry using on-line data. *Journal of Criminal Justice Education, 21*, 300–321.

Holt, T. J. (2012). Examining the forces shaping cybercrime markets on-line. *Social Science Computer Review*. DOI: 10.1177/0894439312452998

Holt, T. J., Bossler, A. M., & May, D. (2012). Low self-control, deviant peer associations, and juvenile cyberdeviance. *American Journal of Criminal Justice, 12*, 378–395.

Holt, T. J., Burruss, G. W., & Bossler, A. M. (2010). Social learning and cyber deviance: Examining the importance of a full social learning model in the virtual world. *Journal of Crime and Justice, 33*, 15–30.

Holt, T. J., & Graves, D. C. (2007). A qualitative analysis of advanced fee fraud schemes. *International Journal of Cyber Criminology, 1*, 137–154.

Holt, T. J., & Kilger, M. (2008). Techcrafters and makecrafters: A comparison of two populations of hackers. *WOMBAT Workshop on Information Security Threats Data Collection and Sharing*, 67–78.

Holt, T. J., & Kilger, M. (2012). *The social dynamics of hacking* (Know Your Enemy Series). The Honeynet Project. Retrieved August 18, 2012, from https://honeynet.org/papers/socialdynamics

Holt, T. J., & Lampke, E. (2010). Exploring stolen data markets on-line: Products and market forces. *Criminal Justice Studies, 23*, 33–50.

Holt, T. J., Soles, J., & Leslie, L. (2008). *Characterizing malware writers and computer attackers in their own words*. Presented at the 3rd International Conference on Information Warfare and Security, April 24–25.

Hookway, N. (2008). Entering the blogosphere: Some strategies for using blogs in social research. *Qualitative Research, 8*, 91–113.

Ianelli, N., & Hackworth, A. (2005). *Botnets as a vehicle for online crime*. Pittsburgh, PA: CERT Coordination Centre.

Jordan, T., & Taylor, P. (1998). A sociology of hackers. *Sociological Review, 46*, 757–780.

Mann, D., & Sutton, M. (1998). Netcrime: More change in the organization of thieving. *British Journal of Criminology, 38*, 201–229.

Meyer, G. R. (1989). *The social organization of the computer underground*. Master's thesis, Northern Illinois University.

Miller, D., & Slater, D. (2000). *The Internet: An ethnographic approach*. New York: Berg.

Morris, R. G. (2011). Computer hacking and the techniques of neutralization: An empirical assessment. In T. J. Holt & B. Schell (Eds.), *Corporate hacking and technology-driven crime: Social dynamics and implications* (pp. 1–17). Hershey, PA: IGI-Global Press.

Motoyama, M., McCoy, D., Levchenko, K., Savage, S., & Voelker, G. M. (2011). An analysis of underground forums. *IMC'11*, 71–79.

Newman, G., & Clarke, R. (2003). *Superhighway robbery: Preventing e-commerce crime*. Cullompton, NJ: Willan Press.

Peretti, K. K. (2009). Data breaches: What the underground world of "carding" reveals. *Santa Clara Computer and High Technology Law Journal, 25*(2), 375–413.

Rajab, M. A., Zarfoss, J., Monrose, F., & Terzis, A. (2006). A multifaceted approach to understanding the botnet phenomenon. *IMC'06*, 41–52.

Rogers, M., Smoak, N. D., & Liu, J. (2006). Self-reported deviant computer behaviour: A big-5, moral choice, and manipulative exploitive behaviour analysis. *Deviant Behaviour, 27*, 245–268.

Schell, B. H., & Dodge, J. L. (2002). *The hacking of America: Who's doing it, why, and how*. Westport, CT: Quorum Books.

Silvermann, D. (2011). *Interpreting qualitative data: Methods for analyzing talk, text, and interaction* (3rd ed.). Thousand Oaks, CA: Sage Publications.

Skinner, W. F., & Fream, A. F. (1997). A social learning theory analysis of computer crime among college student. *Journal of Research in Crime and Delinquency, 34*, 495–518.

Symantec Corporation. (2012). *Symantec Internet security threat report* (Vol. 17). Symantec Corporation. Retrieved May 25, 2012, from http://www.symantec.com/threatreport/

Taylor, P. (1999). *Hackers: Crime in the digital sublime*. London: Routledge.

Thomas, D. (2002). *Hacker culture*. Minneapolis: University of Minnesota Press.

Thomas, R., & Martin, J. (2006). The underground economy: Priceless. *;login: The Usenix Magazine, 31*, 7–17.

Turgeman-Goldschmidt, O. (2008). Meanings that hackers assign to their being a hacker. *International Journal of Cyber Criminology, 2*, 382–396.

Wall, D. S. (2001). Cybercrimes and the Internet. In D. S. Wall (Ed.), *Crime and the Internet* (pp. 1–17). New York: Routledge.

Wall, D. S. (2007). *Cybercrime: The transformation of crime in the information age*. Cambridge: Polity Press.

SECTION

The Criminal Justice System and Social Networking

CHAPTER

Further Examining Officer Perceptions and Support for Online Community Policing

Adam M. Bossler
Georgia Southern University

Thomas J. Holt
Michigan State University

Contents

Police Officer Support for Online Community Policing 170
Methods 173
Measures 174
  Dependent Variables 174
  Independent Variables 175
    Perceptions of the Police Response to Cybercrime 176
    Support for Cybercrime Investigation 176
    Impact of Cybercrime on Policing 176
    Previous Significant Factors Supporting Online Community
    Policing 183
    Controls 183

Results and Discussion   184
Conclusions   190
References   193

Over the last three decades, scholars have developed a substantial body of research considering the impact of technology on all aspects of society, including crime (Brenner, 2008; Newman & Clarke, 2003; Wall, 2001, 2007). The evolution of technology and its general societal adoption have enabled the development of entirely new forms of crime dependent upon computers and the Internet, such as the creation and dissemination of malicious software programs (Bossler & Holt, 2009) and computer hacking (Holt, 2007). The ability to regularly connect with others in near real time has also enhanced offenders' ability to engage in traditional forms of crime and deviance, such as harassment (Holt & Bossler, 2009), prostitution and sex offenses (Durkin & Bryant, 1999; Holt & Blevins, 2007; Holt, Blevins, & Burkert, 2010), and music and media piracy (Higgins, 2005). Property-driven cybercrimes such as hacking and data theft create tremendous financial harm for individuals, corporations, and the economy as a whole (Higgins, 2005; Newman &003; Wall, 2007). Person-driven crimes like harassment and stalking cause significant emotional and psychological harm to victims and their families (Wolak, Finkelhor, & Mitchell, 2012).

The societal changes afforded by technology create many challenges for law enforcement agencies, particularly at the local level (Bossler & Holt, 2012; Goodman, 1997; Holt, Bossler, & Fitzgerald, 2010; National Institute of Justice (NIJ), 2008; Stambaugh et al., 2001). Sheriffs and local law enforcement agencies are the primary point of contact for victims of crime. They are therefore expected to serve as first responders at various crime scenes (Bossler & Holt, 2012; Goodman, 1997; Holt et al., 2010; NIJ, 2008). Cybercrime cases often require some degree of specialized training in order to recognize and properly seize evidence, though such resource allocations may not be possible for small agencies that are understaffed or funded (Goodman, 1997; NIJ, 2008; Stambaugh et al., 2001). Victims of cybercrime may not know to contact local police agencies for aid, and if they do, the scope of the Internet enables offenders to be well outside of the bounds of an agency's jurisdiction (Holt, 2003). These challenges may lead some patrol officers and managers in local agencies to ignore cybercrime cases, or make them a very low priority due to other demands on their time and resources (Bossler & Holt, 2012; Goodman, 1997; Senjo, 2004; Stambaugh et al., 2001).

Despite the investigative hurdles, local law enforcement agencies are increasingly drawn into cybercrime incidents due to citizen awareness of various offenses (Holt et al., 2010). As a result, scholars argue that local agencies may be able to employ more traditional investigative techniques, such as online stakeouts, reversals, and stings of offenders who may operate within their jurisdiction or in nearby towns, with solid cooperative agreements regarding investigation and prosecution (Chu, Holt, & Ahn, 2010; Grabosky, 2007; Hinduja, 2007; Newman & Clarke, 2003; Wall & Williams, 2007). A small group of scholars and practitioners have also encouraged the development of programs designed to engage the much larger population of Internet users in their community to aid in policing and reporting of illicit activity in online spaces (Brenner, 2008; Jones, 2007; Swire, 2009; Wall, 2001; Wall & Williams, 2007). Leveraging the size, scope of knowledge, and general awareness of Internet users could dramatically increase the investigative capabilities of law enforcement and provide actionable intelligence that could generate successful criminal cases (Jones, 2007; Wall, 2001; Wall & Williams, 2007).

There are no clear strategies that have emerged to integrate online community members into policing initiatives, though some argue that the philosophy of community-oriented policing and the strategies derived from it would have the best potential to maximize this sizable resource (Jones, 2007; Swire, 2009). Community-oriented policing is normally thought of as having three essential components. First, the police and community have a shared responsibility to attempt to decrease crime through partnerships that focus on nonarrest strategies (Adams, Rowe, & Arcury, 2002; Bayley, 1998; Mastrofski, Warden, & Snipes, 1995; Skogan, 2006; Skogan & Hartnett, 1997). Second, the community and police collaboratively identify solutions to the problems that most concern the residents (Cordner, 1999; Miller, 1999; Sparrow, 1988). Finally, organizational transformations that support community engagement and partnerships with the private sector are critical to provide program sustainability (Braga, 2008; McGarrell, Chermak, Wilson, & Corsaro, 2006).

There are few, if any, clearly specified strategies or techniques to apply community policing to online environments. Additionally, there is little research on whether certain officers would even be willing to support the use of community policing to address cybercrime. One of the few studies to address this issue found that officers were more likely to support online policing initiatives on the basis of their perceptions of community policing and the nature of cybercrime rather than any demographic factors or computer skill (Bossler & Holt, 2013). Additional research is needed examining officer perceptions of community policing initiatives online to assess how agencies may more successfully implement any program in the real world. Thus, this study builds from Bossler and Holt (2013) by exploring the predictors of officer support for applying the principles of community policing to online communities, including the importance of actively working with online citizens. A sample of survey responses from line officers in two southeastern cities was collected and used to create binary logistic regression models to consider the relationship between various online policing mechanisms and their agency's support for cybercrime investigation, the impact of these offenses on policing generally, and their demographic background. The implications of this study for law enforcement, researchers, and policy makers will be discussed.

☐ Police Officer Support for Online Community Policing

Though various scholars (Brenner, 2008; Jones, 2007; Wall & Williams, 2007) and police organizations (IACP, 2009) have called for the implementation of community-oriented policing programs to combat cybercrime, there are few such initiatives that are active in the field at this time. There are also no real standards or guidelines for law enforcement agencies to develop such programs, making it difficult to identify how they would operate, effectively incorporate citizens online, or impact any one form of cybercrime. Using real-world community policing programs as a model, it is plausible that law enforcement officers may operate workshops on- and offline to demonstrate the dangers of cybercrimes for community residents, what to do in the event they observe or experience an incident, and the preventive steps they can take to reduce their risk of victimization. These programs would also require law enforcement to closely interact with online citizens to ensure any contacts they make with police are acknowledged, logged, and acted upon when possible to ensure reporting is consistent over time.

The lack of research also leads to questions regarding the most appropriate ways to staff any program designed for virtual spaces, as no major program or philosophical paradigm change can succeed without support of both administrators and line staff. Research on traditional community policing demonstrates that officer support for citizen encounters and relations is affected by several factors, including demographics, experiences, and perceptions of crime (Bayley & Shearing, 1996; Pelfrey, 2004; Skogan & Hartnett, 1997). Line officers often resist the implementation of community policing initiatives due to their programmatic focus on order maintenance and public relations rather than traditional police roles (Adams et al., 2002; Miller, 1999; Reuss-Ianni, 1983; Winfree, Bartku, & Seibel, 1996). When expanded to virtual spaces, community policing programs might be viewed as even more displeasing since they involve technology and nontraditional settings that diverge from the usual experiences and skills of law enforcement in the street.

One of the only studies to address these issues through empirical data was conducted by Bossler and Holt (2013) using a sample of patrol officers in the cities of Charlotte, North Carolina, and Savannah, Georgia. They found that the most influential and consistent predictor of support for the philosophy of online community policing and its components, including actively working with online citizens, was the individual's support for traditional community policing. Officers who understood the importance of community policing principles in general were more likely to believe that those principles could be applied to other settings (Bossler & Holt, 2013). This finding is in keeping with the larger literature on police initiatives, as officers who support new programs tend to accept that there is a serious problem to be addressed (i.e., cybercrime) and that there are new methods to specifically address that problem (Skogan & Hartnett, 1997).

Bossler and Holt (2013) also found that officer perceptions of the Internet in general did not affect their views of online community policing. Instead, officers who felt that the Internet has caused more problems for law enforcement than it has produced beneficial impacts were less likely to want to provide informational workshops to the public on cybercrime. Officers who found cybercrime to be more serious than their counterparts, but not necessarily more frequent or unique, were also more supportive of informational workshops and wanting to work with citizens. Finally, officers who felt that most cybercrimes went unreported to law enforcement were more likely to support both the principles of online community policing and cybercrime informational workshops. This appeared to stem from officer interest in informing the public about the dangers of these crimes, but not necessarily wanting to work with citizens to directly address cybercrimes.

Interestingly, computer proficiency had no relationship to support for online community policing (Bossler & Holt, 2013). Technological skill and experience are necessary to facilitate cybercrime investigations either in online spaces or of forensic evidence (Burns, Whitworth, & Thompson, 2004; Bossler & Holt, 2012; Ferraro & Casey, 2005; NIJ, 2008), but they do not appear to affect officers' willingness to engage the public to combat cybercrime. Demographic characteristics also had minimal impact on officer support for community policing, which contradicts the larger literature on real-world community policing (Lurigio & Skogan, 1994; Miller, 1999; Novak, Alarid, & Lucas, 2003; Paoline, Myers, & Worden, 2000; Skogan & Hartnett, 1997).

Though this initial study provides important direction for policy makers, there are a number of issues that must be explored further to increase our knowledge of the capacity of local law enforcement to investigate cybercrimes. Specifically, Bossler and Holt (2013) did not examine how officers' perceptions of the law enforcement response to cybercrime were related to their perceptions of the applicability of online community policing in the field. General evidence suggests that patrol officers are not interested in serving as the primary point of contact for cybercrime cases, even when they occur and are contained at the local level (Bossler & Holt, 2012). The increased responsibility and training required to investigate these cases may be too much for local officers given their other roles in the community dealing with real-world offenses (Bossler & Holt, 2012). The perceived lack of administrative support for these cases, coupled with substantive resource scarcity, may also be a deterrent for local officers (Bossler & Holt, 2012; Burns et al., 2004; Hinduja, 2004; Holt et al., 2010; Stambaugh et al., 2001). It is not surprising then that officers believe that state or federal agencies should act as the primary investigative agencies (Bossler & Holt, 2012; Burns et al., 2004; Goodman, 1997; Hinduja, 2004; Holt et al., 2010; McQuade, 2006; Senjo, 2004; Stambaugh et al., 2001; Swire, 2009).

In light of the existing literature, there are several hypotheses that can be generated regarding officer support for community-oriented policing initiatives in virtual spaces. First, patrol officers who do not believe that law enforcement is taking cybercrime seriously enough are not going to strongly support online community policing or its constituent components. More importantly, they must believe that upper management both treats cybercrime seriously enough and is taking the proper steps within its own department to address it. Officers know that community policing is a highly intensive philosophy that requires substantial investments from both administrators and line officers to succeed (Skogan & Hartnett, 1997). A lack of upper managerial support will likely produce minimal commitment from officers due to the belief that the initiative will fail.

Officers who support community engagement to address cybercrime may also be more receptive of online community policing at the local level than officers who simply want cybercrime responsibilities to rest with state and federal agencies. These officers may be more willing to explore the merits of community policing online and be willing to attempt to engage citizens. Similarly, officers who believe that cybercrime calls should be directly responded to by cybercrime units would be less likely to support online community policing since they are in favor of relegating responsibility to a specialized unit away from patrol officers and the public.

Officers are also well aware that any paradigm change or program implemented needs to be properly funded with resources. For officers to support the principles and components of online community policing, it is logical that they would support the use of police resources for cybercrime investigation so long as doing so does not drain resources from other priorities (Holt & Bossler, 2012). Similarly, officers who recognize the need to support and recognize officers who investigate cybercrime cases that lead to an arrest may be more willing to support community policing initiatives (Bossler & Holt, 2013). A culture supporting the importance of cybercrime investigations would logically favor the implementation of new online programs that have yet to be widely utilized in law enforcement.

Finally, some officers believe that cybercrime is simply traditional offenses that are committed with the aid of a computer (Holt & Bossler, 2012). Though there is some truth to this statement, it oversimplifies the complexity of many forms of cybercrime and the impact they have on law enforcement investigative techniques (Stambaugh et al., 2001). Thus, officers who recognize the variations in cybercrimes, their severity, and influence on policing tactics may be more willing to support new initiatives to deal with these offenses. These various hypotheses will be tested to better understand the factors that directly affect officer support for online community policing initiatives.

☐ Methods

The data for this study were collected from patrol officers in two cities: the Savannah-Chatham Metropolitan Police Department (SCMPD) in Savannah, Georgia, and the Charlotte-Mecklenburg Police Department (CMPD) in Charlotte, North Carolina. These departments were selected due to their proximity to the authors as well as the fact that they have been used by researchers over the last decade to assess both officer decision making (Alpert, Macdonald, & Dunham, 2005) and community policing techniques generally (Lord, 1996; Rutherford, Blevins, & Lord, 2009). These cities are both in the southeastern United States and share regional commonalities, but differ on several key characteristics. Charlotte is a large city with approximately 687,456 residents within the city limits and over 2 million residents in the combined statistical area. Savannah has a much smaller population of 134,669 residents (U.S. Census Bureau, 2009). Charlotte is an influential banking and financial hub, while Savannah's economy is driven by tourism, shipping, and the military. The racial makeup of the two cities differs significantly as well. Savannah is 57% African American, while Charlotte's largest racial group is White (55%).

The two cities' police departments vary in both size and demographic composition as well. At the time of the survey in spring 2008, the CMPD had over 1,400 patrol officers, while the SCMPD had just under 400 patrol officers. Both departments were overwhelmingly staffed by males (85%), though the CMPD was 78.3% White compared to the 59.4% White composition of the SCMPD. The demographic composition of these police departments, however, is mostly consistent with other similarly sized departments across the country (LEMAS, 2007). The CMPD also had a specialized computer crime task force, but the SCMPD has no such resource. As a whole, the differences and similarities between these two cities and police departments make them a valuable resource to assess attitudes toward any form of policing initiative.

A survey instrument was created using questions adapted from previous studies focusing on computer crime awareness among the general public and law enforcement (Furnell, 2002; Hinduja, 2004; Senjo, 2004; Stambaugh et al., 2001). The survey was distributed to all patrol officers at the rank of sergeant and below in order to capture the attitudes of patrol officers. In the SCMPD, the survey instrument in the form of paper copies was given to the command staff at a weekly departmental meeting in spring 2008. It was then distributed to patrol officers. The command staff returned 144 completed surveys (36% response rate). In the CMPD, the command staff wanted the survey to be uploaded on an internal departmental website for patrol officers to complete for the convenience of the officers and staff. Approximately 9% of all CMPD officers ($N = 124$) completed the survey. These response rates were generally low across both cities, but are consistent with the trend of declining response rates to surveys in general (Bickart & Schmittlein, 1999; Dey, 1997; Sheehan, 2001) and the apathy that law enforcement generally has regarding cybercrime (Burns et al., 2004). The low response rates could limit the representative nature of the data, but are consistent with survey participation rates as a whole and appear practical for use in this analysis.

The majority of the sample was male (87%) and White (84%), resembling the demographic characteristics of police officers in U.S. police departments (LEMAS, 2007). In keeping with the demographics of the two departments, the percentages of male officers in the two samples were equivalent, but the CMPD had more White officers respond than the SCMPD.

☐ Measures

Dependent Variables

Following Bossler and Holt's (2013) analysis of patrol officer support for online community policing, this study used the same three dependent variables in order to further our understanding of law enforcement perceptions of and support for innovative applications of community policing to online environments. Each of the three items assessed different but related issues and did not create a reliable scale ($\alpha = 0.512$). As a result, they were analyzed separately to explore the relationships between these variables.

First, officers were asked to assess their support for virtual community policing principles by rating their agreement on a scale from 1 to 5 (1 = strongly disagree, 2 = disagree, 3 = neutral, 4 = agree, 5 = strongly agree) with the following statement: "The principles of community policing may apply to 'virtual communities' (cyberspace) as well as they do in traditional neighborhoods." The officers were mostly ambivalent about this question, as illustrated by the modal category being "no opinion" (2.4% SD, 11.6% D, 48.2% N, 32.7% A, 5.2% SA).

The second item examined officers' perceptions on whether their police departments should intervene and educate the public on the risks posed by cybercrime. Specifically, respondents were asked to rate their agreement with the following statement: "Our police department should hold information workshops for the public informing them of the dangers of cybercrime and how to decrease their risks" (1 = strongly disagree to 5 = strongly agree). Almost two-thirds of the officers agreed with this statement (3.5% SD, 7.8% D, 29% N, 49% A, 14.3% SA).

The third item assessed how important it was for law enforcement to work with citizens online to address cybercrime. Coordinating and working with citizens to affect behavior in specific spaces, including virtual spaces, is one of the founding principles of community policing. Respondents were asked to rate on a scale from 1 to 5 (1 = not important, 2 = a little important, 3 = somewhat important, 4 = important, 5 = very important) how important it was to work with citizens online to police the Internet. Sixty percent (59.65) of the officers believed that this was important or very important.

Since there was some variation in the responses for each of these three variables, an ordered logistic regression model was created for each variable. The tests of parallel lines for these models indicated that the slope coefficients were not the same across response categories. Therefore, each of the three dependent measures was dichotomized to create binary variables that were used for the creation of both correlation analyses and binary logistic regression models.

Independent Variables

To further the work of Bossler and Holt (2013), we examined five categories of predictors that could be theoretically or empirically linked to support for online community policing: (1) perceptions of the police response to cybercrime, (2) support for cybercrime investigations, (3) perceptions concerning how cybercrime will change police work, (4) previous significant factors supporting online community policing (Bossler & Holt, 2013), including support for traditional community policing, and (5) demographic controls (see Table 10.1 for additional details).

Perceptions of the Police Response to Cybercrime

Four items from the survey were utilized to assess the officers' perceptions concerning if law enforcement takes cybercrime seriously, who is primarily responsible for handling local cybercrime, and their belief that upper management within their own department is appropriately handling the issue. First, officers were asked if they agreed that computer crime is not taken seriously enough by law enforcement (not serious enough). Second, officers were asked to rate their agreement that controlling local computer crime is the responsibility of the local police (local responsibility). Third, they were asked whether most cybercrime calls should be responded to directly by a computer crime unit (cybercrime unit). Finally, they were asked two questions to assess if they thought that upper management in their department treated cybercrime serious enough and is taking the proper steps to address it (upper management) ($\alpha = 0.70$).

Support for Cybercrime Investigation

To assess the officers' support for cybercrime investigations, three items (1 = strongly disagree to 5 = strongly agree) were included in the analyses. First, they were asked if investigating cybercrime drained valuable police resources that should be spent investigating more traditional forms of crime. Second, they were asked to rate their agreement regarding computer stakeouts being just as important as traditional stakeouts. Third, they were asked if a police officer would receive more recognition for catching traditional offenders than computer criminals.

Impact of Cybercrime on Policing

One item from the survey was used to assess the officers' perceptions of whether cybercrime will alter police work. Specifically, officers were asked their level of agreement (1 = strongly disagree to 5 = strongly agree) with the following statement, "Cybercrime will dramatically change police work."

TABLE 10.1 Descriptive Statistics

Variable	Measure	Scale	N	Mean	SD	Min.	Max.
Dependent							
Principles	The principles of community policing may apply to virtual communities (cyberspace) as well as they do in traditional communities	0 = disagree or neutral, 1 = agree	251	0.38	0.49	0	1
Workshops	Our police department should hold information workshops for the public informing them of the dangers of cybercrimes and how to decrease their risks	0 = disagree or neutral, 1 = agree	252	0.64	0.48	0	1
Work online	Please score the following items on importance of how to best make improvements in combating computer crimes: Working with citizens online to police the Internet, 1 = not important, 2 = a little important, 3 = somewhat important, 4 = important, 5 = very important	0 = 1–3, 1 = 4–5	255	0.60	0.49	0	1

(Continued)

TABLE 10.1 Descriptive Statistics (Continued)

Variable	Measure	Scale	N	Mean	SD	Min.	Max.
Independent							
Police Response							
Not serious enough	Computer crime is not taken seriously enough by LE	1 = SD to 5 = SA	252	2.97	0.83	1	5
Local responsibility	Controlling local computer crime is the responsibility of the local police	1 = SD to 5 = SA	253	2.72	0.90	1	5
Cybercrime unit	Most cybercrime reports/calls should be responded to directly by a computer crime unit	1 = SD to 5 = SA	252	3.87	0.85	1	5
Upper management	Average score of 1 = upper management in our department treats cybercrime serious enough; 2 = upper management in our department is taking the proper steps to address cybercrime	1 = SD to 5 = SA	253	2.93	0.61	1	5

Investigation Support

Drains resources	Investigating cybercrime drains valuable police resources that should be spent investigating other crime	1 = SD to 5 = SA	252	2.34	0.92	1	5
Computer stakeout	Conducting a stakeout on the computer is just as important as a traditional stakeout	1 = SD to 5 = SA	252	3.42	0.92	1	5
Recognition	A police officer would be given more recognition for catching a traditional criminal over a computer criminal	1 = SD to 5 = SA	252	3.17	0.90	1	5

Impact

Dramatically alter	Cybercrime will dramatically change police work	1 = SD to 5 = SA	254	3.56	0.82	2	5

Controls

COP	Average of five items' z-scores: 1 = I see community policing as an important tool to decrease traditional crime;	1 = SD to 5 = SA	247	−0.00	0.68	−2.30	1.61

(Continued)

TABLE 10.1 Descriptive Statistics (Continued)

Variable	Measure	Scale	N	Mean	SD	Min.	Max.
	2 = community policing takes away valuable time from real police work (reverse coded); 3 = community policing is more social work than real police work (reverse coded); 4 = police officers should try to solve noncrime problems on their beat; 5 = police officers should work with citizens to try and solve problems in their beat						
Internet LE	The Internet has caused more problems for law enforcement than it has helped	1 = SD to 5 = SA	253	2.53	0.96	1	5

Variable	Description	Coding	N	Mean	SD	Min	Max
Seriousness	Average score on "how serious (based on the financial and emotional harm to victims, and their threat to life, liberty, and personal property) you think the following crime types are": (1) copyright infringement such as software and media piracy, (2) credit card fraud, (3) electronic theft of money from accounts, (4) online harassment, (5) identity theft, (6) pedophilia on the Internet, and (7) viruses and malicious software infection	1 = not serious, 2 = A little serious, 3 = somewhat serious, 4 = serious, 5 = very serious	254	4.15	0.61	1	5
Unreported LE	Most computer crimes often go unreported to law enforcement	1 = SD to 5 = SA	250	3.66	0.80	1	5
Demographics							
Female	Sex	0 = male, 1 = female	260	0.13	0.34	0	1
Black	Race	0 = Non-Black, 1 = Black	253	0.16	0.37	0	1

(Continued)

TABLE 10.1 Descriptive Statistics (Continued)

Variable	Measure	Scale	N	Mean	SD	Min.	Max.
Years of experience	Years of total policing experience (asked as open-ended question)	1 = less than 1 year, 2 = 1–2, 3 = 3–5, 4 = 6–9, 5 = 10–14, 6 = ≥15	263	4.18	1.62	1	6
City	Policed department	0 = Charlotte, 1 = Savannah	263	0.53	0.50	0	1
Cybercrime experience	When was the last time that you responded to a computer crime (cybercrime) case?	0 = never, 1 = over year ago, 2 = within last year, 3 = within last several months, 4 = within last several weeks	257	0.76	1.16	0	4

Previous Significant Factors Supporting Online Community Policing

In order to control for factors found in previous research that were significantly related to support for online community policing (Bossler & Holt, 2013), we controlled for (1) support for community policing (COP), (2) perception on how the Internet affects policing (Internet LE), (3) officer perceptions of the seriousness of cybercrime (seriousness), and (4) officer perceptions of cybercrimes going unreported (unreported LE). The COP scale was created by averaging the z-scores to five items supported in the literature (Bayley & Shearing, 1996; Bossler & Holt, 2013; Pelfrey, 2004; Skogan, 2006; Skogan & Hartnett, 1997) (α = 0.705) (see Table 10.1 for specific items).

To assess their perception of the impact of the Internet on policing (Internet LE), officers were asked to rate their agreement (1 = strongly disagree to 5 = strongly agree) with the following statement: "The Internet has caused more problems for law enforcement than it has helped." Their perception of the seriousness of cybercrime (seriousness) was assessed by averaging the responses to how serious (1 = not serious to 5 = very serious) seven offenses (copyright infringement such as software and media piracy, credit card fraud, electronic theft of money from accounts, online harassment, identity theft, pedophilia on the Internet, and viruses and malicious software infection) were based on the "financial and emotional harm to victims, and their threat to life, liberty, and personal property" (α = 0.85). Finally, officers were asked (1 = SD to 5 = SA) if most computer crimes often go unreported to law enforcement (unreported LE).

Controls

Based on the relationship between specific demographic indicators and support for community-oriented policing found in the literature (Bossler & Holt, 2013; Lurigio & Skogan, 1994; Miller, 1999; Novak et al., 2003; Paoline et al., 2000; Skogan & Hartnett, 1997), this study included measures for sex (1 = female), race (1 = Black), and years of total policing experience (1 = less than 1 year, 2 = 1–2, 3 = 3–5, 4 = 6–9, 5 = 10–14, 6 = ≥15). The study also controlled for the city in which the officer worked (city) (1 = Savannah) and the officers' experiences with previous cybercrime cases (cybercrime case) (see Table 10.1).

☐ **Results and Discussion**

To assess the factors affecting officer attitudes toward community-oriented policing strategies online, correlation analyses were conducted to identify significant univariate relationships between these dependent variables and the various independent variables included (see Table 10.2 for detail). The correlation matrix indicated that officers' perceptions of the law enforcement response to cybercrime were not strongly correlated with their views of online community policing in general. In fact, their views regarding the perception of the response to law enforcement and the need to have cybercrime cases run through a cybercrime unit were not significantly correlated with any of the three dependent measures. Officers who believed that controlling local computer crime was the responsibility of local police and that upper management was treating cybercrime seriously enough and taking the proper steps were more likely to believe that community policing could be applied to cyberspace.

There was also a significant relationship between officers' belief that cybercrime investigation was a drain on agency resources and a lack of support for the principles of online community policing as well as providing informational workshops to the public on cybercrime. Support for computer stakeouts was also positively correlated with all three dependent measures. Finally, the belief that cybercrime would dramatically change police work was positively correlated with support for the principles of online community policing and informational workshops, but not significantly related with the belief that it is important to work with online citizens.

Consistent with the work of Bossler and Holt (2013), the community-oriented policing (COP) scale was positively correlated with all three dependent variables. The perception that the Internet caused more problems for law enforcement than it has helped was negatively related with support for the principles of online community policing and workshops related to cybercrime. Officers who perceived cybercrime to be more serious than their counterparts were more supportive of informational workshops and the importance of working with online citizens. In addition, officers who believed that most computer crimes go unreported to law enforcement were more likely to support the applicability of community policing to online environments and the formation of community informational workshops. Demographic factors were generally unrelated to the three dependent variables with two exceptions. Black officers were more likely to support the principles of community policing applied to online environments. Savannah officers were more likely to support all three online community policing initiatives.

The findings derived from the correlation matrix supported further examination of the predictors with multivariate statistical techniques. Binary logistic regression models were conducted for their support for each of the three dependent variables: (1) the principles of community policing can apply to virtual communities as well (Table 10.3, Model 1); (2) their police departments should hold information workshops on cybercrime (Table 10.3, Model 2); and (3) the importance of working with online citizens to police the Internet (Table 10.3, Model 3). Multicollinearity tests showed no significant problems within any model as the diagnostics indicated that no variance inflation factor (VIF) exceeded 10 or any tolerance level dropped below 0.2.

The three models indicated that officers' support for the idea that local law enforcement should be responsible for cybercrime, as well as how law enforcement is handling cybercrime, is not a strong predictor for any of these dependent variables. In fact, there is only weak evidence indicating that the perceptions of how law enforcement is responding to cybercrime were correlated with support for the principles of online community policing and working with citizens.

Officers who saw that upper management was treating cybercrime seriously and taking proper steps were more likely to believe that the principles of online community policing were viable. This provides support for the notion that community-oriented policing can only succeed if upper management is viewed as prepared and competent. At the same time, officers who viewed upper management to be capable of addressing cybercrime appeared less likely to support working with citizens online. Thus, officer perceptions may be affected by their conception of the agency's ability to address an offense by itself. In this case, they perceive that citizens may not need to be directly engaged because officers may not consider them to be a vital resource for online crime control.

The three models also suggest that officers' views on agency recognition for dealing with cybercrime were not significantly related to support for online community policing. There might be a relationship between the belief that cybercrime investigations were a waste of resources and a lack of support for the principles of online community policing. Respondents who valued computer-based stakeouts were more likely to support the application of principles of community-oriented policing and work with citizens in online spaces. These differences may stem from the perception that tactics may be more easily appreciated than resources needed to engage in a specific type of investigation.

Police officers in these two cities were also more likely to support informational workshops for the public informing them of the dangers of cybercrime if they believed that computer crime was going to dramatically alter policing. This may be a reflection of officers' acknowledgment that the general public needs to understand the threats posed by cybercrime

TABLE 10.2 Correlation Matrix

	1	2	3	4	5	6	7	8	9	10	11	12	13	14	15	16	17	18	19
1. Principles	—																		
2. Workshops	0.35*	—																	
3. Work online	0.21*	0.22*	—																
4. Not serious	-0.12	0.00	-0.10	—															
5. Local responsibility	0.16*	-0.07	.009	-0.06	—														
6. Cyber unit	0.06	-0.00	.003	0.02	0.00	—													
7. Upper management	0.17*	0.01	-0.001	-0.29*	0.13*	0.14*	—												
8. Drain resource	-0.20*	-0.18*	-0.05	0.01	-0.08*	0.01	0.20*	—											
9. Stakeout	0.31*	0.16*	0.29*	-0.05	0.31*	0.03	0.15*	-0.21*	—										
10. Recognition	-0.01	0.08	-0.08	0.14*	-0.04	0.07	-0.02	0.07	-0.12	—									
11. Dramatic	0.15*	0.12*	0.07	0.13*	-0.02	0.25*	-0.05	-0.12	0.29*	0.05	—								
12. COP	0.32*	0.30*	0.27*	-0.15*	0.11	-0.10	0.13*	-0.31*	0.35*	-0.01	0.13*	—							

	1	2	3	4	5	6	7	8	9	10	11	12	13	14	15	16	17	18	19	20
13. Internet LE	-0.14*	-0.21*	0.04	0.13*	0.06	-0.00	0.19*	0.22*	-0.04	0.02	0.02	-0.15*	—							
14. Seriousness	0.11	0.20*	0.29*	-0.10	0.04	0.05	0.12	-0.18*	0.29*	-0.19*	0.10	0.26*	0.00	—						
15. Unreported	0.22*	0.24*	0.04	0.28*	0.08	0.09	-0.12	-0.06	0.14*	0.08	0.18*	0.01	-0.06	0.04	—					
16. Female	-0.09	0.08	0.06	-0.01	-0.19*	-0.16*	-0.12	-0.01	0.08	0.03	-0.03	0.11	0.02	0.08	-0.02	—				
17. Black	0.18*	0.11	0.03	-0.27*	0.02	-0.14*	0.14*	-0.07	0.14*	-0.17*	0.01	0.20*	-0.00	0.08	-0.11	0.09	—			
18. Years of experience	0.01	0.01	0.06	-0.03	0.10	0.03	0.00	0.07	0.06	-0.08	-0.05	-0.18*	0.12	0.03	-0.03	-0.12	-0.01	—		
19. City	0.12*	0.18*	0.13*	-0.11	-0.10	-0.12	-0.08	-0.14*	0.10	-0.03	0.09	0.42*	-0.12	0.13*	-0.01	-0.02	0.25*	-0.22*	—	
20. Cybercrime	-0.01	.06	-0.01	.06	-0.02	-0.17*	-0.18*	-0.13*	0.07	0.08	-0.07	0.11	-0.07	0.03	0.17*	0.15	-0.07	0.05	0.12	

$* \ p \le .05.$

TABLE 10.3 Logistic Regression Models Predicting Support for Online Community Policing

	Model 1: Principles			Model 2: Workshops			Model 3: Online Citizens		
	B	SE	Exp (B)	B	SE	Exp (B)	B	SE	Exp (B)
Police Response									
Not serious enough	−0.403#	0.241	0.669	0.114	0.256	1.120	−0.413#	0.242	0.662
Local responsibility	0.025	0.209	1.025	−0.386#	0.220	0.680	−0.017	0.202	0.983
Cybercrime unit	0.001	0.209	1.001	−0.204	0.217	0.815	0.136	0.207	1.146
Upper management	0.576#	0.341	1.779	0.410	0.339	1.507	−0.745*	0.325	0.475
Investigation Support									
Drains resources	−0.350#	0.205	0.705	−0.233	0.200	0.792	0.229	0.211	1.258
Computer stakeout	0.395#	0.226	1.484	−0.077	0.228	0.926	0.615**	0.216	1.850
Recognition	0.070	0.204	1.073	0.254	0.213	1.289	−0.136	0.185	0.873
Impact on Policing									
Dramatically alter	0.263	0.231	1.301	0.484*	0.233	1.623	−0.025	0.224	0.976

	b	SE	Exp(B)	b	SE	Exp(B)	b	SE	Exp(B)
Controls									
COP	0.712*	0.317	2.037	0.753*	0.308	2.123	0.861**	0.305	2.365
Internet LE	−0.413*	0.193	0.662	−0.575**	0.192	0.563	0.347#	0.184	1.414
Seriousness	−0.044	0.318	0.957	0.690*	0.308	1.995	0.822**	0.294	2.275
Unreported LE	0.784**	0.253	2.189	0.809**	0.261	2.245	0.070	0.233	1.073
Demographics									
Female	0.520	0.519	0.595	0.279	0.488	1.321	0.444	0.507	1.560
Black	0.917#	0.489	2.503	0.503	0.529	1.654	−0.256	0.497	0.774
Years of experience	0.104	0.111	1.110	0.252*	0.112	1.287	0.024	0.104	1.024
City	0.049	0.384	1.051	0.340	0.392	1.405	−0.159	0.374	0.853
Cybercrime experience	−0.097	0.146	0.908	−0.172	0.151	0.842	−0.066	0.143	0.936
Constant	−5.018*	2.378	0.007	−6.205**	2.390	0.002	3.254	2.220	0.039
−2LL	227.045			228.041			247.450		
χ^2 (17)	64.457**			62.169**			52.003**		
Nagelkerke R^2	0.345			0.335			0.283		
N	221			222			221		

$^{**}\, p \leq .01,\ ^{*}\, p \leq .05,\ ^{\#}\, p \leq .1.$

and how to protect themselves. The dissemination of information is, however, quite different from the use of citizen interactions in online spaces or the development of new programs to aid online communities generally.

The various control measures derived from Bossler and Holt (2013) were also significantly related to support for all three of the dependent variables included in these analyses. The most influential and consistent predictor of support for online community policing in general was the officers' views of traditional community policing. Officers who supported the philosophy of community policing were more likely to believe that its tenets could be applied in virtual settings. In turn, they were also supportive of practical programs to engage the community to affect cybercrime.

Officers who believed the Internet caused more trouble for law enforcement were also less likely to believe that the Internet and technology could be harnessed for positive outcomes, particularly community policing in general and informational workshops for the public. Those officers who felt that cybercrimes were more serious than their colleagues were more likely to support the use of educational workshops to educate them of the dangers, as well as believing it is important to work with citizens online. This may stem from their realization that law enforcement must engage the community in order to be an effective partner because of the substantial damage caused by cybercrime. In much the same way, respondents who felt that cybercrimes went underreported were supportive of educational programs, but did not necessarily want to work directly with citizens in online spaces.

The only demographic predictor that was significantly associated with the dependent variables was that more experienced officers supported informational workshops on cybercrime. They may recognize that an informed community is a better prepared community, and therefore favor the implementation of such programs. The other nonsignificant relationships noted suggest that individual characteristics are not as important in shaping individual opinions relative to work experiences that may give greater insights into their value in the field.

☐ Conclusions

Police administrators and scholars have called for local law enforcement to more actively engage in the investigation and prevention of cybercrimes (e.g., Stambaugh et al., 2001). A small, but growing body of scholarship from both researchers (Brenner, 2008; Jones, 2007; Wall & Williams, 2007) and practitioners (IACP, 2009) argues that online community policing initiatives, particularly those that integrate the larger population of Internet users, could enhance the investigative capacity of law enforcement and improve their efficiency in combating cybercrime (Brenner, 2008; Jones, 2007; Wall & Williams, 2007). Little guidance is available regarding how such online programs would operate or how patrol officers and command staff would support their implementation in the field. One of the few studies in this area found that officers' views on the use of community policing principles in a virtual space were significantly related to their support for traditional community policing, their perceptions of cybercrime, and the ways that the Internet affects law enforcement (Bossler & Holt, 2013).

The current study attempted to expand upon the existing literature by exploring the factors that influence officers' support for the application of community policing online as well as practical programs, including citizen training courses on cybercrime and direct engagement with online populations. Using a sample of line officers from two cities, logistic regression analyses were conducted that provided mixed support for these concepts. There were no consistent relationships identified across the three dependent variables, though several of the hypothesized relationships were confirmed. Significant relationships, however, were present for officers' support for community policing and their perception of the law enforcement response to cybercrime, their agency's support for cybercrime investigations, and the impact that these offenses have on law enforcement generally.

Taken as a whole, the findings support the research of Bossler and Holt (2013) that online community policing initiatives to address cybercrimes require careful staffing and promotion to ensure acceptance by officers and management (see also Skogan & Hartnet, 1997). Administrators may select officers for cybercrime tasks based on computer skill or age, but this may actually prove counterproductive to program success. Instead, identifying candidates on the basis of support for community policing initiatives in general, and their recognition of the way in which cybercrimes will affect both the community and law enforcement, may prove more effective. Such a practice will require the use of technical training programs to ensure a high degree of technical proficiency for these candidates (FLETC, 2012; NIJ, 2008; NWCCC, 2012), but these costs will be offset by increased officer acceptance and support for these initiatives in general (see Lurigio & Skogan, 1994; Skogan & Hartnet, 1997). In turn, the use of these programs in the field may be more accepted by the wider law enforcement agency and enable a smoother transition to a new paradigm for policing the Internet.

The findings of this study also call into question how an online community policing program would operate and what it might require to efficiently operate in both real and virtual spaces (see also Bossler & Holt, 2013; Holt & Bossler, 2012). It is clear that online citizen engagement must be a part of any program, as the population of Internet users provides a massive base to identify when and how various forms of cybercrime occur, particularly in more isolated or unknown portions of the Internet that require a good degree of technical proficiency to access (Wall, 2001, 2007; Wall & Williams, 2007). Developing support for reporting behaviors may be difficult to generate, as many view the Internet as a space that should not be regulated (Brenner, 2008; Wall, 2001) and historically designed to be free from any sort of police intervention (Holt, 2007). Any program designed to increase citizen encounters and encourage self-regulation and reporting must carefully consider how to gain support among end users who may not want to actively report on the behavior of others (Brenner, 2008; Wall, 2001; Wall & Williams, 2007). Adapting messages and strategies from community-oriented policing campaigns that were successfully able to incorporate citizens in high-crime areas in the real world may serve as practical models to engage citizens in virtual spaces. In turn, this may increase the likelihood of success and high community involvement.

In much the same way, there is a need to consider how real-world community meetings may be structured to promote reporting among citizens and demonstrate law enforcement's investigative capabilities to the community. Physical meetings at community centers or local facilities could inform the public of prevention tips and guidance on which agencies to contact if victimization occurs and provide officers direct access to citizens as well. Special effort should also be made to reach out to youth populations through school resource officers and other existing programs to ensure that the technological abilities of youth and their likelihood of cybercrime victimization are more fully integrated into any problem-solving strategy (e.g., Holt & Bossler, 2009; Wolak et al., 2012). The promotion of outreach campaigns through social medial sites such as Facebook and Twitter would also help increase exposure of the agency to various online populations.

Additional research is also needed to evaluate any existing programs that have been implemented to understand what impact they have on improving communication between the community and law enforcement and any effects on reporting cybercrime incidents or reducing victimization. Further study is also needed with populations of police officers in small, medium, and large agencies across the United States. The two departments sampled here have been studied in the police literature (Alpert et al., 2005; Lord, 1996; Rutherford et al., 2009) and are demographically similar to other departments (LEMAS, 2007). They may not, however, be representative of all officers across the country in terms of their perceptions of cybercrime and the ways that police may be more effectively integrated into online community management (Burns et al., 2004; Marcum, Higgins, Freiburger, &

Ricketts, 2010). Additional research using both qualitative and quantitative methods is needed to better explore officer perceptions of online community policing, its efficacy, and identify sources for reluctance to work with citizens online.

☐ References

Adams, R. E., Rohe, W. M., & Arcury, T. A. (2002). Implementing community-oriented policing: Organizing change and street officer attitudes. *Crime and Delinquency, 48*, 399–430.

Alpert, G. P., Macdonald, J. M., & Dunham, R. G. (2005). Police suspicion and discretionary decision making during citizen stops. *Criminology, 43*, 407–434.

Bayley, D. H. (1998). *What works in policing.* New York: Oxford University Press.

Bayley, D., & Shearing, C. (1996). The future of policing. *Law and Society Review, 30*, 585–606.

Bickhart, B., & Schmittlein, D. (1999). The distribution of survey contact and participation in the United States: Constructing a survey-based estimate. *Journal of Marketing Research*, 286–294.

Bossler, A. M., & Holt, T. J. (2009). Online activities, guardianship, and malware infection: An examination of Routine Activities Theory. *International Journal of Cyber Criminology, 3*(1), 400–420.

Bossler, A. M., & Holt, T. J. (2012). Patrol officers' perceived role in responding to cybercrime. *Policing: International Journal of Strategies and Management, 35*, 165–181.

Bossler, A. M., & Holt, T. J. (2013). Assessing officer perceptions and support for online community policing. *Security Journal.* Retrieved June 13, 2013, from DOI: 10.1057/sj.2013.23

Braga, A. A. (2008). Pulling levers focused deterrence strategies and the prevention of gun homicide. *Journal of Criminal Justice, 36*, 332–343.

Brenner, S. W. (2008). *Cyberthreats: The emerging fault lines of the nation state.* New York: Oxford University Press.

Burns, R. G., Whitworth, K. H., & Thompson, C. Y. (2004). Accessing law enforcement preparedness to address Internet fraud. *Journal of Criminal Justice, 32*, 477–493.

Chu, B., Holt, T. J., & Ahn, G. J. (2010). *Examining the creation, distribution, and function of malware on line.* Washington, DC: National Institute of Justice. Retrieved June 2, 2013, from www.ncjrs.gov/pdffiles1/nij/grants/230111.pdf.

Cordner, G. W. (1999). Elements of community policing. In L. K. Gaines & G. W. Cordner (Eds.), *Policing perspectives: An anthology* (pp. 137–149). Los Angeles: Roxbury.

Dey, E. L. (1997). Working with low survey response rates: The efficacy of weighting adjustments. *Research in Higher Education, 38*, 97–114.

Durkin, K. F., & Bryant, C. D. (1999). Propagandizing pederasty: A thematic analysis of the online exculpatory accounts of unrepentant pedophiles. *Deviant Behavior, 20*, 103–127.

Federal Law Enforcement Training Center (FLETC). (2012). *Internet Investigations Training Program (IITP).* Retrieved September 1, 2013, from http://www.fletc. gov/training/programs/investigative-operations-division/economic-financial/ internet-investigations-training-program-iitp/?searchterm=cybercrime

Ferraro M. M., & Casey, E. (2005). *Investigating child exploitation and pornography: The Internet, law, and forensic science.* San Diego: Elsevier.

Furnell, S. (2002). *Cybercrime: Vandalizing the information society.* Boston: Addison-Wesley.

Goodman, M. D. (1997). Why the police don't care about computer crime. *Harvard Journal of Law and Technology, 10,* 465–494.

Grabosky, P. (2007). *Electronic crime.* Upper Saddle River, NJ: Prentice Hall.

Higgins, G. E. (2005). Can low self-control help with the understanding of the software piracy problem? *Deviant Behavior, 26,* 1–24.

Hinduja, S. (2004). Perceptions of local and state law enforcement concerning the role of computer crime investigative teams. *Policing: An International Journal of Police Strategies & Management, 27,* 341–357.

Hinduja, S. (2007). Computer crime investigations in the United States: Leveraging knowledge from the past to address the future. *International Journal of Cyber Criminology, 1,* 1–26.

Holt, T. J. (2003). Examining a transnational problem: An analysis of computer crime victimization in eight countries from 1999 to 2001. *International Journal of Comparative and Applied Criminal Justice, 27,* 199–220.

Holt, T. J. (2007). Subcultural evolution? Examining the influence of on- and off-line experiences on deviant subcultures. *Deviant Behavior, 28,* 171–198.

Holt, T. J., & Blevins, K. R. (2007). Examining sex work from the client's perspective: Assessing johns using online data. *Deviant Behavior, 28,* 333–354.

Holt, T. J., Blevins, K. R., & Burkert, N. (2010). Considering the pedophile subculture online. *Sexual Abuse: Journal of Research and Treatment, 22,* 3–24.

Holt, T. J., & Bossler, A. M. (2009). Examining the applicability of lifestyle-routine activities theory for cybercrime victimization. *Deviant Behavior, 30,* 1–25.

Holt, T. J., & Bossler, A. M. (2012). Police perceptions of computer crimes in two southeastern cities: An examination from the viewpoint of patrol officers. *American Journal of Criminal Justice, 37,* 396–412.

Holt, T. J., Bossler, A. M., & Fitzgerald, S. (2010). Examining state and local law enforcement perceptions of computer crime. In T. J. Holt (Ed.), *Crime online: Correlates, causes, and context* (pp. 221–246). Raleigh, NC: Carolina Academic.

International Association of Chiefs of Police. (2009). 2008 IACP community policing awards: Presented at the 115th Annual IACP Conference. *The Police Chief, 77*(3). Retrieved August 14, 2013, from http://policechiefmagazine.org/magazine/ index.cfm?fuseaction=display_arch&article_id=1749&issue_id=32009

Jones, B. R. (2007). Comment: Virtual neighborhood watch: Open source software and community policing against cybercrime. *Journal of Criminal Law and Criminology, 97,* 601–630.

Law Enforcement Management and Administration Statistics (LEMAS). (2007). *Local police departments, 2007, NCJ 231174.* Retrieved September 1, 2013, from http://bjs.ojp.usdoj.gov/index.cfm?ty=pbdetail&iid=1750

Lord, V. B. (1996). An impact of community policing: Reported stressors, social support, and strain among police officers in a changing police department. *Journal of Criminal Justice, 24,* 503–522.

Lurigio, A. J., & Skogan, W. G. (1994). Winning the hearts and minds of police officers: An assessment of staff perceptions of community policing in Chicago. *Crime and Delinquency, 40,* 315–330.

Marcum, C., Higgins, G. E., Freiburger, T. L., & Ricketts, M. L. (2010). Policing possession of child pornography online: Investigating the training and resources dedicated to the investigation of cyber crime. *International Journal of Police Science & Management, 12,* 516–525.

Mastrofski, S. D., Worden, R. E., & Snipes, J. B. (1995). Law enforcement in a time of community policing. *Criminology, 33,* 539–563.

McGarrell, E. F., Chermak, S., Wilson, J. M., & Corsaro, N. (2006). Reducing homicide through a "lever-pulling" strategy. *Justice Quarterly, 23,* 214–231.

McQuade, S. (2006). Technology-enabled crime, policing and security. *Journal of Technology Studies, 32,* 32–42.

Miller, S. (1999). *Gender and community policing: Walking the talk.* Boston: Northeastern University Press.

National Institute of Justice. (2008). *Electronic crime science investigation: A guide for first responders* (2nd ed., NCJ 219941). Washington, DC. Retrieved September 1, 2013, from https://www.ncjrs.gov/pdffiles1/nij/219941.pdf

National White Collar Crime Center (NWCCC). (2012). *National White Collar Crime Center online course registration.* Retrieved August 30, 2013, from http://www.training.nw3c.org/ocr/courses_desc.cfm?cn=STOP

Newman, G., & Clarke, R. (2003). *Superhighway robbery: Preventing e-commerce crime.* Cullompton, UK: Willan Press.

Novak, K. J., Alarid, L. F., & Lucas, W. L. (2003). Exploring officers' acceptance of community policing: Implications for policy implementation. *Journal of Criminal Justice, 31,* 57–71.

Paoline, E. A., Myers, S. M., & Worden, R. E. (2000). Police culture, individualism, and community policing: Evidence from two police departments. *Justice Quarterly, 17,* 575–606.

Pelfrey, W. V. (2004). The inchoate nature of community policing: Differences between community policing and traditional police officers. *Justice Quarterly, 21,* 579–601.

Reuss-Ianni, E. (1983). *The two cultures of policing: Street cops and management cops.* New Brunswick, NJ: Transaction Books.

Rutherford, S. L., Blevins, K. R., & Lord, V. (2009). An evaluation of the effects of a street crime unit on citizens' fear of crime. *Professional Issues in Criminal Justice, 3,* 21–36.

Senjo, S. R. (2004). An analysis of computer-related crime: Comparing police officer perceptions with empirical data. *Security Journal, 17,* 55–71.

Sheehan, K. B. (2001). E-mail survey response rates: A review. *Journal of Computer Mediated Communication, 6*(2). Retrieved June 14, 2010, from http://www.ascusc.org/jcmc/vol6/issue2/sheehan.html

Skogan, W. G. (2006). *Police and community in Chicago: A tale of three cities.* New York: Oxford University Press.

Skogan, W. G., & Hartnett, S. M. (1997). *Community policing. Chicago style.* New York: Oxford University Press.

Sparrow, M. K. (1988). *Implementing community policing.* Washington, DC: U.S. Department of Justice.

Stambaugh, H., Beaupre, D. S., Icove, D. J., Baker, R., Cassady, W., & Williams, W. P. (2001). *Electronic crime needs assessment for state and local law enforcement* (NCJ 186276). Washington, DC: National Institute of Justice. Retrieved August 20, 2013, from https://www.ncjrs.gov/pdffiles1/nij/186276.pdf

Swire, P. (2009). No cop on the beat: Underenforcement in e-commerce and cyber-crime. *Journal of Telecommunications and High Technology Law, 7*, 107–126.

U.S. Census Bureau. (2009). *Annual estimates of the population of metropolitan and micropolitan statistical areas: April 1, 2000 to July 1, 2008.* Retrieved August 20, 2013, from http://www.census.gov/popest/data/historical/2000s/vintage_2008/index.html

Wall, D. S. (2001). Cybercrimes and the Internet. In D. S. Wall (Ed.), *Crime and the Internet* (pp. 1–17), New York: Routledge.

Wall, D. S. (2007). *Cybercrime: The transformation of crime in the information age.* Cambridge: Polity Press.

Wall, D. S., & Williams, M. (2007). Policing diversity in the digital age: Maintaining order in virtual communities. *Criminology and Criminal Justice, 7*, 391–415.

Winfree, L. T., Bartku, G. M., & Seibel, G. (1996). Support for community policing versus traditional policing among nonmetropolitan police officers: A survey of four New Mexico police departments. *American Journal of Police, 15*, 23–50.

Wolak, J., Finkelhor, D., & Mitchell, K. (2012). *Trends in law enforcement responses to technology-facilitated child sexual exploitation crimes: The Third National Juvenile Online Victimization Study (NJOV-3).* Durham, NH: Crimes Against Children Research Center. Retrieved August 1, 2013, from http://cola.unh.edu/sites/cola.unh.edu/files/research_publications/CV268.pdf

CHAPTER 11

Prosecution and Social Media

Joseph D. Losavio
Johns Hopkins University

Michael M. Losavio
University of Louisville

Contents

Jurisdiction and Laws on Information, Free Speech, and Crimes   201
Prosecution of Social Media Use as a Criminal Offense   202
Illegal Use of Social Media   203
     Cyberstalking   205
     Cyber Threats   206
Investigations and Prosecutions Using Social Media as Evidence of
a Criminal Offense   208
     Investigations   209
     Prosecutions   211
Use of Social Media by Those in the Criminal Justice System—
Police, Prosecutors, and Judicial Officers   212
Future Issues   213
     Will New Criminal Statutes Be Needed?   213
     Transnational Law Enforcement?   214

Should Law Enforcement Expand and Formalize Training and
Investigative Practices With the Proper Use of Social Media?   215
How Will Personal Autonomy in Social Media Evolve?   216
Conclusion   216
References   217

All media are social: They connect people, usually for the better. *Social media* represents networked systems for vast, immediate, and democratic sharing of information on a scale never before possible.

But they also create unprecedented opportunities to hurt others or violate the law. Cyberbullying and humiliation through social media have led to teenage suicides. Parolees and those under restraining orders may violate the law by "friending" or "poking" people with whom they have been ordered to have no contact (Jackson, 2011). In turn, social media postings may be used as evidence of those and other crimes, such as cyberstalking, online threats and harassment, child pornography, and sexual assault. Social media creates new opportunities for law enforcement and the administration of justice in the investigation of crime and promotion of public safety.

The International Association of Chiefs of Police found 88% of departments responding to their survey used social media for one or several purposes (IACP, 2011). A 2012 survey by LexisNexis Risk Solutions found similar levels of law enforcement social media use, with 67% feeling it helped solve crimes more quickly; 50% of departments used social media weekly, but only 10% said they had formal agency training on its use (LexisNexis, 2012).

This chapter examines these and other aspects of the use of social media in the administration of justice through case studies, case law, and statutes.

Kaplan and Haenlein defined *social media* as

a group of Internet-based applications that build on the ideological and technological foundations of Web 2.0 [content is continuously created and published in a highly collaborative fashion], and that allow the creation and exchange of User Generated Content [creative, noncommercial content published to multiple people]. (Kaplan and Haenlein, 2010)

They suggest the primary types of social media are collaborative projects, weblogs, content communities, social networking sites, virtual game worlds, and virtual social worlds. Of these, social networking sites of varying types have garnered significant attention.

Boyd and Ellison define social network sites as

web-based services that allow individuals to (1) construct a public or semi-public profile within a bounded system, (2) articulate a list of other users with whom they share a connection, and (3) view and traverse their list of connections and those made by others within the system. The nature and nomenclature of these connections may vary from site to site. (Boyd and Ellison, 2007)

Social media and network sites are about information, whether text, video, or sound, and the movement of that information to others easily and inexpensively. So easy, in fact, that even a child can do it. This alone indicates the dangers in social media misuse as more and more children (and unsuspecting adults) go online via social media.

Information is central to the administration of justice, and the use of social media in criminal justice can be categorized in three main areas:

1. Prosecution *of the use of social media* as a criminal offense

2. Prosecution *using social media as evidence* of a substantive criminal offense

3. The *use of social media by those in the criminal justice system* and the ethical implications of that use, from virtual block watch to anticorruption and transparency tools in e-government

Social media can be analyzed in the context of information and communication technologies (ICTs) generally and the laws applicable to them. ICT encompasses the diverse computing systems available for consumer use, ranging from cellphones, tablets, and notebook computers to servers and cloud systems of massively networked computers. It includes the communication systems of the vast interconnected systems of the Internet, cellular telephones, satellites, and other systems.

Social media requires a means of content creation for the user and a way to transmit and communicate the information, such as cellphones for sending tweets via Twitter and pictures via Instagram. Some social media systems also use a storage and hosting service for more permanent posting and distribution of social media content, like Facebook, Reddit, and YouTube.

Criminal statutes and evidence rules may apply to the use of social media or to the particular computing or communication system used to create, post, and transmit social media. The information or communication technology used for social media must be matched to the elements of the crimes and rules to verify a violation that can be proven in court. This can be both confusing and potentially damaging to an investigation where that match is not made.

Statutes relevant to online misconduct prohibit, among other things, unauthorized use of some social media systems, wire fraud, stalking, and online harassment. These are informed by case law in the United States and Great Britain—the decisions of courts—that may interpret the application of these statutes. Constitutional case law in the United States may define how statutes may be applied under the limits of the U.S. Constitution and the Bill of Rights.

Evidence rules define how purported proof of acts or omissions is set out by legislatures and courts. The proper procedures for legally obtaining that evidence may differ for each jurisdiction and technology, depending on the circumstances and the technology, such that using the wrong procedures might damage the investigation. Evidence of social media misconduct must be connected to a particular suspect to the degree required for conclusions that a person is a suspect, more likely than not committed a crime, or did commit the crime beyond a reasonable doubt. A major challenge in all investigations with electronic evidence, especially social media, is reliably connecting the particular use of social media, such as a tweet or online posting, back to a particular individual. Fake social media postings can create special evidence problems for law enforcement in knowing who really created the postings.

Complex issues with social media are seen in their mixed role in the investigation of the 2013 Boston Marathon bombing. The ability to widely distribute information across the multitude of platforms available on social media is credited as part of the reason the two suspects were identified (Voice of America, 2013; CBS News, 2013). Massachusetts State Police Colonel Tim Alben posted, "This is a very serious situation we are dealing with. We would appreciate your cooperation" (Voice of America, 2013; CBS News, 2013). Within minutes of the FBI's release of the suspects' images, Facebook newsfeeds and trending Twitter topics flashed the images on computer and cellphone screens while traditional broadcast newsrooms were still preparing to go live for special reports. Suspect Tamerlan Tsarnaev's YouTube page revealed his support of religious terrorism (Voice of America, 2013; CBS News, 2013). The first official word that suspect 2 in the Boston bombing was captured came not in a press conference but from a tweet from the Boston Police Department (Voice of America, 2013; CBS News, 2013).

But at the same time some social media users crossed the line from engaged civilians to self-deputized detectives. They used the social media site Reddit as a platform to conduct their own investigations (Ulanoff,

2013). Several times the wrong person was identified as a suspect, with accusations that spread quickly over other social media platforms before they were refuted by authorities. This was dangerous for those wrongfully accused and raised questions as to the negative impact of social media technology (Bensinger & Chang, 2013).

Professional media such as the British Broadcasting Company (BBC) noted the two-sided benefit/detriment from social media in the Boston bombing, pointing out its flaws and benefits (Dyer, 2013). Yet the system has demonstrated its capacity for self-correction and analysis. After the FBI released official crime scene photos, Reddit users took down the erroneous information on suspects earlier uploaded and then crowd-scoured photos to find clearer pictures of the Tsarnaev brothers at the scene that the authorities had not yet identified (Dyer, 2013).

Social media is a powerful tool for law enforcement, for investigation and informing or collaborating with the public. But the Boston attack shows unmediated social media use has risks.

The role of social media and electronic artifacts will grow even more with the evolution of the Internet of Things and the Smart City, systems where, more and more, people and the things they use are instrumented and connected into a vast information resource. Cases and case studies show the possibilities and concerns in such a resource as social media continues to evolve and develop.

☐ Jurisdiction and Laws on Information, Free Speech, and Crimes

Our focus is on the law of the United States, but the possible impact of substantive and procedural laws of other jurisdictions should always be considered. Social media is created with internetworked communications technologies, often using the Internet, whose use may span municipal, county, state, provincial, and national boundaries. The legal right and jurisdiction of a particular authority to take action regarding the use of social media may depend on

1. Where the user is

2. Where the information is sent, posted, or otherwise made available

3. Where that information is viewed or accessed

The substantive and procedural laws that may apply to the use of social media depend on these factors. A person posting on a service in San Francisco, California, that is accessed in Memphis, Tennessee, may be required to defend himself or herself in a Memphis court. Postings that are legal in the United States may be illegal in foreign countries, and vice versa, but absent special treaty agreements, transnational enforcement may be difficult. Online activities legal in a user's home country but illegal in another may leave law enforcement in the latter country with no practical means of prosecution. But if that user should ever visit that country, even if only for a connecting flight elsewhere, law enforcement may arrest and prosecute for the alleged crimes. Issues relating to jurisdiction over social media usage, as with cybercrime, may require special attention in prosecutions. Cross-border execution of search orders and extradition of suspects may be needed. Given the transnational power of social media, the particular laws of a nation as to the freedom of information and speech may also impact prosecution.

The United States has broad protections for the free exchange of information incorporated in its founding Constitution through the First Amendment. Other countries have fewer protections for such exchanges, such that social media use that is noncriminal in the United States may be a crime in other countries. The United States will not extradite a resident to another country solely for alleged crimes the enforcement of which would violate the First Amendment, but it may not be able to block prosecution if that resident travels abroad outside of U.S. jurisdiction.

The broad protections of the First Amendment are not absolute. Information, speech, or writings that further any prohibited activity are not protected and may be punished. And if a sufficiently compelling reason exists to limit certain forms of information, such as the prevention of the sexual exploitation of children, that informational conduct may be regulated even as to content. Criminal laws generally develop to protect life and person, personal rights and liberties, and property. Regulation of social media usage will reflect how the primary objectives of social media—information and its exchange—might injure people in these areas.

☐ Prosecution of Social Media Use as a Criminal Offense

Social media is a subset of ICT via personal computing technologies. Criminal law evolves in response to injuries from new technologies

(Rasch, 1996). Social media, information and communication systems, and computing systems injure via information and may create new means of injury and new means for the facilitation of traditional offenses, such as fraud and identity theft (Brenner, 2004). Social media, as with other computing and ICT systems, makes it possible to injure others in ways that were traditionally beyond the skills or resources of the average person (Rasch, 1996, note 9). Some types of conduct and injury with information were different enough from traditional offenses and injuries that it was not possible to prosecute them under traditional laws. This led to new, *sui generis* criminal laws to address certain of these types of misconduct (U.S. Computer Fraud and Abuse Act of 1984). This is a subset of what is called cybercrime (Losavio et al., 2012).

☐ Illegal Use of Social Media

Under the First Amendment to the Constitution of the United States, people have a right to send and receive information from others without government interference. This is not absolute, but where speech falls under the First Amendment, the government must show a compelling need that may be met with narrow restrictions in order to limit that right. Examples of speech that do not fall under the protection of the First Amendment are fraud, obscenity, and criminal facilitation.

For example, the Connecticut State Police threatened to prosecute social media users because of postings made about the Sandy Hook elementary school shootings (Sandy Hook Video Vault, 2013). Without a showing that the social media statements were part of an effort to carry out a crime, they are protected speech no matter how offensive. Protected statements might include those calling the shooting a hoax or questioning official competence. Unprotected statements on social media that could be prosecuted include harassment or threats against victims, their families, witnesses, or others, or false statements of other attacks under way or being planned.

A broad Indiana state prohibition on the use of social media by convicted sex offenders did not survive a court challenge. In *Doe v. Prosecutor* (2013) the convicted sex offender challenged in federal court Indiana Code §35-42-4-12, which prohibits certain sex offenders from "knowingly or intentionally us[ing]: a social networking web site" or "an instant messaging or chat room program" that "the offender knows allows a person who is less than eighteen (18) years of age to access or use the web site or program" (Sex Offender Internet Offense, 2008). A first offense is a misdemeanor punishable by up to 12 months in jail; subsequent offenses are felonies.

The federal Court of Appeals struck down this "blanket ban on social media" as too broad an infringement of the First Amendment and the right of a person, even a convicted felon, to receive and send information to others. The court did note that this did not restrict the ability to limit Internet usage as a condition of parole or supervised release after a conviction (*United States v. Holm*, 2003) and opined a narrower ban on use might be legal.

Other social media use may still be criminal, such as with traditional crimes where information is the tool for the offense. Some uses of social media are in themselves criminal, such as usage that furthers criminal objectives via social media. Examples include the following:

1. Harassment

2. Harassing communications

3. Stalking (18 USC §2261A)

4. Threats (18 USC §875(c))

5. Fraud

6. Sexual solicitation of a minor

7. Digital contraband (child pornography, obscenity)

8. Conspiracy

The use of social media to threaten or intentionally cause emotional distress to someone may be subject to criminal penalties. Efforts to mislead and defraud someone of something of value through misleading information transmitted via social media may be a crime. Sexual importuning of juveniles may be a crime. The transmittal or display of child pornography and obscene materials is an actionable crime. All of these offenses rely on the transmittal of information in some form and may be committed without social media, but social media offers new, easy, and powerful avenues for these offenses, sometimes in new and more dangerous ways.

Cyberstalking

18 USC §2261A, the federal antistalking statute, makes it a crime to, with the intent to harass or cause substantial emotional distress to a person in another state using any interactive computer service, engage in a course of conduct that causes substantial emotional distress to that person. Most states have similar antistalking statutes that cover such action within their state.

In *United States v. Sayer* (2012) the defendant was charged with cyberstalking and identity theft relating to postings about his ex-girlfriend. The District Court summarized the alleged conduct from the government's filings as

> the government's contention is that, after the defendant's former girlfriend changed her name and moved from Maine to Louisiana to escape him, the defendant, still in Maine, created fictitious internet advertisements and social media profiles using [the victim's] name and other identifying information. The fictitious internet postings included [the victim's] address and invited men to come to her home for sexual encounters. The Defendant also posted video clips to several adult pornography websites depicting sexual acts [the victim] had consensually performed with him during their relationship. The Defendant edited the clips so they also displayed [the victim's] name and actual address. As a result of the Defendant's actions, numerous men arrived at [the victim's] Louisiana residence seeking sexual encounters, terrifying her and causing her to fear that she would be raped or assaulted.

The District Court denied the defendant's request to end the case on First Amendment grounds and throw out the evidence from social media sites. In denying the motion to dismiss, the court cited Supreme Court opinions that did not bar prosecution of speech used to facilitate criminal acts (*Giboney v. Empire Storage & Ice Co.*, 1949).

> None of this activity is speech protected by the First Amendment. Yes, emails and websites involve communication and in that sense are speech. But bribery, extortion, conspiracy, fraud, identity theft and threats also all involve communication, and speech in that sense, and yet they are crimes not protected by the First Amendment. Instead, the Supreme Court has long recognized that "speech or writing used as an integral part of conduct in violation of a valid criminal statute" is not protected.

The ongoing and pervasive conduct in this case helped establish the necessary criminal intent and misconduct that justified the prosecution.

Cyber Threats

It is a federal crime to communicate a threat: "Whoever transmits in interstate or foreign commerce any communication containing any threat to kidnap any person or any threat to injure the person of another, shall be fined under this title or imprisoned not more than five years, or both" (18 USC §875(c)). In *United States v. Stock* the defendant was indicted for posting the following on Craigslist about a local police officer:

> I went home loaded in my truck and spend [*sic*] the past 3 hours looking for this douche with the expressed intent of crushing him in that little piece of shit under cover gray impala hooking up my tow chains and dragging his stupid ass down to creek hills and just drowning him in the falls. But alas I can't fine [*sic*] that bastard anywhere.... I really wish he would die, just like the rest of these stupid fucking asshole cops. So J.K.P if you read this I hope you burn in hell. I only wish I could have been the one to send you there. (*United States v. Peter Adrian Stock*, 2012)

The defendant argued he really was not making a "true threat" and asked the case be dismissed. The District Court denied that request. The defendant pled guilty to transmitting threatening communications and was sentenced to a year's imprisonment (Office of the U.S. Attorney, 2012; Pittsburgh Post-Gazette, 2012).

By contrast, an online fraud perpetrated against a Missouri teenager via the MySpace social networking site ended in that child's suicide after the person she thought was an online friend criticized her. The woman who coordinated the fraud, the mother of one of the girl's classmates, was tried for various violations in Los Angeles, California, the home of MySpace, but was acquitted by the jury of the felony charges. The misdemeanor convictions were later dismissed by the judge, finding that violating the terms of service of MySpace by using a false name was not illegal (*United States v. Drew*, 2009).

The hazards of social networking sites relating to child sexual exploitation are significant. For example, a 48-year-old defendant used the social networking features of the Jango.com music site to connect with a 15-year-old girl, moved to MySpace, and emailed to extend the relationship; this eventually led to the girl running away with the defendant (*United States v. Watkins*, 2012). Such misuse is specifically made a crime by 18 USC §2422(b), which provides:

> Whoever, using the mail or any facility or means of interstate or foreign commerce, or within the special maritime and territorial jurisdiction of the United States knowingly persuades, induces, entices, or coerces any individual who has not attained the age of 18 years, to engage in prostitution or any sexual activity for which any person can be charged with a criminal offense, *or attempts to do so*, shall be fined under this title and imprisoned not less than 10 years or for life.

Federal sentencing law set out in the U.S. Sentencing Guidelines recommends an increased punishment for use of such services if

> the offense involved the use of a computer or an interactive computer service to ... persuade, induce, entice, coerce, or facilitate the travel of the minor to engage in prohibited sexual conduct. (U.S. Sentencing Guidelines, 2012)

Other aspects of criminal liability for the use of social media relate to its use for the illegal possession and distribution of some types of information.

The ability of sites like Facebook and tools like Instagram to distribute visual images makes them potential tools for the distribution of obscene materials and child pornography, the information contraband equivalent of heroin and meth. The possession of child pornography (any visual depiction of a minor engaging in sexually explicit conduct) is itself a felony under federal law in the United States and most other countries (Certain Activities Relating to Material Constituting or Containing Child Pornography, 1996).

Other violations may relate to criminal copyright infringement and the distribution of trade secrets, copy protection circumvention technologies, and access devices, including passwords, that represent efforts to protect property interests in information and information systems. Table 11.1 details some of these digital contraband statutes and objects.

Social media may be used to connect with and communicate with like-minded individuals, which may form a foundation for a conspiracy to commit a crime. Indeed, social media may allow for the kinds of connections between people that otherwise would be exceptionally difficult to make. This in turn becomes a source of evidence of the offense.

In *United States v. Valle* (2013) the defendant was charged with conspiracy to kidnap, torture, murder, and eat eight women; the evidence included emails and chat discussions online, as described by the federal district court:

I. Nature of Charges and Expected Defense

The Government contends that through emails and internet "chats" the Defendant conspired with three others to kidnap eight women. (Indictment (Dkt. No. 9); Jan. 11, 2013 Waxman Ltr.) The Government represents that in these electronic communications the Defendant and his alleged co-conspirators "discuss, in graphic detail, plans to kidnap, torture, kill and cannibalize specific and identified women" (Jan. 29, 2013 Waxman Ltr. at 1). The few electronic communications that have been disclosed to the Court discuss acts of extreme violence, generally in a sexual context. See, e.g., id. It appears that the "chats" the Government intends to introduce at trial occurred over sexual fetish websites that cater to individuals interested in violent sexual fantasy, sado-masochism, and bondage, as well as topics such as rape, genital mutilation, dismemberment, and cannibalism (Jan. 28, 2013 Tr. 15; Dec. 12, 2012 Gatto Decl. United States v. Valle, 12 Cr.-4711 (2d Cir.) (Dkt. No. 10-1) at ¶ 20). The Government may introduce at trial images and videos that the Defendant downloaded to his computer showing acts of violence, including staged torture and staged videos of women being hunted in the woods (Jan. 28, 2013 Tr. 7, 9).

The defense at trial will be that the Defendant had no criminal intent, and that his "chats" over the internet reflect nothing more than sexual fantasies. Defendant intends to assert [*3] that he suffers from a psychological condition known as "paraphilia" (Jan. 7, 2013 Gatto Ltr. (Dkt. No. 33) at 4–5). This condition allegedly causes the Defendant to "derive[] sexual excitement from the imagined psychological or physical suffering [of women] (including the abduction and binding) of ... female 'victim[s].'"

After deliberating 16 hours over four days, the jury found Valle's social media use and other conduct established that he was guilty of conspiracy to kidnap and the illegal use of federal databases. (Gregorian, 2013)

☐ Investigations and Prosecutions Using Social Media as Evidence of a Criminal Offense

The information rendered in social media may serve as evidence of criminal actions, either in the social media usage itself, its use to further a criminal activity, or simply capturing information relevant to an investigation or prosecution. This happens within a continuum of evidentiary use that runs from an initial indication of some fact relevant to an investigation to evidence sufficient to show guilt beyond a reasonable doubt.

TABLE 11.1 Digital Contraband

Contraband	Statute
Child pornography	Possession, receipt, 18 USC §2251
Obscene materials	Possession, distribution, 18 USC §1460
Creative content distributed in violation of copyright laws	Copying, distribution, 18 USC §2319
Trade secret information	Distribution, 18 USC §1831
Technology for circumvention of copyright protection technologies	Distribution, Digital Millennium Copyright Act
Access devices, including passwords	Possession, distribution, 18 USC §1029

Investigations

A criminal investigation involving social media is subject to the same procedural and evidence rules as any other investigation, such as the Fourth Amendment protections against unreasonable searches and seizures. Further, as it involves electronic information stored on the computer servers of private companies, additional legal issues and rules may apply to investigators. Violation of these rules may or may not affect the usefulness of the evidence and may or may not subject the investigator to civil or criminal liability.

Yet it is the *social* nature of social media that makes it a good source of evidence that may often limit the privacy protections of the Fourth Amendment under the U.S. Constitution. That social aspect relates to the public or semipublic posting and publication of information. The Fourth Amendment protects those areas of activity were a person has a reasonable expectation of privacy, barring unreasonable searches and seizures and requiring search warrants in many situations. That expectation of privacy begins to vanish once information is publicly posted or distributed to others.

Openly accessible social media postings may be perused by law enforcement or other parties just as if they were walking down a street. The information of interest they find may, at the least, be used to focus investigative resources. Or it may be sufficient to justify the issuance of a search warrant or other investigative legal order to give police the power to search and seize evidence from computers, smartphones, or homes.

Social media have provided a wealth of information in a variety of investigative settings. The explosion of smartphone use gives many a video camera in the palm of their hands. Social media permits the broad publication of those video and photo objects. The MS-13 transnational criminal gang, for example, has cliques who posted information on MySpace (*United States v. Palacios*, 2012).

In one case the victim of a home invasion and carjacking conducted her own investigation to try and identify her assailants (*United States v. Pierce*, 2012):

> Suspecting that her friend Stephanie Chaney's boyfriend might be involved in the invasion, Thomas began her own investigation. She "called around" to some friends and found out that Chaney's boyfriend, Mike Pierce, had an account on the social networking website, MySpace.Com. (Gov't Ex. 5. at 22). Thomas found Pierce's page, and when she and Baskin looked at it, they immediately recognized him from his picture. (*Id.*). Thomas was interviewed again on August 3, 2009. At that time, Thomas told the officers that she saw Pierce's face when he was holding her hair, and she recognized him from his MySpace page. (Gov't Ex. 4 at 23–24).

This led to the defendant's arrest. In another case a Google Hello chat list and transcripts were admitted into evidence to establish the defendant's knowledge of the illicit nature of child images being exchanged online (*United States v. Rubinstein*, 2012).

In 2005 a surprise football win by Penn State over Ohio State led Penn State fans to rush the field in celebration. Penn State police used Facebook pages set up by students who participated to find the fans and charge them with criminal trespassing (White, 2011).

The status of a social media site as semipublic may impact the propriety and legality of getting access to the information on the site.

In some states, neither the prosecuting attorney nor his or her investigator may ask to be a friend of someone under investigation without fully revealing his or her identity. But a police officer could use subterfuge to gain friend status so as to access information that could be used with few limitations. If permission to access a social networking site is not given, there may be other legal options. If a particular site has cross-links to another site, then legal access to that other site to obtain the information would be legally permissible by a police investigator.

But hacking a social networking site without legal access may carry risks and, in some cases, be illegal. Although the evidence might still be used in a prosecution, the person doing the hacking might be subject to civil and criminal penalties. Further, as that person might be a witness in the prosecution, his or her credibility may be attacked for breaking the law to obtain the evidence.

Prosecutions

The effective use of social media evidence must contend with the ease with which electronic information is created, changed, deleted, copied, and renamed. Forensic use of social media evidence requires the authenticity of that evidence be established and includes the issue of integrity, that the evidence is in its original form and has not been materially changed. The trial use of social media evidence is subject to the same rules of admissibility and weight as any evidence. It is about how reliable the evidence is and what it may or may not show as to a defendant's guilt.

Establishing the reliability of social media evidence must address issues of

1. Authenticity

2. Hearsay

3. Weight

Authenticity is a minimal but important threshold factor where there must be evidence sufficient to support a finding that the item is what it is claimed to be. This evidence may be from a witness with knowledge or an expert's opinion that something is what it is claimed to be. Social media evidence, as with many forms of electronic and information evidence, may be authenticated with either internal features of the information or external artifacts, like metadata, that show what it is.

Hearsay is another reliability filter. Essentially, the rule on hearsay prohibits out-of-court statements being used as evidence, except for the statements of a defendant and certain other exceptions. As social media evidence may often be out-of-court statements, one of the exceptions would need to apply for that evidence to be used.

The weight of the evidence deals not with its admissibility, but the weight a finder of fact, such as a judge or a jury, should give to that evidence in making a decision on guilt or innocence. Even if social media evidence is admitted, its reliability may still be challenged for that final finding. By lessening the weight of that evidence, it may not be sufficient to establish guilt.

☐ Use of Social Media by Those in the Criminal Justice System—Police, Prosecutors, and Judicial Officers

The administration of justice in a democratic society functions best on transparency and communication with the citizens it protects. Social media offers great potential benefits for that by prosecutors, police, and the courts. Yet social media may be unforgiving if its users forget that it is a public medium and that they are bound by the same ethical and practical rules as with any media.

The U.S. Attorney for the Eastern District of Louisiana, the chief federal prosecutor for that region, resigned in 2012 under a cloud of scandal (Horwitz, 2012). Two assistant U.S. Attorneys had admitted to posting negative comments about a defendant on the local newspaper's website during that defendant's trial. There have been a variety of cases of lawyers and judges making inappropriate comments on social media. Examples include a lawyer who was disciplined for blogging a judge was an "evil, unfair witch," a public defender calling a judge clueless and posting confidential case details, and a member of a jury blogging about the case during the trial (Schwartz, 2009). Police officers have been attacked and impeached during trial or otherwise embarrassed for their social media postings. This led police departments to develop new policies as to what officers may do on social media that restrict comments on pending investigations and prosecutions (Goode, 2011).

But social media can also bring law enforcement and the community together to promote public safety.

The 2011 IACP survey of law enforcement's use of social media found 88% use social media in one form or another. Of those, 71% use social media for investigative purposes. This was followed by use for intelligence (56%), community notification of crime problems (50%), community outreach (47%), and crime prevention activities (45%) (IACP, 2011).

Former Broward County, Florida, Sheriff Al Lamberti frequently used social media to help prevent and solve crime in his community. His Facebook fan page proved a useful tool for solving crimes the department wouldn't normally have the resources to deal with. This included a sting operation to catch people committing coupon fraud after the sheriff's office received several tips via Facebook (Popken, 2011).

His most well known use of social media in support of law enforcement was posting to his 10,000-plus Facebook fans a suspect description and vehicle make and model to help solve an air conditioner theft spree. That led to several 911 calls and an arrest days later.

Some police departments in large cities are using YouTube to post surveillance videos of unsolved crimes. The faces of bystanders are blurred and the departments have disabled comments but provide a phone number and email address to any would-be tipsters to maintain anonymity (Arndt, 2012). In one case a pair of burglars broke into a car in a restaurant parking lot in Connecticut and stole an employee's purse. She reported the crime and the police posted a picture from a surveillance video on their Facebook page; the suspects were identified within three hours (NBC Connecticut, 2013). Social media has helped with investigations of crimes that saved resources for other investigations.

These technologies have helped with investigations of violent crimes. Tucson, Arizona, police used social media to quickly distribute information on a missing child. The Philadelphia Police Department used YouTube to catch a woman who boarded a bus and punched a passenger 10 times; since 2011 Philadelphia police have solved 85 cases through tips developed through social media (USA Today, 2012). New Jersey police used social media to apprehend a thief who stole $27,000 in gold (NJ.Com, 2012). Each of these cases demonstrates the efficiency in investigation made possible by the link to the community social media offers law enforcement.

Lastly, social media technologies hold tremendous potential as anti-corruption and transparency tools in e-government (Kuriyan, Bailur, Gigler, & Park, 2011). Where police-community relations have frayed, social media offers a means to mend them. Where police conduct may create issues with the community, social media can return open government to its operations and support needed reform.

☐ Future Issues

Will New Criminal Statutes Be Needed?

This is an evolving area of practice built on changing technologies and changing perceptions of rights and obligations. The regulation of social media misuse under substantive and procedural criminal law will require consideration of:

1. How evolving types of social media and social media misuse may fit into traditional ways within elements of crimes

2. How social media misuse supports and facilitates new, unexpected ways, the traditional criminal, requiring special attention to the technical facts of computers and networks

3. How social media misuse, and the related technologies, may fall outside of existing law, and thus may need new statutes for public safety

Law and procedure must evolve to address changes in the technology and the ways criminals create new ways to hurt others.

Transnational Law Enforcement?

An important issue for the future is that of the transnational impact of social media and how criminal use of social media across borders may be policed. The primary transnational legal code applicable to computer-mediated crime is the Council of Europe's Convention on Cybercrime (2001). As of September 15, 2013, 40 countries, including the United States, the United Kingdom, and Japan, have ratified it (Chart of Signatures, Ratifications and Accessions, 2013). It details technical definitions for electronic information systems (Convention on Cybercrime, Chapter I, Article 1) and outlines the special substantive criminal and procedural categories of law for handling electronic information offenses (Chapter II). These include principles and rules for international cooperation, such as the extradition of suspects and mutual assistance in investigations, information sharing, and the preservation of electronic evidence (Chapter III). How those rules and principles are to be effectively applied will continue to evolve.

Social media misuse may fall under its categories of content-related offenses, copyright offenses, and device-related offenses (Chapter III, Section 1, Titles 2, 3, & 4). Offenses against data and systems include access to a computer without or in excess of authorization and unauthorized interception of data, computer-related forgery of data, and computer-related fraud for economic benefit (Chapter II, Section 1, Articles 2–8). The computer-related forgery requirement of the convention appears on its face to be broader than common law forgery of instruments because it deals with the alteration of data with the intent it be acted on. Informatics data are acted upon when processed, so alteration of data may do more than simply promote a fraud; it may interfere with system operations. A good example of this is the Stuxnet malware.

Content-related offenses under the convention at this time address only child pornography with an option to not punish simple possession of child pornography or simulated material (Chapter II, Section 1, Article 9, §§1–4). Punishment of activity of a racist and xenophobic nature is an optional item under the convention (Optional Protocol, 2001). How this is reconciled with the differences in national laws will continue to be a challenge. The First Amendment protections of the United States only apply as far as its border. The greater tolerance for sexually oriented materials of other countries may similarly conflict with laws of the United States.

Should Law Enforcement Expand and Formalize Training and Investigative Practices With the Proper Use of Social Media?

Given the great usefulness of social media for law enforcement, focused and directed training on the use of social media by law enforcement may be needed. Stuart (2013) notes that given the benefits of its use and the risks of mistakes with social media, police departments ensure their officers understand these factors and establish criteria to govern their use in order to maximize the benefits and reduce the risks. He notes issues that range from aid in the apprehension of fugitives to risks of online conduct unbecoming of an officer; at least one criminal was found to have maintained files on over 30 police officers of information acquired from Facebook (Public Intelligence, 2011).

The Global Justice Information Sharing Initiative (2013) sets out guidance and recommendations for developing policies on the use of social media in intelligence and investigation. It suggests that policies must be articulated as to authorized use of such media, proper documentation and analysis, and controls over possible misuse of the information obtained, whether unintentional or not; these policies are just as important as those for patrol or other detective work (Global Justice Information Sharing Initiative, 2013, pp. 1, 19). The New York Police Department, the Georgia Bureau of Investigation, and the Dunwoody Police Department have all developed social media policies for officers that reflect these needs (Global Justice Information Sharing Initiative, 2013, pp. 29–41).

These, along with the other problems in social media use discussed, indicate social media policies for investigation and prosecution should be implemented in clear and detailed rules.

How Will Personal Autonomy in Social Media Evolve?

Lastly, social values are changing with these new technologies. Social media offers new ways to connect, as seen in the valuable ways police departments use it to inform their communities. Yet it may create risks that more of people's lives are set out for scrutiny than ever before. The U.S. Department of Homeland Security systematically monitors and tracks social media via its *Publicly Available Social Media Monitoring and Situational Awareness Initiative System of Records* (Privacy Act of 1974, 2011). This again presents the conflict between security and liberty that exists within the political life of the United States. This too will evolve with the changing technologies, their uses, and the law's response.

☐ Conclusion

The vast new prosecutorial possibilities in an interconnected information society were discussed by the U.S. Supreme Court in the 2012 case of *United States v. Jones* (2012). That case dealt with the secret placement of a GPS tracking and transmission device on a suspect's automobile that relayed the information to a computer system to record and display his activities in public. It would have been perfectly permissible for officers to have followed the suspect as he drove about town.

But the Supreme Court found this an impermissible search subject to the Fourth Amendment's requirement of probable cause for criminal activity and the issuance of a search warrant by a neutral magistrate. It did so applying a traditional trespass analysis relating to the placement of the tracking device without permission, avoiding a direct ruling on the implications of new technologies on privacy.

But five justices, in a concurring opinion, opined that there was reasonable expectation of privacy relating to the GPS tracking at issue. Justice Alito, joined by Justices Ginsburg, Breyer, and Kagan, found that the suspect's reasonable expectation of privacy in his activities were violated by the long-term tracking at issue in the case, though short-term tracking would be acceptable (*United States v. Jones*, concurring opinion Alito, Ginsburg, Breyer, and Kagan, 2012). Justice Alito further noted this was an area particularly ripe for legislative action to define the privacy rights of people in this new information age.

Justice Sonia Sotomayor specifically called for a reevaluation of the concept of privacy and third-party data collection in this new age of electronic data collection and analysis (*United States v. Jones*, concurring opinion Sotomayor, 2012). The power of data collection and analytics, as seen with simple GPS data, was such that

> the net result is that GPS monitoring—by making available at a relatively low cost such a substantial quantum of intimate information about any person whom the Government, in its unfettered discretion, chooses to track—may "alter the relationship between citizen and government in a way that is inimical to democratic society." (*United States v. Cuevas-Perez*, 640 F. 3d 272, 285 (CA7 2011))

These concerns equally apply to the vast, interconnected world of social media. Whether due to constitutional, legislative, or simply ethical principles, the prosecutorial use of social media must be careful not to undermine the trust between citizens and law enforcement that is a foundation of the administration of justice in a democratic society.

☐ References

Additional Protocol to the Convention on Cybercrime, concerning the criminalization of acts of a racist and xenophobic nature committed through computer systems.

Arndt, E. (2012, October 2). *Using social media to fight crime*. Security InfoWatch. Retrieved April 13, 2013, from http://www.securityinfowatch.com/ article/10797383/using-social-media-to-fight-crime

Bensinger, K., & Chang, A. (2013, April 20). Boston bombings: Social media spirals out of control. *Los Angeles Times*. Retrieved September 15, 2013, from http://articles.latimes.com/2013/apr/20/business/la-fi-boston-bombings -media-20130420

Boyd, D., and Ellison, N. (2007). Social network sites: Definition, history, and scholarship. *Journal of Computer-Mediated Communication, 13,* 210–211. Retrieved September 15, 2013, from http://onlinelibrary.wiley.com/ doi/10.1111/j.1083-6101.2007.00393.x/full

Brenner, S. (2004, June). Cybercrime metrics: Old Wine, new bottles? *Virginia Journal of Law & Technology, 9*(13), 10. (Citing British Embassy, Bangkok, Internet fraud: Information and guidance, June 2004)

CBS News. (2013, April 20). *Social media and the search for the Boston bombing suspects*. Retrieved September 15, 2013, from http://www.cbsnews. com/8301-18559_162-57580603/social-media-and-the-search-for-the -boston-bombing-suspects/

Certain activities relating to material constituting or containing child pornography. (1996), 18 USC §2252A (U.S.) (2013).

Computer Fraud and Abuse Act of 1984, 18 USC §1030 (U.S.) (2012).

Council of Europe Convention on Cybercrime, ETS No. 185, opened for signature November 23, 2001. Retrieved September 15, 2013, from http://conventions.coe.int/Treaty/en/Treaties/Html/185.htm

Council of Europe Convention on Cybercrime, Chapter I, Article 1, November 23, 2001, ETS No. 185.

Council of Europe Convention on Cybercrime, Chapter II, November 23, 2001, ETS No. 185.

Council of Europe Convention on Cybercrime, Chapter II, Section 1, Articles 2–6, November 23, 2001, ETS No. 185.

Council of Europe Convention on Cybercrime, Chapter II, Section 1, Article 7, November 23, 2001, ETS No. 185.

Council of Europe Convention on Cybercrime, Chapter II, Section 1, Article 8, November 23, 2001, ETS No. 185.

Council of Europe Convention on Cybercrime, Chapter II, Section 1, Article 9, November 23, 2001, ETS No. 185.

Council of Europe Convention on Cybercrime, Chapter II, Section 1, Article 9, §4, November 23, 2001, ETS No. 185.

Council of Europe Convention on Cybercrime, Chapter III, November 23, 2001, ETS No. 185.

Council of Europe Convention on Cybercrime, Chapter III, Section 1, Title 3, November 23, 2001, ETS No. 185.

Council of Europe Convention on Cybercrime, Chapter III, Section 1, Title 4, November 23, 2001, ETS No. 185.

Council of Europe Convention on Cybercrime, Chapter III, Section 1, Title 2, November 23, 2001, ETS No. 185.

Council of Europe Convention Committee on Cybercrime. Chart of signatures, ratifications and accessions to the convention. Retrieved September 15, 2013, from http://conventions.coe.int/Treaty/Commun/ChercheSig.asp?NT=185&CM=1&DF=&CL=ENG

Doe v. Prosecutor, 705 F.3d 694 (7th Cir. 2013) (U.S.).

Dyer, J. (2013, April 27). *Social media and the Boston bombings.* BBC Radio. Retrieved September 15, 2013, from http://www.bbc.co.uk/programmes/p017cr7p

Giboney v. Empire Storage & Ice Co., 336 U.S. 490, 498 (1949).

Global Justice Information Sharing Initiative. (2013, February). *Developing a policy on the use of social media in intelligence and investigative activities: Guidance and recommendations.* Retrieved September 15, 2013, from http://it.ojp.gov/default.aspx?area=globalJustice

Goode, E. (2011, April 6). Police lesson: Social network tools have two edges. *New York Times.*

Gregorian, D. (2013, March 12). 'Cannibal cop' Gilberto Valle faces life in prison after jury finds him guilty of conspiracy to kidnap and illegal use of databases. *New York Daily News.*

Horwitz, S. (2012, December 6). New Orleans U.S. Attorney resigns amid scandal over anonymous online postings. *Washington Post.* Retrieved September 15, 2013, from http://articles.washingtonpost.com/2012-12-06/politics/35650115_1_federal-investigation-attorney-general-james-cole-prosecutor

International Association of Chiefs of Police. (2011). *2011 survey of law enforcement's use of social media tools.* Retrieved September 15, 2013, from http://www.iacpsocialmedia.org/Resources/Publications/2011SurveyResults.aspx

Jackson, S. (2011, May 25). Woman arrested for Facebook "poke." *Huffington Post*. Retrieved September 15, 2013, from http://www.huffingtonpost. com/2009/10/09/shannon-d-jackson-woman-a_n_315877.html

Kaplan, A., & Haenlein, M. (2010, January–February). Users of the world, unite! The challenges and opportunities of social media. *Business Horizons*, 53(1), 59–68. Retrieved September 15, 2013, from http://www.sciencedirect.com/ science/article/pii/S0007681309001232

Kuriyan, R., Bailur, S., Gigler, B.-S., & Park, K. R. (2011). *Technologies for transparency and accountability*. Open Development Technology Office. Retrieved September 16, 2013, from http://www.iq.undp.org/img/Procurements/75642405-Technologies-for-Transparency-and-Accountability-Implications-for-ICT-Policy-and-Recommendations.pdf

LexisNexis. (2012, July 18). *Role of social media in law enforcement significant and growing*. Press release. Retrieved September 15, 2013, from http://www. lexisnexis.com/media/press-release.aspx?id=1342623085481181

Losavio, M. M., Keeling, D. G., Borisevich, G., Chernyadyeva, N., Frolovich, E., Pastukhov, P., Polyakova, S., & Dobrovlyanina, O. (2012). A comparative review of cybercrime law and digital forensics in Russia, the United States and under the Convention on Cybercrime of the Council of Europe. *Northern Kentucky Law Review, 39*(2), 267–326.

NBC Connecticut. (2013, January 2). *Police use Facebook to ID Waterford robbery suspects*. Retrieved September 16, 2013, from http://www.nbcconnecticut.com/ news/local/Police-Use-Facebook-to-Solve-Crime-in-Waterford-185325142. html

NJ.Com. (2012, November 16). *Social media helps Gloucester Township Police solve 2 crimes*. Retrieved September 15, 2013, from http://www.nj.com/camden/ index.ssf/2012/11/social_media_helps_gloucester.html

Office of the U.S. Attorney. (2012, March 6). *Jeannette man pleads guilty to posting threat against police chief on Craigslist*. Press release. Retrieved September 15, 2013, from http://www.fbi.gov/pittsburgh/press-releases/2012/jeannette-man-pleads-guilty-to-posting-threat-against-police-chief-on-craigslist

Pittsburgh Post-Gazette. (2012, June 30). Craigslist threat gets man year in prison. Retrieved September 15, 2013, from http://www.post-gazette. com/stories/local/neighborhoods-east/craigslist-threat-gets-man-year -in-prison-642653/

Popken, B. (2011, October 31). How a sheriff uses his 10,000 Facebook fans to solve crimes. *Consumerist*. Retrieved September 15, 2013, from http:// consumerist.com/2011/10/31/how-sheriff-al-lamberti-uses-his-7200 -facebook-fans-to-solve-crimes/

Privacy Act of 1974, 76 Fed. Reg. 5603 (February 1, 2011).

Public Intelligence. (2011, February 23). *Arizona Fusion Center warning: Police officers targeted on Facebook*. Retrieved September 17, 2013, from http://public intelligence.net/ules-arizona-fusion-center-warning-police-officers-target-ed-on-facebook/

Rasch, M. (1996). Criminal law and the Internet. In *The Internet and business: A lawyer's guide to the emerging legal issues*. Computer Law Association.

Sandy Hook Video Vault. (2013, March 6). *CT state police threaten prosecution of social media users for Sandy Hook posts!* Retrieved September 15, 2013, from http://sandyhook.ustart.info/ct-state-police-threaten-prosecution-of-social-media-users-for-sandy-hook-posts

Schwartz, J. (2009, September 12). A legal battle: Online attitude vs. rules of the bar. *New York Times.* Retrieved September 15, 2013, from http://www.nytimes.com/2009/09/13/us/13lawyers.html

Sex Offender Internet Offense. (2008). Indiana Code §35-42-4-12(d).

Stuart, R. D. *Social media: Establishing criteria for law enforcement use.* FBI Law Enforcement Bulletin. Retrieved September 17, 2013, from http://www.fbi.gov/stats-services/publications/law-enforcement-bulletin/2013/february/social-media-establishing-criteria-for-law-enforcement-use

Ulanoff, L. (2013, April 18). *Mashable op-ed, "Boston bombings: Truth, justice and the wild west of social media.* Retrieved September 15, 2013, from http://mashable.com/2013/04/18/boston-bombings-wild-west-of-social-media/

United States v. Adrian Peter Stock, Criminal No. 11-182, U.S District Court for the Western District of Pennsylvania, Memorandum Opinion of January 23, 2012, Judge Fischer.

United States v. Damien Michael Pierce, Case No. 3:11cr08-WKW, U.S. District Court, M.D. Alabama, Eastern Division, Recommendation of Magistrate Judge Coody of March 9, 2012.

United States v. Drew, 259 F.R.D. 449 (C.D. Cal. 2009).

United States v. Holm, 326 F.3d 872, 878-79 (7th Cir. 2003), holding total Internet ban as a condition of supervised release was too broad.

United States v. Israel Palacios, a/k/a Homie, No. 09-5174, U.S. Court of Appeals for 4th Circuit, April 30, 2012.

United States v. Jones, 565 U.S., 132 S. Ct. 945 (2012), concurring opinion of Justice Sotomayor.

United States v. Lavi Rubinstein, No. 11-12175, U.S. Court of Appeals for the 11th Circuit, April 19, 2012 (unpublished).

United States v. Sayer, Dist. Court, D. Maine 2012, docket#CriminalNo.2:11-CR-113-DBH.

United States v. Valle, 12 CR 847, Southern District of New York, 2013 U.S. Dist. LEXIS 14864, Memorandum Opinion and Order of February 2, 2013.

United States v. Watkins, 667 F.3d 254 (2nd Cir. 2012).

USA Today. (2012, June 29). Police use YouTube, Twitter to solve crimes, get word out. Retrieved September 16, 2013, from http://usatoday30.usatoday.com/news/nation/story/2012-06-20/police-youtube-twitter-crime/55930126/1

U.S. Sentencing Guidelines, §2G1.3(b)(3)(A).

Voice of America. (2013, April 26). Multi, social media play huge role in solving Boston bombing. Retrieved September 15, 2013, from http://www.voanews.com/content/multi-social-media-play-huge-role-in-solving-boston-bombing/1649774.html

White, W. (2011, October 17). *Internet communications: Social networking for better or for worse.* Legal Issues in Higher Education, University of Vermont. Retrieved September 15, 2013, from http://learn.uvm.edu/wordpress_3_4b/wp-content/uploads/Internet-Communications.pdf

12

CHAPTER

Corrections and Social Networking Websites

Catherine D. Marcum

Appalachian State University

George E. Higgins

University of Louisville

Contents

Restricting Internet Use for Sex Offenders	222
Cellphones and Social Networking	224
Constitutional Rights and Social Networking	226
The First Amendment	226
The Fourth Amendment	227
Summary	228
References	228

The U.S. corrections system has a long of history of dealing with challenges when it comes to effectively managing inmates. Inmates have a variety of physical health issues, such as high blood pressure, cancer, or even the common cold. Multitudes of inmates have been diagnosed with some form of mental illness, which requires individualized attention and treatment. However, more imperative to this text, the corrections systems have had to learn how to manage changing technology, whether it is an amenity to inmates or an issue of tracking contraband. Maintaining control is the main concern within prison walls, and innovation has made it more difficult to maintain that control.

While general use of the Internet and technology has become a controversial issue of contention when it comes to individuals under the supervision of the corrections system, the use and abuse of social networking websites by inmates and staff has recently come into the media spotlight. While literature and media coverage on this particular topic is scant, as it is a new phenomenon, it is important to include what is available for the purposes of this book. This chapter will examine three particular categories of issues now faced by our corrections system as a result of the Internet social networking websites and the current attempts to maintain control: restricting Internet use for sex offenders, cellphones and social networking, and constitutional rights and social networking.

☐ Restricting Internet Use for Sex Offenders

When an individual is placed on probation or parole, it is expected that he or she will have restrictions and requirements while finishing his or her sentence. For example, all offenders are expected to report to a probation or parole officer on a regular basis, stay out of legal trouble, and attempt to obtain gainful employment. Special conditions may include frequent urinalysis, mental health treatment, and restrictions on living arrangements. Sex offenders are often given special conditions during supervised release, and since the emergence of technology, many states have placed restrictions on use of the Internet and eventually social networking websites.

The practice of placing Internet use restrictions on sex offenders originated with the courts as a special restriction for those placed on parole or supervised release (Wynton, 2011). Generally, the ban was placed on access to computers or a complete ban on all Internet use, rather than just a social networking site. Congress gave authorization to federal courts to impose special conditions (such as Internet use restrictions) as long as doing so was reasonably related to the nature of the offense and history of the defendant (18 USC §3583(d) (2006)). For example, if the defendant used the Internet to stalk and harass a minor, restriction of Internet use would be reasonably related to the offense. The restrictions must also deter future criminal behavior, assist in rehabilitating the offender, and protect the general public. However, and possibly most importantly, the restrictions must not deprive "liberty than is reasonably necessary" to achieve the above-mentioned goals.

With that said, the federal appellate courts have been unsupportive of unconditional bans on computer and Internet use (Wynton, 2011). This is even true if the offender was convicted of possession of child pornography, even if there is a past history of sexual abuse of minors. In order to receive computer restrictions, the offender must have also engaged in online conduct that resulted in exploitation of an underage person (*United States v. Freeman*, 2003). If this is lacking, courts have supported the use of filtering and blocking software or unannounced inspections of the offender's computer rather than complete ban of use. With cases that violated a minor in some fashion, such as sexual solicitation of a minor or distribution of child pornography to a minor, harsher restrictions can be imposed. However, still then absolute bans are usually replaced with exceptions that allow Internet use for legitimate purposes, such as work or school research. The few cases that have implemented lifetime bans of the Internet have set precedent, as they are not the norm (*United States v. Fortenberry*, 2009).

This hesitancy to ban ultimate restriction of the Internet is possibly the evolving viewpoint by the federal courts that use of the Internet is a basic freedom, as it has become an integral part of daily life in regard to communication and information gathering. In *United States v. Sofsky* (2002), the court said a total ban of Internet use is as unjustified as a complete ban of the postal system for a person convicted of mail fraud. In other words, both offer the potential for illegitimate purposes (i.e., criminal behavior), but also a multitude of legitimate opportunities, such as banking, shopping, and email for communication with family.

Some states have taken a different approach to Internet restrictions compared to the federal system, with some imposing Internet restrictions on sex offenders without differing treatment dependent upon the circumstances. For example, North Carolina implemented legislation in 2008 making it a Class I felony for registered sex offenders (despite the category of sex offense or seriousness of the offense) to access social networking websites. Indiana and Nebraska passed laws that banned sex offenders convicted of crimes against children from using the Internet to prey on new victims, which included forbidding the offenders to use social networking websites (i.e., Facebook, Twitter). Furthermore, Nebraska's law includes individuals who have completed probation or parole, and also bans the use of chat rooms or instant messaging services (Neb. Rev. Stat §28-322.05(1)).

Some states have enforced court-required social networking bans as a condition of probation or parole. For example, New York and Texas require that registered sex offenders who have committed a crime against a child, used the Internet for commission of a crime, or are at great risk of reoffending will receive such a condition for probation or parole (N.Y. Penal Law §65.10 (4-a)(b), 2011); Tex. Gov't Code Ann. §508.1861(a) (1)-(3), 2010). However, in January 2013, the 7th U.S. Circuit Court of Appeals concluded that while states can impose limits on social media use as a condition of probation or parole, a "blanket ban" of the Internet is a violation of the First Amendment. Two other states, Nebraska and Louisiana, struck down similar laws in 2012 (Smith, 2013).

A groundbreaking law in Louisiana is the first of its kind, according to sponsor State Representative Jeff Thompson. Signed into law June 2012 by Governor Bobby Jindal, it requires sex offenders state their criminal status on social networking pages. This legislation builds on current policy that requires offenders to notify neighbors and school districts of their residency near them (Martinez, 2012). While the above-mentioned law is thus far ruled as constitutional, several federal courts have already reviewed the constitutionality of placing identifiers on sex offenders once they are no longer under government restrictions. In *Doe v. Shurtleff* (2009), a Utah law requiring registered sex offenders to disclose Internet identifiers was ruled a violation of the First Amendment. The court insisted that there was no support from the state to justify why a sex offender should have to give up First Amendment rights if he or she has completed a prison term and is not on further supervision (parole or probation). In other words, no matter if he or she is a repeat offender, a complete ban of the Internet is an overly broad punishment.

South Carolina recently passed a law penalizing state offenders' use of social media websites, such as Facebook, to harass crime victims. Current inmates, or their accomplices, are not allowed to utilize the media to contact victims with the intent to harass, intimidate, or make threats. Violators will face 30 days in jail, a $500 fine, or both (Smith, 2012).

☐ Cellphones and Social Networking

Cellphones as contraband are a growing problem within the corrections system. Smartphones, PDAs, and other forms of cellular telephones are used to access the Internet and post to social networking pages. Inmates are often bold enough to post the location of their cell block, which is simply a way to flaunt possession of the contraband. The California Department of Corrections and Rehabilitation is one of the state systems that has stressed cellphones as its top contraband issue, and has made it a priority to punish offenders responsible for these offenses. In October 2011, legislation was passed making it a misdemeanor to possess a cellphone in a state prison or attempting to introduce one. The penalty for inmates can involve up to 90 days' credit forfeiture, while staff, contractors, and other visitors to a prison who introduce the contraband face a $5,000 fine.

Inmates in several Georgia prisons were using cellphones to coordinate a nonviolent strike in December 2010. Frustrated with living conditions and low pay for prison work, inmates stated they would refuse to do chores or shop at the prison commissary until better pay, food, and educational opportunities were provided. Utilizing text messaging and other social networking techniques, inmate organizers were proud of their coordination efforts. One leader in the strike, an inmate named Mike at Smith State Prison in Glennville, Georgia, informed the media that there were several men in each participating prison who had cellphones and were functioning as the point person. Cellphones were smuggled in by visitors or guards, and often sold for a hefty price to the inmates (Wheaton, 2010).

CASE STUDY

An investigation by a newspaper in Oklahoma revealed that dozens of Oklahoma inmates, including convicted murderers, were active on Facebook while incarcerated despite restrictions against such behavior. Smuggled cellphones have allowed inmates to make comments and post pictures (selfies) on the social networking website without detection by prison officials. Some of the inmates posted under created nicknames, such as Itzme Fbthaone Brown, while others like Logan Lee and Clifford Putnam posted under their actual names. Putnam, a convicted murderer, has posted more than 200 photos since June 2012.

Some of these social networking inmates simply rant about their incarceration or make comments on current events. Many inmates proposition women or insult former girlfriends. Other inmates, however, use their time on Facebook to report what is going on inside the prison walls. Inmate Jordan Lalehparvaran, serving time for assault and battery with a dangerous weapon, posted he had stopped a prison race riot and deserved a Nobel Peace Prize. De'Ontel Harris posted a picture of himself in the "hole" (aka solitary confinement) smoking marijuana (Knittle & Clay, 2013).

Criminological research has repeatedly reported that prisons and jails are overcrowded and there is a high inmate-to-staff ratio. However, it appears as if this behavior is a blatant way of mocking the correctional staff. What can we as a corrections system due to punish and prevent this behavior?

☐ Constitutional Rights and Social Networking

As citizens of the United States, we are all entitled to rights guaranteed to us by the Constitution. Even individuals under some form of correctional supervision are entitled to basic constitutional rights, although there may be limitations and restrictions due to security issues within a prison facility or community. With that said and as discussed previously, it is difficult for complete bans of these rights to be placed on those under correctional supervision. This section will discuss how the Supreme Court has applied the First and Fourth Amendments to Internet and social networking usage by offenders.

The First Amendment

This continued ban of Internet restrictions, and often specifically restrictions on the use of social networking websites, has forced us to consider if constitutional rights are violated when these restrictions are implemented. The First Amendment guarantees us the protection of freedom of speech, press, assembly, and address. While it does not directly state the right of freedom of association, the "right to associate for the purpose of engaging in those protected by the First Amendment" is protected (*Roberts v. U.S. Jaycees*, 1984). In other words, our right to gather together and communicate with others in some form to practice religion or discuss a new piece of proposed legislation in a peaceful fashion is protected. Furthermore, this association does not have to be for the purpose of expressing a certain message, such as support for a political candidate or promotion of a new film. It can merely be to discuss issues, express opinions, and explore philosophies (*Boy Scouts of Am. v. Dale*, 2000).

Social networking websites allow users to associate in methods akin to those offline, as well as in different ways. Based on the reasons discussed above, Wynton (2011) asserts that speech on social networking websites should therefore be protected as well. Individuals do not have to log on to Facebook to post information about one certain topic in order for it to be protected. They can post opinions and thoughts about whatever they choose, which is essentially what is done now. Social networking websites also allow for users to create communities to share information and ideas.

The Supreme Court has begun to recognize the importance of social networking websites as a place to express opinions and associate with others. *Citizens United v. Federal Election Commission* (2010) allowed the court to explain that while television advertisements are an effective way to spread a political message, Internet sources are also a useful tool in providing information to individuals about campaigns and candidates. Furthermore, in *Christian Legal Society v. Martinez* (2010), the court noted that social networking websites lessened the necessity for other methods of communication, like newsletters and bulletin boards. Members of a social networking website like Facebook or Twitter can build and maintain networks with friends and strangers to share information. Even smaller social networking websites aimed at specific interests or groups are considered places to expressively associate.

The Fourth Amendment

The Fourth Amendment guarantees us protection against unreasonable search and seizure of our property. In other words, it states that we should have some expectation of privacy when it comes to our personal possessions. However, there has been a question regarding the protection of contents on a computer, specifically those obtained online. For example, in 2009, a federal district court examined the constitutionality of amendments to the Nebraska Sex Offender Registration Act. A particular amendment of interest required registered sex offenders to consent to a warrantless search of any of their computers, as well as the installation of monitoring software. This amendment was ruled unconstitutional, as the court stated it should not apply to individuals who were not on some form of court-monitored supervision. There was no case support that justified that an individual who had completed his or her punishment should not have the same Fourth Amendment protections as those persons never convicted of a crime.

Application of the Fourth Amendment has been an issue for not only offenders in the corrections system, but also potential employees desiring to work in corrections. Applicants for government positions expect to participate in a background check as a part of employment screening. It is not unusual to have one's criminal history, employment background, or credit check run as a condition of hiring. However, official and unofficial checks of social networking websites have become more prevalent. Agencies can gain a sense of an applicant's character based on the information and pictures posted on a social networking website. For example, an individual who posts pictures of drug use and illegal behaviors would not be an ideal corrections officer.

As of April 1, 2011, the Department of Public Safety and Correctional Services (DPSCS) in Maryland adopted a revised policy in regard to hiring of correctional officers. They are now asked to participate in a voluntary screening of all postings on their social media services, although no login or password information is requested. During the first year's screening, the DPSCS found this to be an effective tool in finding quality employees and eliminated some of the applicants based on content found on their social media services. However, no applicants were immediately disqualified as a result of denying access to the screening (Associated Press, 2011).

There have also been issues regarding the constitutionality of accessing social networking websites for individuals currently employed by the corrections system. In October 2012, a Huntsville, Texas, corrections officer was reinstated after being fired in May for violating state policy. Sergeant Heath Lara was fired for friending an inmate on Facebook. Lara appealed his termination, stating he was unaware that Gary Wayne Sanders was serving time in the prison complex and that other officers were also friends with him on Facebook. He knew him previously as a high school classmate. Texas legislation bars fraternizing between offenders and correctional officers, but is not expanded to social media (McDonough, 2012).

☐ Summary

As stated previously, this chapter is not lengthy with research, case studies, and statistics, as this phenomenon is just beginning to be an issue with corrections. However, the purpose of this entire book is to provide an accurate and up-to-date picture of social networking and criminality as it stands today. With the second edition of this book, it will be interesting to see how current events, legislation, and Supreme Court decisions have changed the face of social networking in corrections. As an offender goes through the criminal justice system, the corrections portion is the last stop, and we will begin to see a filtering of these offenders into our system more and more.

☐ References

Associated Press. (2011, April 1). State prisons agency revises social media policy for applicants. *Baltimore Sun*. Retrieved February 10, 2012, from http://weblogs.baltimoresun.com/news/crime/blog/2011/04/state_prisons_agency_revises_s.html

Boy Scouts of Am. v. Dale, 530 U.S. 640 (2000).

Christian Legal Soc'y Chapter of the Univ. of Cal., Hastings Coll. of the Law v. Martinez, 130 S. Ct. 2971 (2010).

Citizens United v. Fed. Election Comm'n, 130 S. Ct. 876 (2010).

Doe v. Shurtleff, No. 1:08-CV-64 TC, 2008 WL 4427594 (D. Utah Sept. 25, 2008), vacated as moot, 2009 WL 2601458 (D. Utah Aug. 20, 2009).

Knittle, A., & Clay, N. (2013, September 22). Oklahoma inmates access Facebook with smuggled cellphones. *The Oklahoman*. Retrieved September 26, 2013, from http://newsok.com/oklahoma-inmates-access-facebook-with-smuggled-cellphones/article/3885598

Martinez, M. (2012, June 21). *New La. law: Sex offenders must list status on Facebook, other social media*. CNN Tech. Retrieved February 13, 2013, from http://www.cnn.com/2012/06/20/tech/louisiana-sex-offenders-social-media/index.html?iref=allsearch

McDonough, M. (2012, October 1). Prison guard reinstated after investigation shows other guards were friends with inmate on Facebook. *American Bar Association Journal*. Retrieved February 13, 2013, from http://www.abajournal.com/news/article/prison_guard_reinstated_after_investigation_shows_other_guards_were_friends/

Neb. Rev. Stat §28-322.05(1).

N.Y. Penal Law §65.10 (4-a)(b) (McKinney Supp. 2011).

Roberts v. U.S. Jaycees, 468 U.S. 609, 618 (1984).

Smith, G. (2012, June 27). New SC law makes it a crime for state prisoners to use social media to taunt victims. *IndependentMail*. Retrieved February 15, 2013, from http://www.independentmail.com/news/2012/jun/27/new-sc-law-makes-it-crime-state-prisoners-use-soci/

Smith, M. (2013, January 23). *Indiana can't kick sex offenders off social media, court says*. CNN Tech. Retrieved February 13, 2013, from http://www.cnn.com/2013/01/23/tech/sex-offenders-social-media/index.html?iref=allsearch

Tex. Gov't Code Ann. §508.1861(a)(1)-(3) (West Supp. 2010).

United States v. Fortenberry, 350 F. App'x 906, 911 (5th Cir. 2009).

United States v. Freeman, 316 F.3d 386, 387 (3d Cir. 2003).

United States v. Sofsky, 287 F.3d 122, 126-127 (2d Cir. 2002).

Wheaton, S. (2010, December 12). Inmates in Georgia prisons use contraband phones to coordinate protest. *New York Times*. Retrieved February 13, 2013, from http://www.nytimes.com/2010/12/13/us/13prison.html

Wynton, J. (2011). MySpace, yourspace, but not theirspace: The constitutionality of banning sex offenders from social networking sites. *Duke Law Journal, 60*, 1859–1903.

INDEX·

A

Abrams, Jonathan, 5, 6
Academia.edu, 126
Adult dating and matrimonial sites, 126, 127
Age-of-consent laws, 21
Agnew, Robert, 36
Amazon, 83
American Express, 83
Analysis of variance (ANOVA) analyses, 153–154
Anderson, Tom, 6
ARPANET, 4
Ask.fm, 102

B

Bebo, 83
Beverly Hills Internet (BHI), 5
Boston Marathon bombing, 200
Bureau of Justice Statistics (BJS), 70–71

C

CAN-SPAM Act, 60
Catfish, 9
Celerity, 33
Cellphones and social networking, 224–225. *See also* Smartphones
Child pornography, 60, 223
Child Pornography Prevention Act of 1996 (CPPA), 59–60
Children and social media. *See also* Cyberbullying
   children *versus* children, 133
   grooming/trapping of children, 130–131
   pedophilia, 19
   sexual victimization, 129–134
   social development, 96
Christensen, Ward, 4, 5
Classmates.com, 5

Commonwealth Bank, 83
Community-oriented policing, 170, 184
Computer-mediated communications (CMCs), 147, 148, 149
Conrads, Randal, 5
Context collapse, 15–16
Controlling the Assault of Nonsolicited Pornography and Marketing (CAN-SPAM) Act. *See* CAN-SPAM Act
Copyright Felony Act, 113
Corrections and social media
   cellphones and social networking, 224–225
   overview, 222
   sex offenders, use of social media by; *see* Sex offenders, use of social media by
Cox, Damian, 92
Crime and social networking
   overview, 6–7, 28
Cyber threats, 206–208
Cyberbullying, 21
   defining, 97–99
   ease of, through social media, 96–97
   effects of, 103
   legislation, 97
   overview, 97
   prevalence, 100, 103
   prevention, 103–105
   Rebecca Marino case, 92
   school policies and involvement, 104
   severity of, 54, 92, 101
   social media, via, 101–103
   suicides related to, 54, 101, 102
   taxonomy, 101
   traditional bullying, *versus*, 99–100
   vulnerabilities of, 58
Cybercrime. *See also* Policing of cyberspace
   defining, 41
   evil twin attack; *see* Evil twin attack
   impact of on policing, 176
   motivations for, 32

neutralization techniques, relationship
between, 40
offenses, types of, 183
prevention, 33
rational choice theory regarding; *see*
Rational choice theory
seriousness of, 183
Cyberstalking, 21, 34, 37, 205

D

Damage Lab, 157
Data mining, 131
Dating sites. *See* Adult dating and
matrimonial sites
Delayed gratification, 38
Deolf, Chris, 6
Deterrence theory, 32
Deviance
cyber-deviance, 36
social bonds, theory regarding, 37
social learning theory regarding, 35–36
Digital piracy. *See* Piracy, digital
Diners Club, 83
Doe v. Prosecutor, 203
Durkheim, Emile, 36

E

e-government, 213
eBay, 83
eUniverse, 6
Evil twin attack, 81–82

F

Facebook, 6
active users, number of, 72
attractiveness to users, 127
cyberbullying on, 101–102, 102–103
personal information given over,
101–102
popularity, 138
privacy issues, 20
self-image, relationship between, 14,
96
user communication, 13
Favre, Brett, 54
First Amendment, 138–139, 202, 203, 205,
226–227
Fourth Amendment, 227–228
Friendster.com, 5–6

G

Gender gap, online disclosure, 21
GeoCities, 5
Google, 6, 127
Google+, 127
popularity, 138

H

Hacking, 41
age, 154
analysis of variance (ANOVA) analyses,
153–154
demographics, 154, 159
ethics involved in studying, 160
forums, 151
gender, 154
groups, 151–152
overview, 146–147
research regarding, 147
risk, 157–158
Russian Federation, 154, 159
social network analyses, 155–156
sophistication of, 150
subculture of, 150, 159
tactics, 146–147
user profiles, 151, 155–156
HackZona, 152, 156, 157
Harassment, online, 19
Hell Knights Crew, 152, 157

I

Identity theft, 41
aggregation of public data, 73–74
defining, 70
financial motivations for, 73–74
malicious software use, 76–77
market for, 83
perpetrators, 71–72
recovery from, 71
reputation, ruining of, 82
social networks, theft via, 72–73
trends, emerging, 84–85
Identity Theft and Assumption Deterrence
Act, 70
Instagram
sexting over, 102
Interface Message Processors (IMPs), 4
International Association of Chiefs of
Police, 198
International Association of Chiefs of
Police (IACP), 61
Internet

lack of regulation of, 9–10
origins of, 3–4
Internet service providers (ISPs), 5

K

Kleinrock, Leonard, 3
Koobface, 78

L

Lamberti, Al, 212
Lasdun, James, 82
LexisNexis, 62
Lifestyle exposure theory, 33–34
LinkedIn, 126

M

Malware, 76–78, 146, 147, 214
Marino, Rebecca, 92
Massachusetts Institute of Technology
      (MIT), 3
Matrimonial sites. *See* Adult dating and
      matrimonial sites
Mazafaka, 157
Micro-anomie theory, 36–37
MODEM File Transfer Protocol, 5
Multiuser domains (MUDs), 11
Murdoch, Rupert, 6
MySpace, 6, 13, 14, 16
      fraud and suicide case, 206
      pedophilia scare, 19

N

No Electronic Theft (NET) Act, 113
National Crime Victimization Survey
      (NCVS), 114, 115
National Highway Traffic Safety
      Administration (NHTSA), 57
National Incident-Based Reporting System
      (NIBRS), 114
Neutralization theory, 39–40
New Deal era, 38
News Corp, 6

O

Online (song), 22
Open-source data, 153
Overstock.com, 83

P

Paisley, Brad, 22
Palin, Sarah, 82
Patriot Act, 59
PayPal, 83
Pedophilia, 19, 131–133
Phishing, 80
Piracy, digital, 35–36, 39
      defining, 113
      effects of, 116
      integrated theory of, 118–120
      overview, 111–112
      policies regarding, 121–122
      reporting of, 114–115
      self-control, relationship between, 120
      social learning theory (SLT) regarding,
           117–118
      theory of planned behavior (TPB) as
           theory for, 117
      trends in, 115
Policing of cyberspace. *See also*
           Cybercrime; Pedophilia;
           Prosecution and social media
      cellphone mining of evidence, 62, 63,
           92
      cellphone use by incarcerated persons,
           51–52, 64
      demographics of officers, 174
      investigative hurdles, 168, 169
      methods, 173–174
      overview, 61, 168
      police officer perceptions, 176
      police officer support for, 170–173, 191
      predictive, 171
      prevention issues, 61
      research, 170–171
      strategies, 169
President's Identity Theft Task Force, 72,
           73–74, 81
Privacy issues, online, 19–20
      teenage sexuality, issues related to, 60
Profile squatting. *See* Squatting, profile
Progressive New Deal era, 59
Prosecution and social media. *See also*
           Policing of cyberspace
      admissibility of evidence, 211
      complexity of pursuing, 200
      criminal facilitation, 203
      evidence rules, 200
      fraud, 203
      illegal use of social media, 203
      information, laws on, 201
      investigations, 209–211

judicial officers' use of social media, 212

jurisdiction, 201

obscenity, 203

police use of social media, 212, 213

power of social media for law enforcement, 201

procedural law, 202

prosecutions, evidence for, 211

prosecutors' use of social media, 212

self-deputized civilians, dangers of, 200–201

sex offenders, use of social media by, 203–204

statutes, 200, 213–214

sui generis criminal law, 203

transnational enforcement, 214–215

trials, 211

Public safety, 198

Punishment, 32

deterrence theory; *see* Deterrence theory

formal, 33

informal, 33

Puppetnet, 85

R

Rational choice theory, 31–32

Reddit, 200–201

ResearchGate, 126

Revenge porn, 133

Roberts, Lawrence, 3, 4

Role-playing games (RPGs), 11

Routine activities theory, 33–34

RU Hack, 156

S

Self-control theory, 38–39

Sex offenders, use of social media by, 203–204, 222–224

Sexting, 50, 102

Child Pornography Prevention Act of 1996 (CPPA), expansion of, 59–60

compulsive, 58

defining, 53

reasons for, 53–54

Short message service (SMS), 51. *See also* Texting

SIMs, The, 132

SixDegrees.com, 5

Smartphones, 3, 224

Internet use over, increasing, 112

Smishing, 53, 58

Social bonds theory, 37

Social engineering, 81

Social learning theory, 35–36

Social learning theory (SLT), 117–118

Social media. *See also* Social network sites (SNSs); Social networking

communication, impact on, 94–95

corrections and; *see* Corrections and social media

defining, 198

usage, expansion in, 93–94

Social network sites (SNSs), 10. *See also* Social networking; *specific sites*

adult dating and matrimonial sites; *see* Adult dating and matrimonial sites

characteristics of, 128–129

communication opportunities, 12

context collapse; *see* Context collapse

corporate use of, 72–73

demographic patterns, 18–19

identity exploration, 12–13

identity verification, 12

interactive sites for venting frustrations, 127

interactive vlogging sites (IVSs), 127

motivations for using, 17–18

multipurpose popular social networking sites (MPSNSs), 127–128, 129, 130, 133, 134, 136, 138, 142; *see also specific sites*

number of, 12

privacy issues, 20

professional social networking sites (PSWs), 126–127

profiles, 128

social bonding premise, 127–128

Social networking. *See also* Social network sites (SNSs)

children, use by; *see* Children and social media

crime committed through; *see* Crime and social networking

defining, 28, 126

disconnection resulting from, 96

identity on, 9–10, 11–13; *see also* Virtual identity hypothesis

popularity, 6

preference for, over face-to-face, 17, 95–96

size of potential networks, 94–95

social satisfaction stemming from, 95–96

Spam messaging, 50, 52–53

Squatting, profile, 81
Stalking. *See* Cyberstalking
Statutory rape, 21
Steubenville, Ohio, juvenile rape case, 55–57, 62, 92
Stored Communications Act (SCA), 63
Strain theory, 36–37
StudiVZ, 14
Stuxnet, 214
Suess, Randy, 5
Suicides related to cyberbullying. *See under* Cyberbullying

T

Texting. *See also* Sexting
    compulsive/destructive, 53
    criminal cases, involvement in; *see* Policing of cyberspace
    deviance with, 51–52, 54
    driving, while, 53, 57–58
    evolution of, 51
    growth of, 49–50
    history of, 49–50
    origins of, 49, 50
    regulation of, 50
    spam messaging; *see* Spam messaging
Theglobe.com, 5
Theory of planned behavior (TPB), 117
Theory, defining, 29–30
Threats, cyber. *See* Cyber threats
Todd, Amanda, 101
Touchscreens, 3
Transmission Control Protocol/Internet Protocol (TCP/IP), 4
Trolling, 135
Twitter
    attractiveness to users, 127
    cyberbullying over, 101–102
    personal information given over, 101–102
    popularity, 138
    user communication, 13
    virtual identity on, 15

U

Uniform Crime Reports (UCR), 114
United States v. Drew, 206
United States v. Sayer, 205

United States v. Valle, 207, 208
Uniting and Strengthening America by Providing Appropriate Tools Required to Intercept and Obstruct Terrorism Act. *See* Patriot Act

V

Ventyouranger.com, 127
Victimization, through social networking, 19, 21–22, 28. *See also* Cyberbullying
    abuse petitions, 138–139
    avatars, fake, 134–135
    awareness, increasing, 142
    children *versus* children, 133
    children, sexual, 129–134
    cyber-aided violence, 137
    data mining, 131
    effects of, 103
    fake profiles, use of, 130
    grooming/trapping of children, 130–131
    monitoring of sites, 138–139
    prevention, 142
    revenge porn; *see* Revenge porn
    risks, via day-to-day activities, 33–34
    sexual messages, sending of, 135–136
    suicides; *see under* Cyberbullying
women, of, 134–138
Virtual identity hypothesis, 13–14

W

Weiner, Anthony, 54
WiFi
    speed of, 3
WordPress, 127
Worms, 78. *See also* Malware

Y

Youth Internet Safety Surveys, 98
YouTube, 127, 132, 133, 135, 213

Z

Zloy, 157
Zuckerberg, Mark, 6